'This wonderful book is the first to solve a near-universal problem: communicating strategic ideas is just as hard and just as important as coming up with them in the first place, and both are visual activities. The question is not "Do you understand?" but "Do you see?"'

**William Duggan, Professor at Columbia University and author of *Strategic Intuition* and *The Seventh Sense***

'This book shows how to draw an organization's strategy so you see what's been considered, what's not been considered, and how things are related. Strategy building is presented as a fun and involving learning process. The approach is revolutionary in that it enables not only the development but also the easy sharing of strategic understanding.'

**Roger L.M. Dunbar, Emeritus Professor, Stern School of Business, New York University**

'I am delighted that at last someone has grasped this idea and come up with a way to help us demonstrate strategic plans and ambitions in a creative new way. A drawing can encapsulate what 10,000 words can't do. By harnessing our innate creativity we can improve strategic communication, comprehension and implementation. This book could provide a vital new tool to help hard-pressed leaders to demonstrate strategic vision and deliver real strategic impact.'

**Vikki Heywood CBE, Chair of The Royal Society for the Encouragement of the Arts, Manufactures and Commerce and former Executive Director of the Royal Shakespeare Company**

'As a time-pressed executive it was a delight to find a book that I can dip into to find the best strategic frameworks – those that have proved the test of time and academic scrutiny as being truly useful in the workplace. Even better for an inveterate scribbler: endorsement that a picture and "permission to play" with ideas visually really does say a thousand words and more!'

**Sarah Mitson, Global Business Director, TNSGlobal**

'This is an invaluable resource for any executive wanting to improve engagement in strategy development and communication. The accessible layout means that the book itself can play an active and inspiring role in strategy discussions.'

**Matt Thomas, Director, Braxton Associates, Strategy Consultants and Divisional Chief Executive, Meyer International Plc**

'At last a book that grasps the implications of recent psychology: people think visually as well as verbally. The authors provide powerful visual devices that will both help managers conceive better strategies and enable their people to execute them more effectively.'

**Richard Whittington, Professor of Strategic Management at Saïd Business School, Oxford University and author of *Exploring Strategy***

'A powerful approach to make strategy more engaging again! *Strategy Builder* is a landmark book and is destined to make an important impact to the field of strategy, strategizing and strategic management. Executives across the board (and students of strategy) will find the core message of this book counterintuitive and compelling. The idea of "drawing" strategy may seem like child's play, yet all great strategists and philosophers know that it is through such "serious play" that we're allowed to see things differently so that we can see different things.'

**Robert Wright, Professor of Strategy at Hong Kong Polytechnic University**

*Thanks to Mairead, and to Kay*

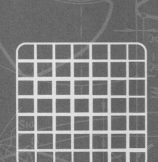

# STRATEGY BUILDER

How to create and communicate more effective strategies

## STEPHEN CUMMINGS & DUNCAN ANGWIN

Illustrations conceived by Stephen Cummings & Duncan Angwin, drawn by Rebecca Walthall

**WILEY**

*Library of Congress Cataloging-in-Publication Data is available*

A catalogue record for this book is available from the British Library.

ISBN 978-1-118-70723-4 (hardback)    ISBN 978-1-118-70718-0 (ebk)
ISBN 978-1-118-70716-6 (ebk)

Cover Design: Wiley

Cover Image: © PGMart/Shutterstock.com

Illustrations conceived by Stephen Cummings and Duncan Angwin, drawn by Rebecca Walthall

Set in 10/12pt Rockwell Std Light by Aptara, New Delhi, India
Printed in Singapore by Markono Print Media Pte Ltd

# CONTENTS

# STRATEGY BUILDER TEAM

## Authors

**Stephen Cummings**
**Professor of Strategy at Victoria and ICMCI Academic Fellow**

Other books I've been involved with include *Recreating Strategy, Images of Strategy, Creative Strategy, Handbook of Creativity and Management* and *Strategy Pathfinder* with Duncan, but Duncan and I have been discussing how to build *Strategy Builder* since we worked together at Warwick Business School. The following team of people enabled us to do the original idea for a book about drawing strategy justice.

**Duncan Angwin**
**Professor of Strategy at Oxford Brookes University**

My other books include *Mergers and Acquisitions, Implementing Successful Post-Acquisition Management, Practicing Strategy, Exploring Strategy* and *Strategy Pathfinder* with Steve. Whilst at the University of Warwick we began thinking about how managers actually 'do' strategy effectively. We hope this book will help people in the practice of creating and communicating strategy. For more information please visit www.duncanangwin.com.

## Illustrators

**Rebecca Walthall**
**Information design, Visory**

Rebecca is a graphic designer and illustrator from New Zealand. She specialises in projects that require her to distill complex information and concepts into easily digestible visual material. She believes that there is no such thing as being 'unable to draw' – like anything it just takes a little bit of practice.

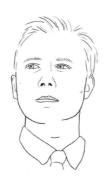

**Simon Collins, Hadley Smith**
**Principals, Visory**

We were both previously students of Stephen's but have (hopefully) pulled ourselves up by the bootlaces to become something approximating colleagues. A few years ago we saw the opportunity to help organizations 'do strategy better' by making it visual, accessible, even beautiful. We started Visory to do just that.

## App Development

**Craig Catley**
**CEO, StrategyBlocks**

I've been involved in the enterprise software market for 20 years, specifically in sales and marketing management and I am Founder & Director of StrategyBlocks, driving international market growth and product development strategy. My key technology interests focus on business analytics and performance improvement solutions.

**Chiwai Chan**
**Developer, StrategyBlocks**

A Software Developer with StrategyBlocks for over 5 years, my primary area of responsibility is the development of the engines, servers and databases of our products. In this role I'm directly involved in the development of key product functionality.

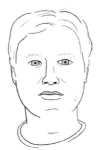

**Glenn Murphy**
**Developer, StrategyBlocks**

I was born in Canada and worked as a software developer for Cognos Inc. in Ottawa for 7 years, before they were acquired by IBM. In 2007, I dropped everything and moved to New Zealand for a change of lifestyle and became the lead front-end developer for a new startup company called StrategyBlocks.

## Production

**Holly Bennion**
**Executive Commissioning Editor, Wiley**

Holly commissions new projects for Wiley Business books and Capstone Publishing, a Wiley brand, publishing high-profile books to inspire people in business, including innovative new titles in personal development and career success.

**Jenny Ng**
**Development Editor, Wiley**

Jenny is responsible for developing content at Wiley on the Capstone and business lists, helping authors to turn their material into the best products they can be!

**Tessa Allen**
**Senior Production Editor, Wiley**

I work on Wiley's Business, Finance, Accounting, and Capstone titles. I'm proud to be working with such talented authors and colleagues – and being surrounded by gorgeous books isn't too bad either. With all of its visual and graphical elements *Strategy Builder* has been both interesting to work on and a real challenge.

And special thanks to: Rosemary Nixon, David Wilson, Robin Wensley, John McGee, Peter Doyle, Haridimos Tsoukas, Rob Grant, Eric Cassells, Matt Thomas, Gibson Burrell, Harminder Singh, Peter McKiernan, Roger Dunbar, Richard Dunford, Chris Smith, Chris Bilton, Urs Daellenbach, Sally Davenport, Sally Riad, Adam Martin, Sophia Lum, Luisa Acheson, Megan Key, Noelle Donnelly, Bob Galliers, Jane Parker, Colin Campbell-Hunt and Sebastian Green.

And our many inspirational students at Victoria University, Oxford Brookes University, Saïd Business School, Oxford University, Georgetown University, Chinese University Hong Kong, Tongji University Shanghai, Melbourne Business School, University of Warwick, ENPC Paris, EHTP Casablanca, Mediterranean School of Business, Tunisia and Vlerick Business School, Belgium.

# PART ONE
# THE CONCEPT

Misunderstood strategy may be the biggest problem facing most organizations today. If the people implementing a strategy don't 'get it', confusion, dysfunction and sub-optimization result.

Over the past five years and across eight different countries we've conducted experiments into whether the way you communicate strategy make a difference? The answer: yes. Whether you are African, American, Asian, Australasian or European, an MBA student, an executive or a young entrepreneur, communicating strategy in pictures is by far the most effective way. Those shown a diagrammatic portrayal of a strategy recall with 70% accuracy; those shown a textual rendition of the same strategy underperform dramatically, recalling less than 30%.[1]

And it isn't just in simple reproduction that pictures add value. Those shown the strategy as text who sought to aid their recall by drawing were more than one and a half times more accurate than those who just recalled the strategy by writing. Something kinetic happens when you draw that stimulates other senses. Seeing a picture of a strategy helps, but drawing it is even more powerful.

But what might be most shocking to anybody interested in strategy was the discovery that there is little to no correlation between the amount that can be accurately recalled about a strategy and a person's confidence in acting on it. This suggests that there may be many people in organizations who don't know what their strategy is, but who are confidently implementing it anyway (which could explain why many organization's strategies appear confused in practice).

Despite the power of drawing, organizations still express strategy in the form of text. The strategic plans that sit unloved on corporate shelves, and the presentations inflicted upon staff that summarize these plans, are almost always presented as words and numbers. Surveying the websites of the Fortune 100 companies, The 100 Best Places to Work and the 50 Most Respected Companies revealed that only one used a diagram to express their strategy – one out of 250.

It seems we're building and communicating strategy all wrong. Strategy Builder outlines a revolutionary way that you can do it right. If strategy is about winning (and in our experience this is the most compelling definition of strategy), then picturing a strategy is the best way to figure out and communicate how you and your organization can win.[2]

## The clue in the corner

It could be a bit dispiriting to dwell on the effect that the word 'strategy' has on most people in most organizations most of the time. Talking and writing about strategy tend to put people off making it. Thinking about when you last talked strategy in your organization probably conjures up bad memories: 100-page documents that you haven't read (you suspect that nobody else has read them either); hours spent arguing about whether 'purpose' or 'values' or 'philosophy' is the best word to describe something that nobody is sure they understand and the wording of which can't be agreed upon in any case; convoluted mission statements designed by committees of 'yes men'; numerical bamboozlement; strategy 'away days' just when your backlog is at its largest. It's no surprise, then, that many feel disengaged from or by strategy, or that a recent study found that 95% of people have little idea what their organization's strategy is.[3] We believe that this lack of clarity about and involvement with strategy is one of the main reasons that organizations underperform.

However, we've been teaching strategy and advising companies about it for long enough to know that people don't inherently dislike strategy. On the contrary, most people will agree that having a good strategy is a great feeling. It focuses the mind, energizes, provides a sense of purpose and relieves anxiety. It's more the way that strategy is currently developed and communicated that turns people off.

Rather than dwelling on this problem, we decided to build a strategy book by first trying to identify places where people weren't disengaged, when they actually felt good about talking strategy, when they were as interested in it as we know people can be.

Gradually, such a place occurred to us. A large clue had been standing there in every classroom in which we have taught and in the offices where we have consulted in Asia, Africa, Australasia, Europe and the Americas for decades. Where do we see people get engaged about discussing and making strategy? Often it happens around whiteboards…

Whiteboards may now be one of the lowest-tech devices in the room, but think about what happens in a meeting at that moment when eyes move from the pre-prepared PowerPoint presentation and the thick documents to the whiteboard as somebody seizes the pen and starts to write on it: some keywords, some arrows or a flow of processes. Things change gear. As others seek their turn with the pen or to inform the scribe with their insights, things open up. Change is possible. Cufflinks are released. Sleeves are rolled up. Strategy is happening, in real time. The material and the social – things and people – work together as the whiteboard provides a vehicle for collectively figuring out how stuff fits together and where new value can be created. That moment is uplifting. It's game on. People are building something.

The same is true in the classroom. We spend a lot of time preparing slides and writing cases, but most MBAs really get into strategy when we stop lecturing and start scribing ours and their thoughts on a case and facilitating and recording their debates, uncertainties and insights into frameworks on a humble whiteboard. Of course, it's not the whiteboard, but rather what people do with it, that makes strategy engaging. And what they do is they draw, connecting words, images and insights. If this is done well that drawing is a collective experience. So, this engagement could happen on a whiteboard or a flipchart, sheets of paper, an iPad or the back of an envelope.

Pinpointing this moment leads to an excellent foundation upon which to build a book that could help managers become more engaged in strategy-making. We have come to believe that while strategy may be developed in the now conventional ways (conversations, number crunching, the writing of documents, files of PowerPoints), collectively generated graphical representations are an unrecognized but powerful approach. Educational theorists since Piaget and Brunner have shown how people learn most effectively through the combination of three modes: the concrete doing of things, the pictorial representations of things, and the symbolical description of things in text or numbers.[4] People generally learn an organization's strategy by working in that organization, or they have it communicated to them in words and numbers. But the kind of pictorial representations and translations that whiteboards provide space for are useful ways of connecting the everyday activities in an organization with the high-level words and numbers from the strategic plan. They facilitate the substitution of actually being in concrete situations in ways that promote useful abstractions and group communication.[5]

However, if we do not recognize the importance of and potential for drawing pictures in strategy development soon, the connection that they can provide could become a missing link as technological developments and busy schedules discourage us from thoughtful drawing. There are a number of emerging opportunities for a new way of developing and communicating strategy. And drawing as the basis of building strategy has a number of key strengths. Seizing these opportunities and acting on these strengths before it is too late is what the Strategy Builder is about and we do so in three simple steps:

1. By encouraging people to draw strategy – which may be as simple as stepping up to a whiteboard and using arrows to depict how you currently relate to your customers.

2. By showing how many of the greatest strategy frameworks developed over the past 50 years can be used and combined in creative and playful ways to tell really engaging strategy stories.

3. By distilling from these frameworks five easy-to-remember foundations that can enable you and your organization to draw a compelling strategy that can be communicated on a single page.

# OPPORTUNITIES FOR A NEW WAY OF DEVELOPING STRATEGY

People like strategy. But they don't like conventional modes of communicating it. As a consequence, the people who have to implement strategy feel disengaged from it – this is a big reason why organizations underperform. If we identify this as the problem, we can also see a number of opportunities to fix it. We list these opportunities on the 'high engagement' device below and explain them in the paragraphs that follow.

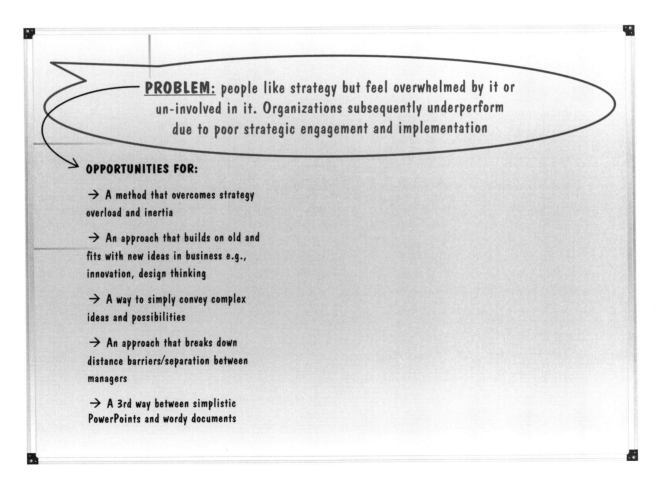

**PROBLEM:** people like strategy but feel overwhelmed by it or un-involved in it. Organizations subsequently underperform due to poor strategic engagement and implementation

**OPPORTUNITIES FOR:**

→ A method that overcomes strategy overload and inertia

→ An approach that builds on old and fits with new ideas in business e.g., innovation, design thinking

→ A way to simply convey complex ideas and possibilities

→ An approach that breaks down distance barriers/separation between managers

→ A 3rd way between simplistic PowerPoints and wordy documents

## 5. The need for a third way between the oversimplicity of PowerPoints and the overcomplication of the typical strategic plan

Let's start with that last opportunity listed on the whiteboard first and work backwards. While the term 'death by PowerPoint' may be an exaggeration (nobody has actually been killed, to our knowledge), millions of people are numbed by PowerPoint presentations every day.[6] That 95% of employees may be unaware of or do not understand their company's strategy is largely, we believe, due to the way that strategies are communicated. Most strategy is disseminated in large wordy documents (referred to by some humorists as SPOTS – 'strategic plan on top shelf'), and, given that hardly anybody actually reads these documents, in PowerPoint presentations containing bulleted text summaries.

This convention is not surprising given that the 20th-century technology used to generate these documents – typewriters, standard office computer software – was much friendlier to those who use words and numbers than to those who adopt individualized graphics. The same is true for lecture materials. And once the files that people learn strategy from are set in text formats, they are often difficult for others to question or manipulate or otherwise get involved in discussing. Subsequently, students and managers are more apt to learn frameworks and strategies by rote (if at all) and 'cut and paste' what they see on their PowerPoints or their laptops, rather than actually drawing, questioning and building upon them. As a consequence, we believe that learning about strategy, and strategy itself, are under threat of becoming more a veneer than an organic and engaging pursuit.

The danger of losing the ability to get behind the veneer and tinker with strategy can be related to Mathew Crawford's arguments in the book, *The Case for Working with Your Hands*.[7] Here, Crawford criticizes the privileging of knowledge work over manual work without recognizing how one aids the other. He relates it to an 'engineering culture [that] has developed in recent years in which the object is to "hide the works"'. When appliances break, they are replaced not repaired.

Toasters come with screwheads with odd angles designed to foil the most intrepid home-handyperson and dire warnings for those who seek to go behind the casing. Cars can only be repaired if one has access to the manufacturer's diagnostic computer program. The user need not worry about maintenance or understanding or development. But what we are losing by obscuring the workings, Crawford argues, is the intellectual engagement that hands-on understanding provides: 'Without the opportunity to learn through the hands, the world remains abstract, and distant, and the passions for learning will not be engaged.'

If the 'workings' remain under the bonnet or the thinking behind the PowerPoints is not probed, we lose the confidence in our ability to really understand, tinker with and contribute to the working of things. The son helping a parent to check a car's oil by finding the appropriate picture in the manual and comparing it to reality is no longer just a passenger: he receives an education that may cause him to ask questions that spark new trajectories of thought. A manager sketching her company's strategy in front of a group of colleagues and inviting contributions is far more likely to engage her audience in a fruitful debate and spark new ideas than if she had e-mailed them a consultant's generic rendition.

To borrow a phrase from Crawford, managers and management students who fail to explore and tinker with concepts and ideas never become 'masters of their own stuff': this leaves them vulnerable, susceptible to being told how things are and what to do without having the confidence to question their advisors' logic. Just as the person who has no idea how a car works is disempowered when talking to a car mechanic, so too the employee who has not explored how management ideas may be constructed and developed. Given that it is difficult to physically experience a strategy in its entirety across an organization, drawing may be the closest we can get to 'hands on' experience. As such, drawing is an excellent way of overcoming the vulnerability, susceptibility and lack of mastery or control in our field: a great way to learn through the hands and discuss what is emerging with others – a great way to bring strategy to life.

Twenty-first-century technology provides an opportunity here. Many people we have spoken to recently have admitted experiencing an epiphany as they realize it is so much easier to scan, manipulate and send a sketch they did than to try and redraw it using popular software. And perhaps the most engaging new devices we've encountered in classrooms are document cameras that allow you to draw on a piece of paper and have it projected behind you – just like on a huge whiteboard. Others promote new presentation formats like Prezi, which make it easier to keep the big picture in view and not get bogged down in detail. Continued reliance on 20th-century technology threatens our ability to experience strategy 'through the hands' by drawing it, and thus the quality of strategy development itself. Embracing 21st-century technology to develop and communicate strategy is an opportunity to recapture the engagement that people experience when they feel they are involved in the workings of strategy.

## 4. A need to reduce the distance or separation between managers and other stakeholders

These days, lecture theatres are bigger, large organizations are bigger, and these changes in scale have changed the way that senior managers relate to employees and that professors relate to students to discuss strategy. In organizations, the scale has encouraged the broadcasting of strategy in the difficult-to-digest forms listed in the previous paragraphs. Hence, most people in most organizations are not in any way engaged in contributing to strategic discussions. Recently, a CEO from a large financial organization told us the purpose of the leadership programme that he wanted us to facilitate was to counteract a culture where employees thought that *strategy was something that happened to them*, rather than something they were a part of. Students, too, are now less likely to actually work through strategy problems and cases with their professors present. Lectures are given. PowerPoint slides are sent and downloaded. Textbooks go unscribbled upon. In fact, not only is it the new normal to not make notes on textbooks, there is also financial benefit. Amazon and others will pay a premium for unmarked copies of texts to sell on to the following year's class.

The good news is that technology and social views have evolved to the point that they could encourage more interactive thinking and building. One CEO recently revealed to us that perhaps the best thing he did upon joining his new organization was to send out a blanket e-mail to all staff with the simple question, 'Any ideas?' He got 290, and a cross-sectional committee selected the best 30 for implementation. 'Most of the good ones my exec team never would have thought of,' he said.

Web 2.0 presents new opportunities for people to engage in live 'open-strategy' discussions. There are now dozens of apps that replicate the experience of drawing on a whiteboard while making it easier to share these drawings with others. The most innovative thing about the latest edition of a strategy textbook called *Strategy Pathfinder* that we co-author is also the simplest: the insertion of blank spaces where students can draw their interpretations of key ideas and frameworks on the pages. Students report that these drawings help their revision immensely, particularly when they get together to discuss them with others in study groups. Related to this, we've noticed a trend towards involving not only the C-suite in corporate strategy discussions but representatives of lower-level employees, directors and even key customers. Not everybody in this broader group may absorb the numbers or have time to read all of the supporting documents, but they might perhaps relate to good diagrammatic summaries?

## 3. An opportunity to seek other ways to convey complex ideas and possibilities

Aristotle: 'It is impossible to even think without a mental picture.' Albert Einstein: 'If I can't picture it I can't understand it.' Karl Weick: 'How can I know what I think until I see what I say?' Scan any field and you'll often find that those most admired for making complex phenomena understandable appreciate the utility of pictures. Most companies, though, don't seem to get this – yet.

While most executives would claim to run complex businesses, few, if any, seek to represent their strategies in anything other than numbers and text. Recently, we examined the websites of 250 organizations: those of the global Fortune 100, the 100 'Best Places to Work' and the World's 50 Most Respected Companies. Almost all of these sites contained some expression of what the organization's strategy was, but only one sought to use a picture to do this (Procter & Gamble – you will see it in Part 3 of this book).

In professions like medicine, architecture, design and military practice, realizing ideas graphically has always been and still is an essential skill. And even in traditional academic disciplines like science, there is a desire to utilize the communicative power of graphical illustration. The recent book, *The Where, the Why, and the How*, assigned 75 artists to make illustrations of key scientific concepts that would aid understanding, an approach motivated by looking through old scientific charts and diagrams where, even though the knowledge was nascent, the descriptions seemed somehow richer and more inspiring.[8] In sports, a field of endeavour that business people like to associate themselves with and glean

analogies from, drawing and developing strategy are completely integrated (see the following box on drawing strategy in sports).

Despite the threat we can see posed by business people not associating strategy development with drawing, we can also discern an emerging opportunity. Some of the most interesting and innovative executives we have encountered over the past decade are fans of conveying strategic thinking graphically. For example, in a recent edition of *Fortune* magazine profiling Ford CEO Alan Mulally, the journalist was so taken aback and impressed by his drawing of Ford's strategy, scribbled with his own hand in preparing for the interview, that he asked if they could reproduce it in the magazine.[9] The picture is a vivid illustration of the power of a simple graphic to communicate strategy. Individual strategy drawings like Mulally's are described in more detail in the final part of *Strategy Builder* to help inspire your own creative strategy drawings.

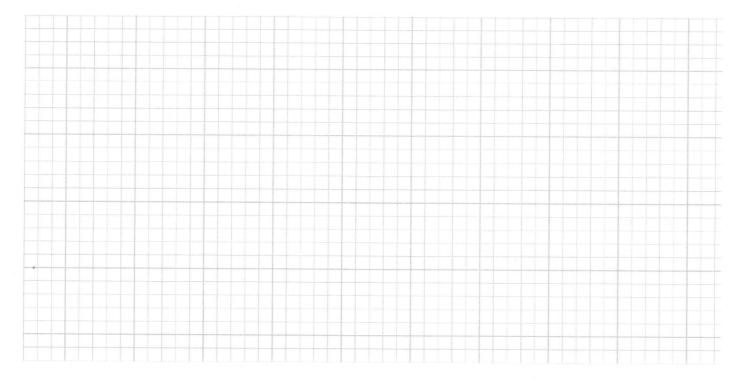

## Drawing Strategy in Sports

Football (i.e. soccer) history novices are often surprised by the fact that a seemingly minor club, Preston North End, easily won a number of the earliest incarnations of the English Football League Championship. However, a major step in the history of this sport was the assigning of specialist roles or positions and then thinking about the subsequent interrelationships. Preston did well because they were ahead of the curve on this.

At a time when defending was seen by some in England to be unmanly, and all went into attack bar the goalie plus perhaps one other player (there 'to keep the goalkeeper in chat' according to one scathing journalist who thought he too should hare up the field), Preston lined up in a 2-3-5 formation. They strategized in this way under the influence of one James Gledhill, a teacher and doctor from Glasgow (in Scotland at this time the game was guided more by strategy than by notions of proper manly conduct). In a series of lectures, Gledhill, as David Hunt put it in his history of the Preston club, 'showed them by blackboard what might be done by a team of selected experts'. In 1887 Preston won the title without losing a game, beginning a never-since-matched 42-game winning streak.[10]

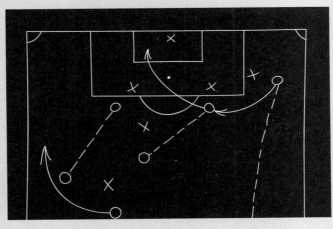

A few years earlier, the fledgling sport of American football was given a significant boost. In 1875, a pair of Princeton men, W. Earl Dodge and Jotham Potter, returned from a Harvard–Yale match and tried to convert their classmates to the game. They encountered considerable resistance, but joined forces with fellow student Tommie (Woodrow) Wilson. Wilson was a sports nut and already a persuasive communicator. He developed, in the words of a classmate, 'clear-cut notions of how the game should be played and insisted upon them'. He worked out these views as he, Dodge and Potter strategized, developed ideas and concocted plays by sketching them on tablecloths during their meetings. Over time, Dodge, Potter and Wilson convinced the college to adopt the rugby-like Harvard–Yale game and then, in late 1876, issued invitations to student sports representatives from Harvard, Yale and Columbia to attend a meeting in Springfield, Massachusetts, to discuss the future of the game. This was the birth of the Intercollegiate Football Association.[11]

To this day, a coach visualizing plays and communicating them graphically is still a common and a positive image. While one of soccer's strategic pioneers, Vittorio Pozzo, claimed to have learned some of his legendary chalkboarding skills at a business school (Zurich's International School of Commerce in the early 1900s), the image of a business person using a board is, unfortunately, decidedly uncommon.[12]

## 2. Recognizing that what they teach in business school can, and should, change to embrace forgotten and new insights

Business schools in the 20th century sought to model themselves on recently established academic disciplines such as economics and psychology, rather than on what could be considered closer cousins, professions such as medicine, law and architecture.[13] Ideas in these disciplines are conveyed in words, numbers, algorithms and equations, and so it has transpired in the study of business too. But there is now a growing appreciation that the way in which business schools and their curricula are configured is as much for historical as it is for fundamental reasons – and consequently, we need not be beholden to current norms. For example, the first serious attempts to standardize higher-level business education happened in the US in the middle of the 20th century, by which time economics was a well-established university subject on whose coat-tails it was possible to hang other things. But in earlier attempts to establish business schools, economics was not so prominent. For example, on January 8, 1869, when Washington College President (and former General) Robert E. Lee presented a plan for a business school, the curriculum was made up of the following subjects 'to be studied in equal parts' as shown on the whiteboard on the following page.

Many of these subjects appear familiar, but others, like history and drawing, suggest that a business school could offer courses that are in keeping with the concerns of the day, rather than those chosen by people enamoured by economics in the 1950s.[14] Indeed, in what might be a case of history repeating itself, the current vogue for 'design thinking' in today's world has business schools all over the world looking at how they might encourage their students to think like designers as well as economists. And this, we believe, represents a significant opportunity for furthering new approaches to representing strategy (we return to General Lee's plan and this idea of encouraging more drawing in business schools at the end of the book).

## 1. An opportunity to find a way through the framework and idea overload and inertia

In the past, strategic management has been about expressing ideas in ways other than numbers and text. Indeed, some of its earliest and most famous developments in the field are frameworks: the industry life cycle, the value chain and the five forces of industry. It used to be that strategy's leading thinkers were engaged in developing frameworks that others could use to critique and think through strategic options. However, the key performance indicators for strategy academics have changed, and the best and brightest are now engaged in developing numerical and textual representations and are focused on the detailed performance equations and micro-behavioural aspects of strategy that suit publication in the top academic journals.

But this hasn't stopped others developing frameworks, and now there are hundreds. In response, many books with titles like *101 Management Models* and *80+ Strategy Frameworks* seek to reproduce all of these. However, many of these frameworks do the same sort of thing in slightly different ways. Others leave out related elements or connections. In any event, we have more and more frameworks, fewer of high quality, and it is difficult for managers to understand how they relate to one another.

Educational theorists have long known that people have difficulty holding more than seven elements in their working memory, so 80+ as a number is not helpful. It is information overload that can make people less likely to make decisions and take strategic action rather than encouraging this. One of the reasons that SWOT (strengths, weaknesses, opportunities, threats) continues to be ranked as the most popular management framework in international surveys is that it is one of the few that most people remember well enough to actually use. This is a shame, as strategy has a lot more to offer which could, with a little thought and organization, be provided to intelligent (but busy) managers to help them express strategic ideas in a more effective way.

# A 19th-century Business School curriculum for the 21st century?

Mathematics

Geography

Technology

Economy

Modern languages

Book-keeping and penmanship

Correspondence and correct English

Law

History  and biography

Geometry  and drawing

# SEVEN STRENGTHS OF DRAWING STRATEGY

Connecting all the opportunities outlined in the previous chapter is the simple fact that most people like to build things (and currently most feel that they're not engaged in building strategy). This facet of human nature goes a long way to explaining the appeal of some of today's most famous brands, from LEGO (building models), Facebook and LinkedIn (building personal profiles), to Minecraft and SimCity (building virtual worlds), and Pinterest (building hobbies) and Homebase – or its DIY (home-handyperson) equivalents around the world. And it's common sense that if you were going to build something important and reasonably complex, without the instruction manual or prompts such as those provided by these companies, you would work it out by drawing it first. However, while picturing a strategy may be starting to make sense in light of what we have discussed so far, there are other, more scientific, reasons why you should be drawing strategy in order to build it better. We outline seven strengths of drawing strategy: seven strengths which, as we illustrate on the whiteboard below, respond to the opportunities for a new approach to making and communicating strategy.

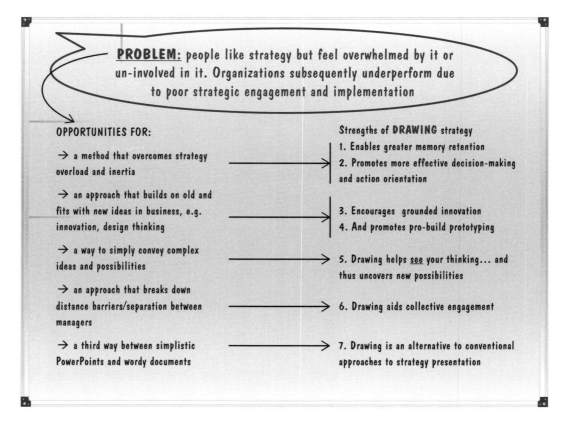

**PROBLEM:** people like strategy but feel overwhelmed by it or un-involved in it. Organizations subsequently underperform due to poor strategic engagement and implementation

**OPPORTUNITIES FOR:**

→ a method that overcomes strategy overload and inertia

→ an approach that builds on old and fits with new ideas in business, e.g. innovation, design thinking

→ a way to simply convey complex ideas and possibilities

→ an approach that breaks down distance barriers/separation between managers

→ a third way between simplistic PowerPoints and wordy documents

**Strengths of DRAWING strategy**

1. Enables greater memory retention
2. Promotes more effective decision-making and action orientation

3. Encourages grounded innovation
4. And promotes pro-build prototyping

5. Drawing helps <u>see</u> your thinking... and thus uncovers new possibilities

6. Drawing aids collective engagement

7. Drawing is an alternative to conventional approaches to strategy presentation

# 1. Drawing strategy aids memory retention (and more)

A strategy is only as good as its implementation. Therefore, good strategy development requires effective communication to ensure that all who are involved in delivering on a strategy know what it is they are supposed to be delivering. In short, strategies that aren't remembered don't work. People understand this problem. A recent survey asked executives about the areas relating to strategy in their organizations requiring greater strength or emphasis. At the top of the list for 79% of respondents was the need to more effectively communicate their strategy internally.[15]

Drawing strategy could help, because pictorializing makes things easier to remember. Psychological tests have shown that pictures are more easily recalled, receive more processing attention and act as more effective stimuli than words and numbers, particularly when people are busy, multi-tasking or distracted.[16] A drawing's superiority over text and numbers in memory stimulus is the result of its greater *mimetic* and *synaesthetic* qualities.

Strategic planning documents, presented as text, can only go left to right and top to bottom – they are not *mimetic*. They can't, in other words, mimic other directions. With graphical representations, three pathways to market can be drawn as three arrows, going 'upmarket' can be shown as going up the page – above where we might draw the standard offering now – and by representing things in this way the drawing will be more closely linked with our experience of the world. As Karl Weick put it: 'People who examine [only] the numbers are unable to reconstruct [in reality or in their minds] the actual events that produce those numbers.'[17] People who draw can.

For example, you may know a little about Napoleon's Russian campaign that led to the downfall of a mighty army and, eventually, of Napoleon himself as well. But the details are probably hazy. Charles Joseph Minard's diagram, considered 'the most impressive statistical graph ever produced', is an excellent example of how a drawing can deliver a complex story in a simple and memorable way (Figure 1.1).[18] The narrowing light line going left to right shows the gradual decline of Napoleon's force from 422,000 men when crossing the Russian border, to 100,000 when it gets to Moscow. The black line traces their continued demise

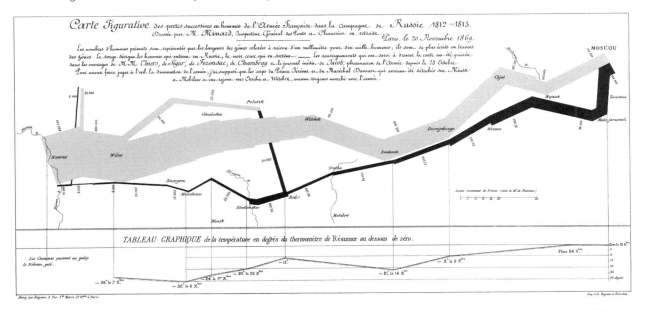

**Figure 1.1.** Picture tells the story: Minard's Napoleonic invasion of Russia. Retrieved from http://en.wikipedia.org/wiki/File:Minard.png

in retreat, set above the declining temperatures of the Russian winter (the thin line at the bottom). Only 10,000 men will cross back into Poland. Napoleon's force is spent. Words alone could not capture this unfolding in a way that enables one to so readily see antecedents and relationships between events and leave such an indelible mark on the memory.[19]

Drawings can add further value by connecting cognition to physiology and engaging other senses or *synaesthesia*. Good drawings develop their relationships with the reader from the initial 'eye contact' onwards to draw in and engage other senses which then start working together to give the picture greater meaning. A good map makes you want to touch the image; find interrelationships; talk to the person next to you about it and hear what they have to say – whether they see what you see. If you've ever been in London, you may recall just how tactile the Tube map is: it invites you to trace your route with your finger, to share your perspective on it with your travelling companions, to annotate it with additions, reminders and doodles particular to individual aims and goals. Recent studies have shown how even doodling can aid recall and involvement.[20] As former General Motors Vice-Chairman

Bob Lutz said: 'I can look at old sketches done in meetings 40 years ago and experience sudden recall of the room, the table, the voices.'[21] Once you have added physically to a map, a drawing or even a blank piece of paper, you have a greater mental and physical connection with it. And this synaesthesia in turn helps you to remember. Just as when you write a shopping list, but forget to bring it with you, the 'muscle memory' of scratching things on a pad helps you to recall what you needed.

Experiments we have conducted reiterate the power of pictures in terms of memory retention. We asked students in our MBA and undergraduate classes in France, Austria, Morocco, New Zealand, Tunisia, the UK and the United States to each open an envelope that had been given to them and take out the page inside. On that page was a simple strategy made up of five elements. The students were asked to read the plan, without consultation, and commit it to memory. They were then asked to place the page back in the envelope, seal it and put it to one side. After varying periods of time focused on another task (ranging from 5 to 30 minutes), subjects were asked to reproduce the strategy as best they could on the back of the envelope, and hand their envelopes back

## KEY FINDINGS FROM TEXT VS PICTURE STRATEGY EXPERIMENT

→ Those shown a drawing of a strategy remember twice as much as those shown the same strategy in written form

→ The recall difference between picture versus text is even greater for those whose first language is not English

→ Even if a strategy is communicated in written form, recalling it in a diagram leads to greater recall: drawing has a positive kinetic effect that helps people connect things up

→ There is a weak correlation between amount recalled and confidence to discuss: it could be that the most confident people influencing strategy in your organization have a poor understanding of that strategy

→ Recall is even better for subjects who are familiar with the archetype being used: in this case it was a simple arrow-shaped polygon, a value chain to us. They were then informed that there were in fact two versions of the plan. One-half of each lecture room had a plan written as five bullet points of text; the other half had the plan represented as a simple picture (a Value Chain) with those points in text arranged on different parts of the diagram. On average across the whole sample of 1,000 subjects (with very little variation across the different countries), those with the text rendition could only remember two of the five elements; those with the drawing could remember nearly four out of five.[22] Interestingly, those who received the strategy as text but reproduced it as a drawing of some kind had far greater recall that those who recorded it in words. And those who received the picture but reproduced it using just text scored far lower than those who recorded it as a picture. This indicates that the memory process is not just photographic. There is something kinetic about drawing that aids recall.

Additional insights came through in the supplementary questions we asked participants before they handed back the envelopes: 'On a scale of 1–5, with five being highest, to what degree to you see clear integration between the elements in the strategic plan you looked at?'; and 'On a scale of 1–5 with five being highest, what would your degree of confidence to discuss that strategy be if you were about to go into a meeting on it?' As we expected, subjects who had seen the picture could recall greater integration. However, there was, to our surprise, little correlation between how much people could accurately recall and their confidence to discuss. Even more curious was the fact that people's confidence went up the longer the interval was between seeing the strategy and reproducing it – as if the length of time helped them forget what they didn't know. We might extrapolate from this that even if people in your organization don't know what your strategy is, they are still out there confidently implementing something – which is even more reason to find ways of enabling people to really understand what they are supposed to be working towards, and doing it often!

## 2. Drawing strategy provides an effective action orientation

A team from the University of Chicago recently discovered that when people discuss potential decisions in a non-native language, irrational biases are reduced. Working in a foreign language created a distance between decision-makers and their preconceived ideas, more than one 'angle' for looking at things, and subsequently encouraged more effective decisions and actions.[23] While it may not be possible for people in your organization to master a second language, this is not necessary to achieve similar benefits. They can already communicate in an alternative mode: graphically.

To illustrate how drawings and words can work together to guide effective decision-making and action, think back to the London Tube map example. The map shown in the cartoon in Figure 1.2 is actually an extremely accurate representation of the Tube map prior to the 1930s. Harry Beck, designer of the map we recognize today

**Figure 1.2.** The bad old days of travelling by Tube: *Punch* cartoon (1909). Sourced from http://britton. disted.camosun.bc.ca/punch.html

(which has become the template for mapping all urban transport systems), works on the principle that you cannot reproduce all of the complexities and possibilities, and even if you could, it would probably confuse, alienate or otherwise bog people down (Figure 1.3).[24] So the map is not fully representative, it is only partially so. But in combination with an individual who can speak and think in English (even only partially, like many tourists), it is a wonderful aid. Similarly, when we present drawings of companies' strategies in Part 2 of *Strategy Builder*, we sometimes err in favour of presenting the most compelling and memorable rendition, rather than sticking religiously to the frameworks 'textbook' layout.

John Luffman's 'Invasion map' of 1803 sought to mobilize action through a simple map in another way (Figure 1.4). It was drawn to encourage the political classes to *do*

*something* about the threat of invasion from Napoleonic forces after France's occupation of the Austrian Netherlands. The invasion map spoke louder than words alone to show the proximate European ports from which French forces could attack.[25] It enabled people to see the decisions that needed to be made, and to discuss them, and oriented and animated action. After a period of strategic inertia, it helped make things happen. (We've traced some of the invasion routes in blue to make the point in these visually saturated times, but 200 years ago Luffman's pencil was all it took.)

These examples illustrate how graphical images are useful not only because they represent reality, but also because they provide another focal point, a new language that can free people stuck in detail and encourage fruitful communication. Such graphical renditions provide

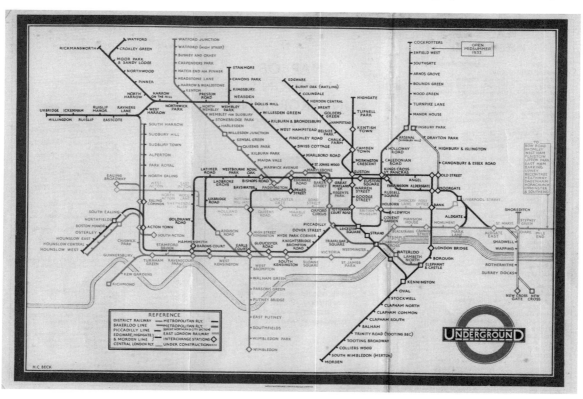

**Figure 1.3.** London in the palm of your hand: Beck's Underground map (1933) © TfL from the London Transport Museum collection

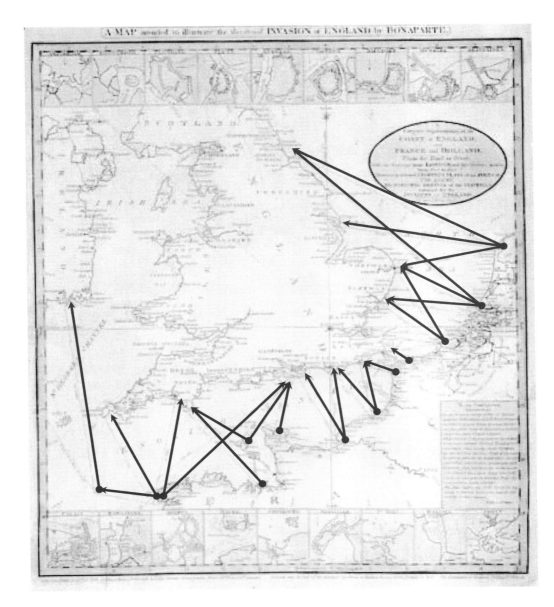

**Figure 1.4.** Fifty ways to be invaded: Luffman's famous 'invasion map' (1803). The invasion lines have been over-drawn in blue. Sourced from http://www.mapforum.com/04/luffman.htm

both the confidence to act and a template for thinking through how this might be done. They can get people moving and make them more agile to adapt as events unfold.

It is interesting to relate this to trends in strategic management thinking. In the early 1990s, a lot of ink was used up debating whether strategy was driven from the top of an organization by executives, or whether it came from the bottom as good ideas emerged through the interactions of employees with one another or with different stakeholders: customers, suppliers and so on.[26] Eventually, it was agreed that this was a false dichotomy. Good ideas that could impact the whole firm could come from the lowest levels if people higher up gave them the space to emerge. In other words, strategy happens both from the top-down and from the bottom-up. Both languages are useful, particularly when used in combination. In fact, exploring both helps to appreciate the work that good middle-managers do in matching resources from lower levels with aspirations from the top (hence, it is good to have a wider cross-section of people engaged in strategy-making). Realizing the value of both perspectives on strategy led Richard Pascale to argue that there is a useful tension between strategy as designed and strategy as emergent, and that subsequently the key strategic capability is agility – the ability to discuss, make, implement, adapt and change plans faster than one's competition.[27]

Drawing strategy can promote this kind of agile thinking, by allowing a more open cross-section of people from an organization to work together to see how high-level visions or corporate philosophy might be enacted by employees relating to different stakeholders, or how a good practice being carried out in one division might be reinforced by, or be spread to, the corporate level. Furthermore, actually drawing out how your firm is relating to customers or suppliers, or how your competitors might react to your actions, encourages action to be taken: it makes it clearer that you can and must develop and adapt a strategy.

## 3. Drawing strategy promotes new thinking that builds on the shoulders of giants

Recent studies have shown how firms' increased tendency to copy best practice from competitors has led to declining margins as products and services become increasingly homogeneous and companies are left to compete on price.[28] Indeed, a similar trend may be occurring in all fields of knowledge. A recent study published in the scientific journal *Science* posited that a proclivity to read and cite only the latest research rather than scan more widely for interesting connections may be behind a decline in breakthrough

thinking.[29] So how do you encourage 'next practice' innovation that doesn't get bogged down in the detail of what is happening today and just reproduce what has gone before, but without straying away from the fundamentals?

It is no coincidence that many of the most innovative new car designs have been conceptualized as they were sketched. The Land Rover's iconic shape was born in 1947. Rover's technical director, Maurice Wilks, was holidaying in Anglesey where he was using an army surplus Willys Jeep as a utility vehicle. Impressed by its abilities, Wilks wondered if a civilian version would boost Rover's stagnant post-war sales. With a stick in the sand, he outlined his concept behind the Land Rover Defender. Similarly, while the story that the Mini took shape on the back of a napkin isn't quite correct (Alec Issigonis only used high-quality Arclight paper), its revolutionary design was worked out in pencil sketches.[30]

One powerful aspect of thinking strategically and innovatively by drawing in this way is that it can be detached from 'the database' of the past while still being grounded. An experienced draftsperson or engineer with a clean sheet can draw unhindered by the weight of what is currently in vogue, while her knowledge of the fundamentals keeps her from going completely off-beam. So often in modern organizations, the ease with which current information is at one's fingertips protracts the research process and often ends up promoting views that are heavily influenced by current 'best practice' fads, stifling real involvement in particular problems and, hence, real innovation.

Arrigo Sacchi, coach of the great AC Milan teams of the late 1980s and 1990s, spoke of his response to a similar problem: how to create an environment in which people work collectively – not as mere robots implementing predetermined plans, or as uncontrolled mavericks.

*Many believe that football is [just] about the players expressing themselves. But that's not the case. The player needs to express himself within the parameters laid out by the manager. And that's why the manager has to fill his head with as many scenarios, tools, movements, with as much information as possible. Then the player makes decisions based on that.*

*Arrigo Sacchi*

Fortunately, strategic management's history is replete with the kinds of things that Sacchi claims managers should provide to players: tools, frameworks and scenarios against which movements may be plotted.[31] Indeed, before we became so enamoured with the detailed performance modelling, strategy research was about developing tools that, as Michael Porter said, 'highlighted omitted variables, the diversity of competitive situations, the range of actual strategic choices, and the extent to which important parameters are not fixed but continually in flux… Frameworks identify the relevant variables and the questions which the user must [then] answer in order to develop [their own] conclusions'.[32] Managers could provide links to their own and the giants of their field's experience, without stifling meritocracy and creativity, by encouraging and leading, drawing upon the simple dimensions provided by strategy's best frameworks (although, as indicated in the 'opportunities' for a new approach outlined earlier, we may need a more helpful way of organizing these frameworks). Indeed, as per the drawing vs text experiment that we described on the whiteboard on page 14, those who were familiar with the Value Chain framework had significantly greater picture recall than those who did not…

## 4. Drawing strategy enables effective prototyping and 'design thinking'

Despite a myriad of more technologically advanced options, ideas, for most designers, are often first articulated in a sketch. According to Gert Hilderbrand, lead designer at BMW: 'We [still] work hands on… If you can put it on a piece of paper in a simple way, it's the best argument. You can easily judge Yes or No immediately. You cannot be cheated.'[33] In other words, the drawing is the fastest and cheapest and most flexible form of prototyping.

Perhaps the biggest 'new idea' to emerge in strategic management recently is 'design thinking', and a key aspect of design thinking is the notion of effectively prototyping management ideas in the way a designer would do with a new product.[34] While those who promote design thinking don't outline one particular method by which this should be done, we believe that drawing a strategy can be a form of prototyping that can engage people and inspire better strategic decisions. One can see how a change in one part of the organization will need to be supported by other parts, how a change in the product mix or bundling offerings might stave off competition, or unwittingly create new opportunities for competitors to exploit.

## 5. Drawing helps you see what you think and enables new possibilities to come into view

In a classic article, Karl Weick outlined how stochastic practices like medicine or management or mechanical engineering are different from many other fields of knowledge. In these fields, effective practice is not about thinking before acting or independently of action, but acting and thinking in unison.[35] As he outlines: 'Medicinal diagnosticians do not follow the sequence: observe symptom, make diagnosis, prescribe treatment. Instead they… observe symptom, prescribe treatment, make diagnosis. They can diagnose… only after they see how [the disease] responds to treatment, not before.' Weick writes of how the action of developing drawings and maps creates meaning, animates debate and facilitates shared diagnoses and action in organizations. Weick goes on to explain that: 'The world of the manager is senseless until [someone] produces some action that can be inspected… you can't make sense of a situation until you have something tangible to interpret.' In this way, drawing strategy not only enables you to prototype and test ideas – the act of drawing what you are trying to do can enable new, unforeseen opportunities to come into view.

When asked to explain the idea that led to 'total football', a strategy that revolutionized soccer, Dutch coach Rinus Michels claimed that: 'In starting, you have no exact idea about the aims after which you are going to strive.' In a sense, he went on to explain, you simply start by trying a few things, and if you are observant and are open to good influences and can connect ideas to one another as things unfold, then a good strategy starts to become clear.[36] There has never been a better articulation of this idea than Alfred Polgar's description in his obituary of famous Austrian footballer Matthias Sindelar: 'In a way he had brains in his legs… and many remarkable and unexpected things occurred to them while they were running.'[37] While we may lack this level of artistry, many of the best strategic ideas we have been a part of have occurred only as a group's emergent thoughts were whiteboarding.

## 6. Drawing can bring people together to enable collective understanding

One such idea was 'What's your problem New Zealand?' WYPNZ? was an idea developed by a group of young scientists as an attempt to better connect their organization (a government-funded entity empowered to help firms apply science to add value to their capabilities) to the commercial realities faced by their clients. New Zealand businesses were invited to submit the biggest problems that they faced that might be solved by the clever application of science. A prize of NZ$1 million (around US$900,000) of free research would be offered to the company judged to have the most interesting (but potentially solvable) problem. The prize was won by a paint company seeking to make a commercially viable paint from sustainable materials. But far more important for everyone else concerned was the fact that the companies that submitted an entry were then invited to sit down with the research organization to discuss their problem so as to improve their submission.[38] In talking with these potential clients, and particularly by getting together and sketching ideas, they became partners rather than customers. Relationships were developed, problems were shared, and confidence that problems could be tackled increased. This created a shared adversity that led to social bonds that would have been difficult to gain through writing a report together or viewing a slide presentation of what the company could do for clients. Many of these companies went on to win grants they would not have done without the greater articulation that came from those meetings.

Indeed, a recent McKinsey study found that only 45% of executives were satisfied with their strategic planning process, while only 23% claimed that major strategic decisions were actually taken within their processes. The remedy proposed was to involve executives in conversations that started with debating the issues rather than the numbers.[39] Drawing with a group can help this kind of approach. It can also help with what the authors of *The Where, The Why and the How* call that 'period of wonder and funny guesses' that used to draw people into a discussion – before people could connect to the internet and use a world of facts to close down debate with 'the right answers' or information overload.[40]

Most strategy communication involves either excessive amounts of predetermined answers or insufficient information, resulting in little shared or collective knowledge being developed, and subsequently low communicative efficiency. Drawing strategy with a small cross-section of employees and other stakeholders can take organizations to higher degrees of communicative effectiveness by allowing a useful amount of information to blend with uncertainty to build into shared knowledge and interest. Simon Collins and Hadley Smith, founders of Visory, a company that helps firms develop graphical representation of key data, claim that the biggest gains from good strategy graphics are often social: 'Pictures enable people to share ideas more easily and have a really productive chat about where their organization is going.' Or, as Confucius apparently put it (although some attribute the saying to Benjamin Franklin), 'Tell me and I'll forget. Show me and I'll remember. Involve me and I'll understand.'

To summarize, another key strength of drawing strategy is that it can help to get you to the communicative high-point expressed in Figure 1.5, Massironi's three-dimensional model of the communication, from *The Psychology of Graphic Images*.[41]

## 7. Drawing strategy can move people beyond the 'boilerplate' and numerical short-termism

Focusing on short-term financial gain at the expense of longer-term and more difficult to measure benefits has for some time been an enemy of strategic thinking.

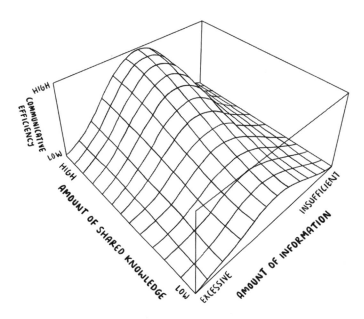

Labels in figure:
HIGH — LOW — COMMUNICATIVE EFFICIENCY
HIGH — LOW — AMOUNT OF SHARED KNOWLEDGE
EXCESSIVE — INSUFFICIENT — AMOUNT OF INFORMATION

**Figure 1.5.** Massironi's Matrix: optimum communication = graphics (adapted from Massironi's *Psychology of Graphic Images*, drawn by Rebecca Walthall)

The focus on short-term numbers may, in fact, be more prominent in strategy research nowadays. Recent studies have noted a significant increase in articles in the highly ranked strategic management journals aimed at developing equations and algorithms that appear to lead to greater performance (despite the fact that, even if such equations were discovered, they would become less valuable as copycatting would lead to them becoming the norm and new sources of advantage would need to be sought).[42] As Richard Whittington recently noted, this performance obsession in research is happening at a time when firms may be inspired to look more broadly at social, environmental and other measures. Indeed, Whittington encourages researchers to worry less about narrowing the focus on financial performance in for-profit companies, or what he calls 'small strategy', and more about the effects of wider issues and impact, or 'big strategy'. Seeing strategy as the big picture and not just the short-term numbers can help with this.[43]

Many of the views being addressed in Britain at present with regard to a revised UK Corporate Governance Code get to the nub of this problem. The Chairman's preface to the revised Code hopes that it 'might be a turning point in attacking the fungus of "boiler-plate" which is so often the preferred and easy option in sensitive areas, but which is dead communication'.[44] Reporting on subsequent discussions, an article in the *Financial Times*, 'Investors want you to tell a better story', argued that the task for leaders in the light of the new code was to recognize that current modes of communicating strategy:

> *drowning in technical measurements – total shareholder returns, earnings per share, economic value added… fail to answer the much more important and basic questions: why do you exist? What are you trying to do?… The task [now] is to communicate the character of your company. Stop hiding behind massaged figures and intricate PowerPoint slides. Tell us a story about your business that people can believe in.*[45]

A good drawing of your company's strategy could help you to paint such a story. As another executive whose drawings we will feature further on in this book put it: 'What got us over getting lost in the short-view was broad agreement on a really simple picture of where we wanted to be in 2030. A picture of what winning would look like for us.'

# WHAT STRATEGY BUILDER DOES

Most people find the way that strategy is communicated and developed off-putting and disengaging. However, this isn't the case when people discuss and draw strategic ideas and developments collectively at a whiteboard. This makes sense: people like being involved in building things. Rather than dwell on strategy's negative connotations, we have identified a range of opportunities for a revolutionary way of developing and communicating strategy. The strengths of drawing make it an ideal vehicle with which to respond to these opportunities.

Drawing can be an alternative to conventional strategy presentation: a third mode of pictorializing strategy that could provide a missing link between overwrought Word documents and oversimplified PowerPoints. Drawing can aid collective understanding in ways that can help break down conventional barriers between people who should feel engaged in strategy development and implementation. The ability to convey complex ideas and new possibilities through drawing has already been proved in other spheres. Drawing's potential for promoting innovation based on proven frameworks and prototyping fits well with new directions in how we teach business, such as design thinking. Finally, the fact that drawings can aid memory retention and promote good decision-making and an action orientation could be a useful way of overcoming the overload and subsequent inertia that can stem from people feeling overwhelmed with information relating to strategic plans, theories and ideas. What is needed is a drawing approach for building strategy that captures the necessary aspects of complexity, the fundamentals of good practice, and allows some creativity while keeping things simple. And this is what the Strategy Builder does. Its strategy for doing so is in four parts:

- Based on our experience of working with proven strategy frameworks over the past 25 years, we have chosen to focus on only the 25 most useful classic and new frames for drawing and discussing strategy, rather than 50, 80+ or 101.

- Strategy frameworks are often presented to a reader in a random fashion or in terms of the chapters in a textbook in which they appear. We have arranged the best frameworks into a logical sequence that will help you build a strategy from the ground up.

- Twenty-five may be a less daunting number than 101, but it is still too many for an active manager to retain. So we have grouped the 25 into five key categories or foundations ('environment', 'positioning', 'resources and capabilities', 'growth options' and 'goal-setting') and created forms that capture the best elements of the frameworks in each category. Distilling in this way means that a builder of effective strategies (i.e. you and your team) only need keep five meta-frameworks in mind: the Environmental Ecosystem, the Positioning Spidergram, the Capability Radar, the Growth Options Heatmap and the Balanced Goals Envelope. Each of the five foundations, the frameworks within each category and the meta-frames are presented in the Strategy Builder in a logical sequence to enable you to build a strategy step by step and see your building taking shape.

- Finally, we show you how you can actually draw with these frameworks, rather than just reproducing them or cutting and pasting them in their generic form. We illustrate this blueprinting method by applying all of the frameworks we have selected and developed to draw the strategies of a range of real-case organizations. Then we provide space and a range of tips to encourage you to draw strategies which are familiar to you using each framework. And, once you feel you have mastered this general approach, the final section of the book shows how you can develop your own individualized drawings based on a set of simple underlying principles, illustrated with reference to drawings by innovative organizations and managers that we have followed and worked with.

**PROBLEM:** People like strategy but feel overwhelmed by it or uninvolved in it. Organizations subsequently underperform due to poor strategic engagement and implementation

**OPPORTUNITIES:**

1. Need a method that overcomes strategy overload and inertia

2. Need an approach that builds on old and fits with new ideas in business e.g., innovation, design thinking

3. Need a way to simply convey complex ideas and possibilities

4. Need a way that breaks down distance barriers/separation between managers

5. Need a third way between simplistic PowerPoints and wordy documents

**Strengths of DRAWING strategy**

1. Enables greater memory retention
2. Promotes more effective decision-making and action orientation

3. Encourages grounded innovation
4. And promotes pre-build prototyping

5. Drawing helps <u>see</u> your thinking... and thus uncovers new possibilities

6. Drawing aids collective engagement

7. Drawing is an alternative to conventional approaches to strategy presentation

## = Strategy Builder

1 → SELECT ONLY the MOST USEFUL CLASSIC AND NEW STRATEGY FRAMEWORKS

2 → ARRANGE THEM INTO CATEGORIES THAT FOLLOW A LOGICAL 'BUILD' PROGRESSION

3 → COMBINE EACH CATEGORY'S FRAMES INTO A SEQUENCE OF EASY-TO-RECALL 'BEST OF' FRAMES

4 → SHOW HOW TO DRAW 'REAL LIFE' STRATEGIES WITH THESE FRAMEWORKS, MAKE IT EASY FOR PEOPLE TO BUILD AND COMMUNICATE EFFECTIVE STRATEGIES

## Liberated by Drawing Strategy

The two-part exercise we use to start our executive programmes on strategy begins with us asking participants to take a piece of paper and outline their firm's strategy on it. Many, even the most seasoned, executives struggle with this task. Almost every participant in every course represents their strategy in words. For some reason (habit, we suspect) this is the default mode of communication in strategy. Subsequently, many find the exercise difficult and frustrating.

Having written their strategy, we then ask the participants to draw it instead. Most find this idea invigorating. Executives, in our experience, certainly go about drawing strategy with greater gusto and it almost always leads to a greater willingness to share their strategies and allows others in the group to probe and discuss them.

Hopefully, many readers will have begun to think about how they might represent their strategies by drawing them and will have found this idea similarly liberating.

What we then move on to do in those programmes – and what we do next in this book – is outline frameworks and tips that can build upon this desire to draw strategically. We start with SWOT, elements of which have been utilized throughout this chapter, and which provides a thread through the middle sections of this book. SWOT is much-maligned, we believe, because people use it poorly and as merely a text tool rather than a drawing framework. We begin the next part of the book showing how you might use it more graphically and more effectively, before moving on to show how you could do likewise with a number of familiar and not-so-familiar strategy frameworks that can help you build and communicate strategies that actually work.

We see an increasing number of CEOs and strategy directors (CSOs) drawing instead upon aspects of frameworks that they feel are particularly relevant to the specific situations of their organizations and their audiences rather than slavishly applying generic models. We believe this is valuable and Strategy Builder shows that drawing strategy in this way engages its users and releases creative possibilities. There is a purpose behind Strategy Builder's design, therefore, as it moves along a continuum from informing or reminding you of the possibilities offered by classic to the most modern strategy frameworks, to inspiring you to relax some of the assumptions of those frameworks in order to allow you to customize to your own situations and to introduce creativity into your thinking. And then, in the final section of the book, we encourage you to create your own customized and engaging strategy blueprints to convey your particular insights to your specific audiences.

# PART TWO
# DESIGN

# PART 2 CONTENTS

## I. ENVIRONMENTAL ECOLOGY

## II. COMPETITIVE POSITIONING

# III. RESOURCES & CAPABILITIES

# IV. STRATEGIC GROWTH OPTIONS

# V. MANAGING PERFORMANCE STRATEGICALLY

# USER'S GUIDE TO THE STRATEGY BUILDER'S FRAMEWORK PROFILES

As the preceding contents pages show, we have selected what are, in our experience (and reflective of a number of recent independent surveys), the 26 best frameworks for developing and communicating strategy graphically. We have arranged each of these into five categories that follow a logical linear progression:

1. Environmental analysis
2. Competitive positioning
3. Capability development
4. Growth options
5. Strategic goal development.

Each of these five Strategy Builder 'blocks' contains five strategy frameworks and each framework is outlined across six pages in this 'design' section of *Strategy Builder*.

**Page 1** introduces and outlines the framework, lists its author and global rating, states when it is best to use it and lists its constituent parts.

**Page 2** describes the historical development of the framework and what the 'key takeouts' are that you should seek to gain by using it.

**Page 3** contains a worked example that actually tells the story of a strategy through the lens of the framework. In our experience, such drawings when seen (or even better drawn) really help managers to understand what a framework is about and its possibilities.

**Page 4** provides space and tips to encourage drawing your own strategy or strategic ideas using the frame in focus with the worked example on the facing page as inspiration.

**Page 5** lists the common pitfalls that users may encounter with the framework, how the framework might be used in conjunction with others for multi-level analysis, how it could be merged with other frameworks for specific purposes; and links to extra information sources.

**Page 6** provides space for you to insert further notes and drawings.

While each of the frameworks are worth knowing in their own right and will add value to any strategist's toolkit, we do not expect that a working manager will be able to recall all of them at any one time. So to aid the development of strategies grounded in the best thinking while on the go we have taken the best or most essential features of the frameworks in each block to create one 'best of' foundational drawing aid for each section. Hence, if you are on the move, as you probably are most of the time, you only need remember our five 'best of' frames to begin to build or remodel and communicate a strategy. These foundations are:

1. The Environmental Ecosystem
2. The Competitive Spidergram
3. The Capability Radar
4. The Growth Options Heatmap
5. The Balanced Goals Envelope.

These five foundations are described at the end of each 'block' section, and in Part 3 of *Strategy Builder* we bring them together into an integrated model for developing and communicating strategy quickly and effectively on a single page.

## Design features

Throughout the six page spreads, we have incorporated a number of features designed to enhance your working knowledge and ability to use and communicate with that framework in order to build more effective strategies. These features include:

### 1. World ratings and rankings

In a notepad in the top right corner of page 1 is a note on how the framework rates in terms of popularity and user satisfaction. This assessment draws on four recent studies:

- A 2009 study published by the United Kingdom's Advanced Institute of Management Research (AIM) entitled *Building a Strategy Toolkit*.

- An Aston University study by Tapinos, Dyson and Meadows on framework usage, published in 2011.

- Bain & Company's annual *Management Tools and Trends* survey (2013).

- He, António and Rosa's (2012) study, 'Strategic tools in China/strategic tools: An investigation into strategy in practice in China', published in the *African Journal of Business Management*, 6(26), 7823–7832.

### 2. Simple, matter-of-fact explanations

The rest of pages 1 and 2 contains a standard diagrammatic interpretation of the framework and three brief descriptions:

- *when* to use it – people often fail to get value from drawing strategy by employing a good framework at the wrong time and for the wrong task;

- *what* it is composed of – a second problem is that users are often unsure about the elements in a framework and the relations between them;

- on page 2, *why* and *how* it was developed – understanding a framework's past provides guidance and insight into how it can best be used in the present.

### 3. A 'real-life' storyboard and storyline

Most people who want to do strategy better are practical and theoretical people, but they tend to be able to understand the theory better if they can see it in practice. On page 3 we go multi-modal to depict a strategy 'storyboard', with a large drawing of the framework creatively applied to depict a strategy or strategic options for a real organization above a 'storyline' that embellishes the picture with a text description.

To illustrate each framework in this way, we've chosen a range of recent and 'classic' strategy examples from the past. And for the most part, we've tried to use organizations whose products or services you will be familiar with and interested in (apart from a few public sector examples, lesser-known and smaller organizations or start-ups to provide a range). We have selected all of our examples because, in our classroom experience, they are excellent instructional and inspirational exemplars.

In some instances we have disguised identities, particularly where the information on which our interpretations are based is not public knowledge or is not in the public domain already, and it is also important to remember that for the most part these are our – or our students' – interpretations of firms' strategies; **they do not necessarily reflect the explicit strategies of the organizations.**

We've also taken some liberties (or been creative) with the frameworks, drawing for the sake of communicating ideas rather than always being truly representative of the framework in question, in much the same way that Harry Beck's Tube map does as we explained in Part 1 of *Strategy Builder*. As always, the problem we are seeking to address, and the number one criterion we use for selection, is as follows: Will this example and this interpretation interest the reader in strategy, help them understand and make them want to engage further?

It is for this reason, too, that the pictures are hand-drawn and done using common items that you might find on your desk or in your briefcase: a pencil, a biro and a highlighter pen.

### 4. Space

Facing page 3 in each four-page spread is space. Most of page 4 is left blank, or rather as blank graph paper to encourage the reader to go multi-modal by drawing as well as reading. American notebook manufacturer FieldNotes' motto is 'I'm not writing it down to remember it later, I'm writing it down to remember it now', and we take the same view here. Drawing while reading about these frameworks makes them 'stick'.

After a lifetime of being told not to draw on books, those of a certain age (like us) may find drawing on these pages difficult at first. But we have found that drawing while reading about strategy is an essential part of the learning process, and once you've drawn on the book once, it gets easier (use a pencil if you are still not comfortable). Moreover, the Strategy Builder website provides access to a specially designed graph paper page that includes blank graph paper above for drawing and blank 'storyline' boxes below for text elaboration, in the form of the template used in page 3, that you can print off, draw on, fold up and place in your book. As authors we would be very pleased if your copy of this book were to become more and more overwritten and overdrawn and stuffed with notes and scribbles and extra pages as it ages.

## 5. Drawing tips: for getting started, enhancing your creativity and key 'take-outs'

Underneath the space for your renditions and ideas on page 4, there is a series of notepaper pages. The first few contain tips for drawing aimed at helping you to get started. The remainder contain a list of ideas to encourage creative developments upon the basic 'shape' of the framework. A further difficulty that users of strategy frameworks often encounter is that somewhere in the process of using them they lose sight of the output. They end up with wrong answers or a lot of extraneous information that adds unnecessary complexity and makes arriving at conclusions further down the track more difficult than it needs be.

## 6. Common pitfalls

Page 5 comprises four elements designed to take your knowledge of the framework further. The first is a list of common mistakes that users of this framework make. Knowing these can help you avoid them.

## 7. Menu suggestions for fruitful combinations

Like food and wine, some frameworks just go well together, but if you're new to the game it can be hard to be cognizant of the best combinations. Here we provide some suggestions for good 'matches'.

## 8. Mutation possibilities

Beyond being used as a set, some frameworks can be effectively mutated or grafted together to provide creative hybrids. So we provide some guidance here on the best grafting options for each framework.

## 9. Signposts towards further knowledge

As strategists we are all attracted to some frameworks, or find them more useful than others (reflective of this are the quotations sprinkled through the pages of this section from famous strategists relating their particular preferences and predilections). So, if you want to explore a particular framework further, we provide a list at the bottom of page 5 of what we consider to be the best classic and recent articles and books on each framework, so that you may advance your knowledge of them further.

These nine features are apparent throughout each of the 25 strategy frameworks covered in this section of Strategy Builder, and are also reflected in the presentation of the five 'best of' tools that we have developed to capture the key elements of our five strategy building blocks. But at the outset we mentioned 26 frameworks: $5 \times 5 = 25$. So what is our 26th player and how does it fit in?

Our 26th framework is strategy's most popular tool: SWOT analysis. We will present it first, ahead of the other main frameworks.

SWOT is, and has been for the past four decades, the most utilized and the most maligned of all ideas in strategic management. It is the most utilized largely because it can be remembered and simply applied. It is the most maligned because it is so often poorly and overly simplistically used, leading to strategic confusion rather than clarity. Rather than throw the baby out with the bathwater, we want to utilize it, only better.

SWOT's biggest flaw, in our opinion, is that it's used as a text list in a linear fashion – not as a dynamic diagram. In our first framework treatment in Strategy Builder we seek to show how it can be used to better effect if expressed graphically.

In this way, SWOT becomes the starting point of this Design section of Strategy Builder, and an opening illustration of how a few drawn lines can add value when building and communicating strategy. Further on, its elements will become a familiar backbone that runs through the five strategy building blocks to follow.

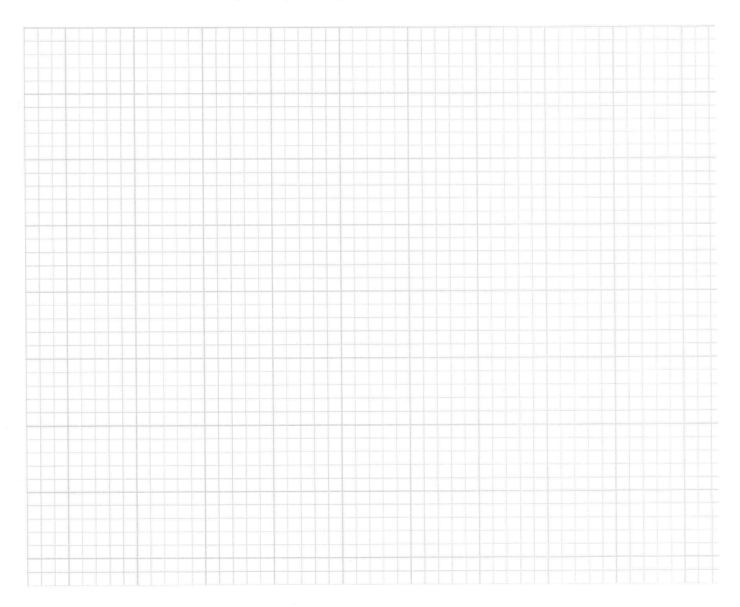

## 1. The Strengths and Weaknesses of SWOT

## AUTHOR: Multiple

# S
# W
# O
# T

**RATINGS:** AIM's most popular strategy tool (used by nearly 80% of all companies surveyed and consistently across all industries), ranked number one in its Practioners' Core Toolkit. The Aston study's most popular strategy tool (used by 65%), and second only to PEST (political, economic, social, technological) in Chinese firms (59%). Other studies name it number one in Australia, New Zealand, Malaysia, Singapore, the UK and Finland. However, AIM found that it rates low for 'implementation' and, while popular, it has middling 'perceived value', indicating that people are unsure what to do with its outcomes. Despite its popularity, detractors claim it is dangerously superficial.

**WHEN TO USE:** Excellent for assessing the fit between an organization and its context. The assumption is that an organization in alignment with its context will survive better than one which is not.

**COMPONENTS:** SWOT summarizes environmental opportunities (i.e. opportunities beyond the firm's boundaries), environmental threats (i.e. threats beyond the firm's boundaries), internal strengths and internal weaknesses.

## DEVELOPMENT:

The historical background of the perennial no. 1 strategy framework is not altogether clear. Some attribute SWOT to the 1965 Harvard Business School book *Business Policy* by Learned, Christensen, Andrews and Guth. However, this only refers to opportunities, risks, environment and problems, and cites Prof. Kenneth Andrewes' lecture notes as inspiration. Another view is that SWOT stemmed from a Stanford study funded by a panel of Fortune 500 companies begun in 1960 and carried out by a team of academics led by Albert Humphrey. By 1960 every Fortune company had a 'corporate planning manager', and 'associations of long range corporate planners' had formed in the USA and in Europe. The Stanford study sought to determine why corporate planning often failed between the thinking and doing of strategy and how to address this. Based on the emerging research findings, team member Otis Benepe defined an eight-step 'chain of logic' as the core of a new system. The first two steps focused on getting the corporate *values* right and conducting a good *appraisal* of the business situation. Finding that a method for determining values was difficult to develop, the team decided to focus on appraisal, developing an approach that began by asking what is good and bad about the present and the future. What was good in the present was 'satisfactory'. Good in the future was an 'opportunity'. Bad in the present was a 'fault'. Bad in the future was a 'threat'. This became SOFT analysis. SOFT was presented at a conference in Zurich in 1964. British delegates Urick and Orr took the framework and changed the F to a W. They then promoted SWOT in Britain where it was used in a number of high-profile cases. This was increasingly applied in the US too. Urick, Orr, Humphrey and Benepe realized that the superficial use of SWOT as a list had little value and developed an additional approach for sorting what came out of a SWOT analysis into the following categories: product (What are we selling?); process (How are we selling it?); customer (To whom are we selling it?); distribution (How does it reach them?); finance (What are the prices, costs and investments?); administration (And how do we manage all this?). While this failed to catch on, their categories are very similar to those used in recent popular books like *Business Model Generation*.

**Key Takeout:**

→ A summary of the key Opportunities, Threats, Strengths and Weaknesses influencing your development of strategy.

In the strategy framework outlines in the following pages we will provide a 'worked example' of each framework in action, applied to a real organization, to help illustrate how it can be used, and inspire you to use it too. Part of this example will be a 'storyline' that explains the flow of the pictures. Here, though, the storyline is up to you. Jot down the key Os and Ts and Ss and Ws that should influence your organization's strategy into the SWOT graphic.

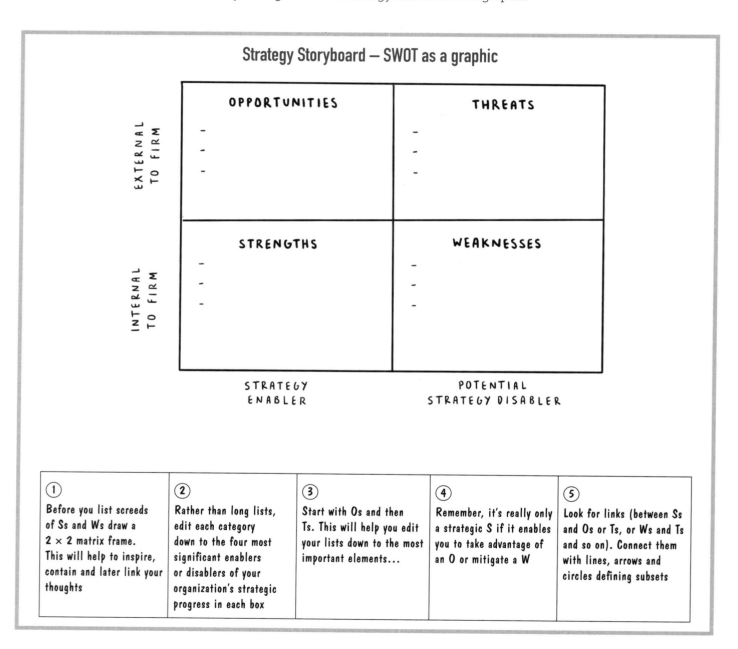

## Strategy Storyboard — SWOT as a graphic

|  | OPPORTUNITIES | THREATS |
|---|---|---|
| EXTERNAL TO FIRM | - <br> - <br> - | - <br> - <br> - |
| INTERNAL TO FIRM | STRENGTHS <br> - <br> - <br> - | WEAKNESSES <br> - <br> - <br> - |
|  | STRATEGY ENABLER | POTENTIAL STRATEGY DISABLER |

| ① | ② | ③ | ④ | ⑤ |
|---|---|---|---|---|
| Before you list screeds of Ss and Ws draw a 2 × 2 matrix frame. This will help to inspire, contain and later link your thoughts | Rather than long lists, edit each category down to the four most significant enablers or disablers of your organization's strategic progress in each box | Start with Os and then Ts. This will help you edit your lists down to the most important elements... | Remember, it's really only a strategic S if it enables you to take advantage of an O or mitigate a W | Look for links (between Ss and Os or Ts, or Ws and Ts and so on). Connect them with lines, arrows and circles defining subsets |

### COMMON PITFALLS:

- While SWOT is a catchy acronym, listing strengths and weaknesses before opportunities and threats can lead to a lot of redundancy and a subsequent lack of time spent on the other two categories or, worse, myopia – seeing the world though one's own eyes rather than for what it is. It is far more useful to do an OTSW, as focusing on current Os and Ts first will make it easier to identify the most relevant Ss and Ws.
- SWOT is mostly used to generate a list – and as Part 1 of this book demonstrated, relationships are hard to see in linear lists, as they don't show relationships between and across points. If there is no interrogation of these relations then there is little value in SWOT.

Both of these pitfalls can be addressed by viewing OTSW in graphical terms: by creating a matrix that sets Os and Ts against Ss and Ws, so that you can discuss relationships and, subsequently, potential strategic developments (as we have done on the previous page). This simple step can turn SWOT analysis from a superficial weakness in a strategic analysis to a strength. And, in general terms, unlike others who argue that SWOT's limitations should consign it to the scrapheap, we believe that SWOT's continued popularity and resonance point to something well worth keeping in a strategy 'framekit'. As we shall see, if used well, it can provide an excellent backbone upon which we can use the best classic and new frameworks to build strategies that can orient and animate your organization.

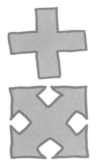

**GOOD IN COMBINATION WITH/MUTATION POTENTIAL:** The major potential for enhancing SWOT is by rendering it graphically (as on the following page) and using it to group and summarize outputs from the other analytical frameworks that we outline in the pages that follow, something that we encourage you to do throughout the remainder of this book and which will come to particular fruition in block IV's summary framework, the Growth Options Heatmap. By contrast, there is little value in adding to SWOT's four dimensions or directly blending its components with other frameworks into new configurations.

### INFO FOR FURTHER READING:

- Piercy, N. and Giles, W. (1989). Making SWOT analysis work. *Marketing Intelligence & Planning*, 7(5/6), 5–7.
- Hill, T. and Westbrook, R. (1997). SWOT analysis: it's time for a product recall. *Long Range Planning*, 30(1), 46–52.
- Pickton, D.W. and Wright, S. (1998). What's SWOT in strategic analysis? *Strategic Change*, 7(2), 101–109.

**FIELD NOTES:**

# ENVIRONMENTAL ECOLOGY

**Purpose:** Environmental ecology frameworks help to analyse the environmental opportunities and threats facing your organization in greater depth.

2. **ESTEMPLE** – Enables evaluation of the impact of past, present and future macro-environmental forces on a firm's strategic development.

3. **The power/interest matrix** – Helps analyse the relative importance of a firm's stakeholders on strategic development and subsequently determine the most appropriate stakeholder relationships for each.

4. **Diamond of international competitiveness** – Can aid in determining the relative strategic environmental advantages of particular nations or regions.

5. **The five forces of industry** – Studying the combined power of the five forces helps to explore whether an industry is an attractive one, with high average margins for competitors operating in it, or not.

6. **The industry life cycle curve** – A depiction of how industries tend to change over time, to exhibit particular opportunities or threats, whether in an uncertain introductory period, high-growth early phase, maturity or decline.

## 2. ESTEMPLE

**AUTHOR:** Duncan Angwin (building upon earlier acronyms such as **PEST** and **PESTLE**)

TIME

DRIVERS OF CHANGE

> ECONOMIC
> SOCIAL
> TECHNOLOGICAL
> ECOLOGICAL
> MEDIA
> POLITICAL
> LEGAL
> ETHICAL

**RATINGS:** AIM rates PESTLE as the ninth most used tool (used by >30%). This rises to 42% for public and not-for-profit organizations. AIM's highest ranking tool for strategy analysis. PEST rated number 10 in the UK by Aston study. He et al.'s (2012) study rates it number one in China (60%), just ahead of SWOT. Like SWOT, ESTEMPLE has much lower ratings for implementation.

**WHEN TO USE:** To evaluate the impact of past, present and future macro-environmental forces on a firm's strategic development.

**COMPONENTS:** The letters stand for the following eight key categories in the macro-environment that can impact on a firm's strategy: economic, social, technological, ecological, media, legal and ethical.

## DEVELOPMENT:

ESTEMPLE is a development and update of PEST (political, economic, social, technological) analysis, which has been widely applied since the 1970s when there was less awareness of the aspects added by ESTEMPLE (e.g. ecological and media impact). PEST was the first widely used generic framework for determining the environmental opportunities and threats with which earlier theorists had claimed a firm's internal strengths and weaknesses should be matched. The provenance of PEST is difficult to discern, but in the late 1960s Francis Aguilar outlined 'ETPS' – for economic, technical, political and social – as sectors of his taxonomy for analysing the business environment. This was later changed to the mnemonic STEP. From the 1980s, several other authors advocated variations, such as PEST and PESTLE. Why the negative sounding PEST has proven to be more popular than STEP, which is no longer heard of, is unclear. There is no implied order or priority in any of the formats; however, it is important, once the opportunities and threats in each category have been outlined, to ascribe a relative value and ranking to each of the categories in terms of their likely impact on the strategy of the firm in question, so that potential strategic actions to take advantage of, or mitigate, environmental forces can be more effectively rated.

## Key Takeouts:

➔ What are the two or three elements in your ESTEMPLE that you think will provide the biggest opportunities for strategic development? And the two or three biggest threats?

➔ Note these Os and Ts and keep them clearly in focus throughout your strategy development process!

# Morocco Oil: Opportunities to be seized (*c.* 2012*)

| | ENVIRONMENTAL DRIVERS | T1 | T2 | T3 | T4 | |
|---|---|---|---|---|---|---|
| E | FAVOURABLE GDP GROWTH. INFLATION DOWN. HIGH INWARD INVESTMENT | ⑤ | ⑤ | ⑤ | ③ | ↘ |
| E | LOCAL CURRENCY APPRECIATING | 0 | -1 | -2 | -2 | ↗ |
| S | HIGHER CAR USE. GROWING AFFLUENCE & DISPOSABLE INCOMES | ② | ② | ③ | ③ | ↗ |
| T | INVESTMENT IN TIGHTER CONTROLS. SPECIFICATIONS. TECHNIQUES | ② | 0 | ① | ① | → |
| E | INCREASING EMISSION RESTRICTIONS. POOR WEATHER AFFECTING CONSUMPTION | -2 | -3 | -3 | -2 | → |
| M | INCREASINGLY ATTACKED SOCIALLY (BIG FOREIGN BUSINESS) & ENVIRONMENTALLY | -2 | -3 | -3 | -2 | → |
| P | STABLE DOMESTIC REGIME & DOMESTIC POLICIES HELPING INVESTMENT | ④ | ④ | ④ | ④ | → |
| P | UNSTABLE MIDDLE EAST INFLATES OIL PRICES | ④ | ④ | ③ | ② | ↘ |
| L | NEW CODES & RESTRICTIONS BUT SLOW TO TAKE EFFECT | -1 | -1 | -2 | -3 | ↗ |
| E | CORRUPTION & LACK OF TRANSPARENCY INTENSIFY COMPETITION & INTERNATIONAL PRESSURES | -2 | -2 | -3 | -3 | ↗ |

◎ POTENTIAL OPPORTUNITY　　▨ POTENTIAL THREAT　　↗ TREND

| ① | ② | ③ | ④ | ⑤ |
|---|---|---|---|---|
| The macro-environment offers Morocco Oil real strategic opportunities | Economic, social and political conditions present strong opportunities for growth | But clouds are gathering — ecological, legal, media and ethical threats loom further into the future | Opportunities, while strong now, may also be declining by T4. Decisive strategic action should be taken | Develop strategy around exploiting E, S and P opportunities and mitigating coming Eth, M, L and Ec threats |

* The identity of this organization has been disguised.

**DRAW YOUR OWN HERE...**

1. Divide the paper in two. Brainstorm the macro-elements that impact on the firm on the right. Write the ESTEMPLE categories that correspond to these on the left. Then consider the remaining ESTEMPLE categories and whether there may be other important elements that relate to these.

2. You don't have to cover all the bases. If, for example, social developments and the legal environment have little impact, just do an ETEMPE.

Creative ideas:

A. Re-order your categories in terms of biggest impact. It may be that TPEEME best captures your macro-environmental opportunities and threats.

B. Some categories may have sub-categories perceived as more important than whole categories — so you could have EESTTEMPLE.

C. Probability of impacts could be displayed for different future time periods.

**COMMON PITFALLS:** Thinking that you have to create a long list for each of the categories. Some categories may not be so relevant for your industry.

Realize that some sub-categories may be more important than other full categories – do not be imprisoned by feeling the categories should be of equivalent importance. Edit so that you are left with just the most important elements, and if you have nothing particularly impactful in a category leave it out.

Not ascribing some kind of values to each of the elements of your ESTEMPLE can lead to an unwieldy mass and paralysis. You need to walk away knowing the main opportunities and threats to the industry.

**GOOD IN COMBINATION WITH:** An 'impact matrix' in order to refine the degree of impact of ESTEMPLE elements and the timing of likely impact. In addition to ranking the categories and their elements in terms of their impact, it's useful to put the findings from your ESTEMPLE into the opportunities and threats part of a SWOT matrix (no. 1). It's also good to begin an environmental analysis at the 'periphery' with an ESTEMPLE analysis at the macro level and then move in towards the organization in focus with a power/interest matrix (no. 3) at the meso level and a five forces of industry (no. 5) at the industry level to complete a holistic environmental analysis.

**MUTATION POTENTIAL:** ESTEMPLE is a simple categorization tool, so the eight categories are not necessarily connected. You can remove categories you believe are not particularly relevant to your analysis and you can add ones that you believe are more appropriate. However, avoid category inflation for the sake of it. Think hard to see if your elements cannot be brought under the existing umbrellas before creating new ones. Eight categories is right at the edge of what people can be expected to hold in their working memory over time.

**INFO FOR FURTHER READING:**
- Aguilar, F.J. (1967). *Scanning the Business Environment* (particularly pp. 69–70). New York: Macmillan.
- Angwin, D., Cummings, S. and Smith, C. (2011). *The Strategy Pathfinder: Core Concepts and Live Cases*. John Wiley & Sons, chapter 1.
- Thomas, H. (2007). An analysis of the environment and competitive dynamics of management education, *Journal of Management Development*, 26 (1): 9–21.

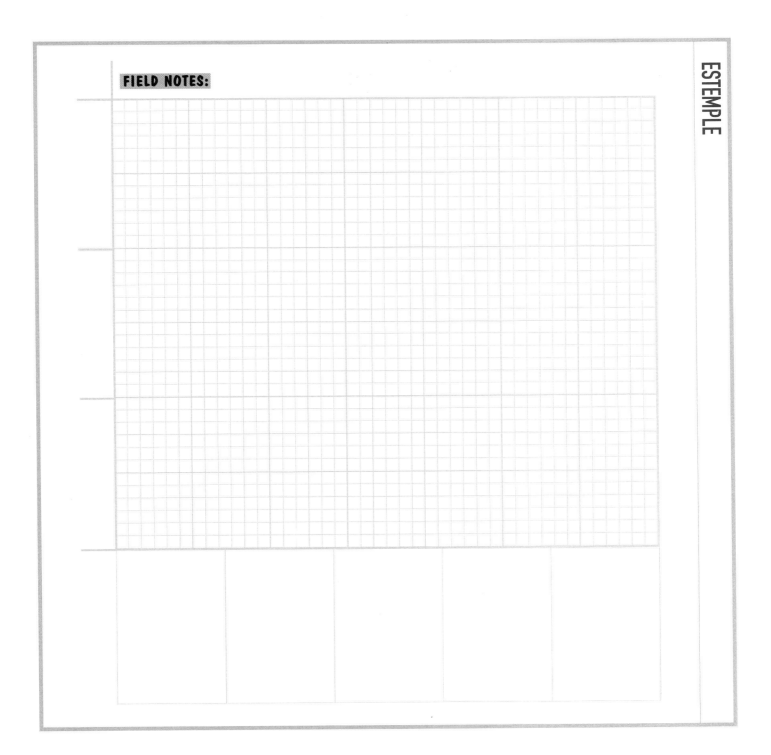

**FIELD NOTES:**

## 3. Power/Interest Matrix

## AUTHOR: Aubery Mendelow

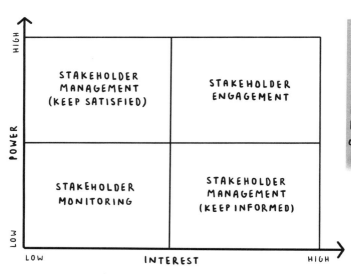

**WHEN TO USE:** To analyse the relative importance of a firm's stakeholders and subsequently determine the most appropriate stakeholder relationships for a strategy to focus on.

**COMPONENTS:** A stakeholder is an individual, group or body that has an interest in, or is affected by, an organization's strategic development. The PI matrix is a 2 × 2 matrix created by combining an x-axis charting a stakeholder's power to influence an organization's strategy and a y-axis charting a stakeholder's interest in influencing that strategy. The most strategically important stakeholders are those with high power and high interest.

## DEVELOPMENT:

Stakeholder analysis has been addressed in strategic management for decades. However, for many firms, this analysis simply entails listing all stakeholders and how the firm would satisfy their concerns. On the principle that you cannot please everybody all of the time, this often stymies rather than aids strategy development. What is needed to make effective strategic choices about how to engage with stakeholders is a way of mapping and ranking them in terms of their relationship to the firm's strategy. In the 1980s, Aubery Mendelow wrote about how strategic planning was limited in its focus on macroeconomic, industry- and resource-based analysis and developed the PI matrix to assist managers in carrying out an analysis of other influences.

The only written record of the PI matrix is a 1991 conference paper, but its intuitive logic and ease of use have seen it picked up by textbooks and in consultancy projects, variations of which include defining the 'keep satisfied' and 'keep informed' groups as only requiring 'stakeholder engagement', but the top right-hand group as requiring 'stakeholder participation'. The PI matrix is an excellent way of ensuring that elements such as employees, unions, governments, directors and shareholders in the 'meso' level between ESTEMPLE and industry forces are taken into account in a constructive fashion in an environmental ecosystem analysis.

**Key Takeout:**
→ Who are the key stakeholders to be closely involved in informing and driving your strategy development process?

## Transport Ministry: Beyond *Yes, Minister* (*c.* 2011*)

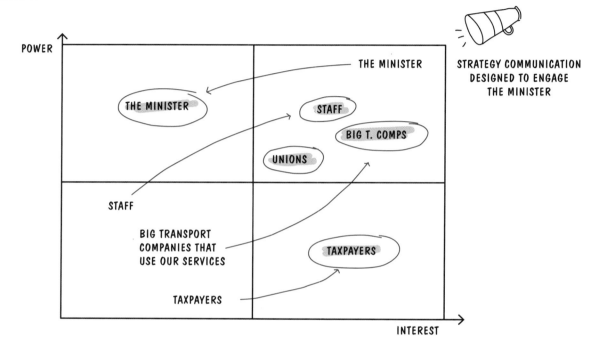

POWER

THE MINISTER

THE MINISTER

STAFF

BIG T. COMPS

UNIONS

STAFF

BIG TRANSPORT
COMPANIES THAT
USE OUR SERVICES

TAXPAYERS

TAXPAYERS

INTEREST

STRATEGY COMMUNICATION
DESIGNED TO ENGAGE
THE MINISTER

| ① | ② | ③ | ④ | ⑤ |
|---|---|---|---|---|
| Over the years the ministry has become less innovative and the staff increasingly disengaged | One source of the problem may be the perception of the key stakeholder in the M's strategy: its govt boss, the Minister of Transport | But the Minister (who has other responsibilities) only has high interest when there's a problem | So the aim should be to keep him in the top left box. This can enable a new way of thinking about stakeholders | Staff and key service users can be more engaged in strategy dev and we can think about better informing taxpayers of how their money is spent |

* The identity of this organization has been disguised.

**DRAW YOUR OWN HERE...**

1. Start with a first draft that puts all stakeholders in the top right box, and then, in a second draft, think carefully about the extent to which each group has the interest and power to influence your strategy and move stakeholders leftwards and downwards accordingly.

2. Once you have placed all stakeholders, rank them within the four boxes, with the most important at the top of the box.

Creative ideas:

Be proactive. Complete your stakeholder map by writing strategies alongside the stakeholder groups. Develop clear strategies to enable top-ranked stakeholders to participate in some way in the firm's strategic development. Develop clear strategies for keeping the top left and bottom right stakeholders informed.

### COMMON PITFALLS:

1. Poor editing. Strategy is about making choices, so edit out all but the most important and influential stakeholders from the top right box.
2. Vanity – just because an individual or group has the power to influence your strategy, you should not assume they will have the desire or time to do so. They may have more pressing strategic concerns of their own. Before placing a stakeholder in the top right box, ask yourself how often they have sought to influence your strategy in the past five years. If the answer is seldom, then they may be better left in the bottom right box.
3. Not considering that stakeholder positions may change over time.

**GOOD IN COMBINATION WITH:** Better used as a stand-alone framework in its generic form, although it can be useful to list clear objectives on an expanded PI matrix so that people can see how the organization will seek to manage stakeholder relations (see the strategy storyboard on the previous page).

**MUTATION POTENTIAL:** If your top two to three stakeholders from the matrix can be seen as part of the industry in which you are operating, you can take these and add them to a five forces of industry (no. 5) analysis to create an expanded seven or eight forces of industry framework that can be viewed and debated as part of a single framework.

### INFO FOR FURTHER READING:

- Low, C. and Cowton, C. (2004). Beyond stakeholder engagement: The challenges of stakeholder participation in corporate governance. *International Journal of Business Governance and Ethics*, 1(1), 45–55.
- Mendelow, A. (1983). Setting corporate goals and measuring organizational effectiveness – a practical approach. *Long Range Planning*, 16(1), 70–76.
- Mendelow, A. (1991). Environmental scanning: The impact of the stakeholder concept. In: *Proceedings from the Second International Conference on Information Systems*, pp. 407–418. Cambridge, MA.

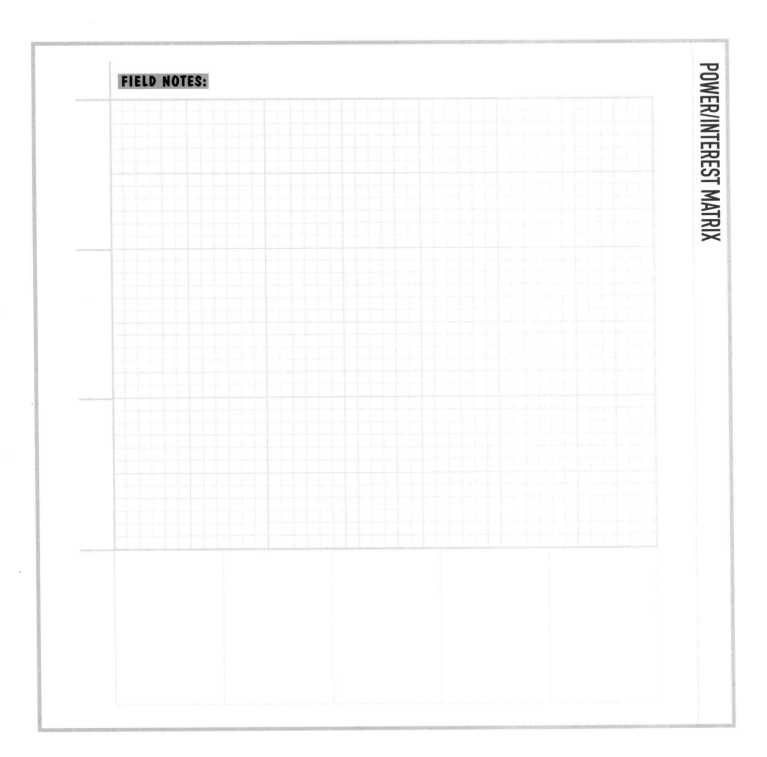

**FIELD NOTES:**

POWER/INTEREST MATRIX

## 4. Diamond of International Competitiveness

## AUTHOR: Michael Porter

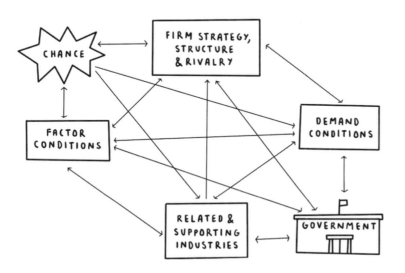

**WHEN TO USE:** To determine the environmental advantages of locating activities in particular nations or regions or to better understand the strategic opportunities and threats of your current location.

**COMPONENTS:** The horizontal line has factor conditions (conditions that aid good production) on the left, and demand conditions (conditions that aid useful buyer behaviour) on the right reflect other Porter frameworks which borrow the classic input–process–output form of the microeconomic theory of the firm. Strategy, structure and rivalry are about the Os and Ts presented by local competitors. Related/supporting industries is about local co-option (see no. 11) and synergies. Government support and the chance benefits afforded by location (e.g. proximity to major markets) make up the six elements of the diamond.

## DEVELOPMENT:

Starting with industry forces (the five forces, no. 5), and an elaboration on the traditional economist's 'black box' of what goes on within the firm to add value (the value chain, no. 7) in 1980's *Competitive Strategy*, then looking 'between' these elements to the choices that rivals face in organizing their value chains (the generic strategy matrix, no. 8) in 1985's *Competitive Advantage*, industrial economist Michael Porter went macro to examine how nations compete. The result was 1990's *Competitive Advantage of Nations*, and its explanations, through the diamond of international competitiveness, of why the Swiss excelled at watchmaking, Silicon Valley at computing and so on.

While the diamond is not as popular as Porter's earlier frames, *Competitive Advantage of Nations* built on the success of the earlier books and Porter was brought in by a variety of governments to identify and support local strategic opportunities for the good of the region's economy.

## Key Takeouts:

➔ What are the main strategic opportunities afforded by your base location?

➔ What other locations may offer advantages for your business?

# Hong Kong: The third financial capital of the world? (*c.* 2013)

**GOOD FORTUNE**
- GEOGRAPHIC LOCATION
- TIME ZONE BETWEEN NY & LONDON

**DEMAND CONDITIONS**
- MATHS OBSESSION
- INTEREST IN GAMBLING CONTRIBUTES TO HIGHLY DISCERNING CUSTOMERS

**FACTOR CONDITIONS**
- GOOD UNIS
- MANY LOCALS STUDY ABROAD
- GREAT EXPAT LOCATION
- GOOD INFRASTRUCTURE

**HONG KONG**
VERSUS
DUBAI, TOKYO, SINGAPORE

**FIRM STRATEGY, STRUCTURE, RIVALRY**
MANY FINANCE-RELATED COMPANIES OF ALL SIZES, CONFIGURATIONS, EAST & WEST ALL COMPETE IN HK

**RELATED & SUPPORTING INDUSTRIES**
MANY INSURANCE, COMMODITY COMPANIES, M&A, CONSULTANCIES, BROKERS HAVE BASES IN HK

**GOVERNMENT**

BLENDED ANGLO-SINO LEGAL/POLITICAL SYSTEM

| ① | ② | ③ | ④ | ⑤ |
|---|---|---|---|---|
| Eventually, the world may only have three main financial centres. New York and London will likely be two... | Candidates for the third include Dubai, Singapore and Tokyo. The above picture reflects a case made by a group of HK MBA students for their town | Obvious advantages are HK being home to many finance comps and HQs for many supporting industry comps | But other advs = East+West governance, geo location and a highly educated & motivated workforce | Less obvious to outsiders may be HK culture's emphasis on maths ed and gambling: understanding risk, reward, hedging etc. is ingrained |

**DRAW YOUR OWN HERE...**

1. Draw your organization in the middle of the diagram — this will make it easier to conceptualize the regional/national impacts on your strategy.

2. Break up the bottom related/supporting industries box into a number of boxes, one for each of the industries that are impacting on your analysis. Then use lines and arrows and symbols to show how they interrelate.

3. Don't worry about connecting all the diamond elements with arrows immediately, as is often the case in textbook versions of the diamond. Only draw links when they indicate relations that promote particular Os or Ts.

Creative ideas:

A. Draw multiple and combined locations/diamonds that tap selected advantages in other regions. Can you locate your operations in more than one location (e.g. production where factor costs are low and relating and supporting industries are favourable, and marketing, design where demand conditions are discerning) and then effectively combine these?

B. Double the demand box. Use demand sophistication in one location to drive demand in another (e.g. using French nationals and expat networks to sell wine in China).

**DIAMOND OF INTERNATIONAL COMPETITIVENESS**

**COMMON PITFALLS:** In the words of Robert Grant's excellent review: 'The breadth and relevance of [the diamond has] been achieved at the expense of precision and determinacy. Concepts are often ill-defined, theoretical relationships poorly specified, and empirical data chosen selectively and interpreted subjectively.' Given this, users can become frustrated if they try too hard to see the boxes and relationships as discrete and distinct or stick rigidly to its prescribed structure.

Falling prey to cultural/geographical stereotypes. The diamond should be used in combination with a good knowledge of, or advice about, the particular workings of the region in focus. In any event, it is best used as a rough guide to stimulate strategic discussion, rather than an exact representation.

**GOOD IN COMBINATION WITH:** Other environmental frameworks, such as ESTEMPLE (no. 2), the PI matrix (no. 3) and the five forces (no. 5), as a final check to scan the environmental ecosystem for opportunities and threats. If market, product or any kind of international expansion is being considered, the diamond can be used in combination with growth options frameworks such as the Ansoff's box (no. 19).

**MUTATION POTENTIAL:** The diamond's elements can be added to a five forces analysis to provide greater depth (factor conditions in addition to suppliers; government as a sixth force; related and supporting industries as another layer around competitive rivalry, etc.) and it is a useful tool for firms to analyse where they might base operations or expand into. But once one places an industry and/or a firm in the middle of the diamond to gauge the impact of the diamond's elements on these, it can become quite detailed, so joining with other frameworks can make things messy. It is perhaps best used as a stand-alone framework whose findings can be added to those from others and summarized in a SWOT.

**INFO FOR FURTHER READING:**
- Porter, M.E. (1990). The competitive advantage of notions. *Harvard Business Review*, March–April, 73–93.
- Grant, R.M. (1991). Porter's 'competitive advantage of nations': an assessment. *Strategic Management Journal*, 12(7), 535–548.
- Davies, H. and Ellis, P. (2000). Porter's competitive advantage of nations: time for the final judgement? *Journal of Management Studies*, 37(8), 1189–1214.

DIAMOND OF INTERNATIONAL COMPETITIVENESS

## 5. Five Forces of Industry

## AUTHOR: Michael Porter

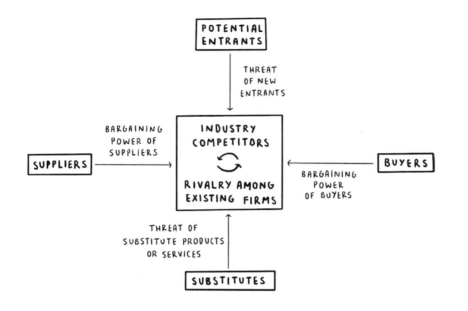

**WHEN TO USE:** 1. To evaluate the profit potential of an industry. 2. To understand which forces have the greatest influence on profitability. 3. To see how a company might influence the forces.

**COMPONENTS:** 1. The intensity of the rivalry caused by the concentration of competitors and the rate of industry growth. 2. Suppliers' power to influence the industry is determined by their strengths (e.g. relative size, ability to switch to other buyers, unique technologies). 3. Customer power (e.g. relative size, ability to switch to alternatives, degree of need). 4. Threat of new entrants: investment, cultural, political, technology barriers to entry /exit from industry. 5. Threat of substitutes to provide aspects of an industry cheaper, faster, more innovatively, healthier, etc.

## DEVELOPMENT:

In 1980's *Competitive Strategy*, Porter introduced what are still the most widely used tools for developing strategies that take advantage of or shape the industry landscape – the five forces of industry – and for analysing the strategic arrangement of the elements that constitute a firm – the value chain (no. 7). The five forces draws on the structure–conduct–performance paradigm in industrial economics to isolate the particular forces that determine an industry's 'attractiveness': an unattractive industry is one in which forces act to drive down average margins (the difference between cost of production and selling prices). It can be useful to think of the five forces as made up of three aspects: power, entry and rivalry. Power relates to the horizontal line: the power that buyers and suppliers have to influence the behaviour of competitors. Entry relates to the vertical line and is about the ease with which new players can move past barriers to entry to enter the competition, or the ease with which buyers can substitute what an industry produces with other alternatives. Rivalry relates to the box in the middle and how fierce or 'gentlemanly' is competition between organizations in the industry. The five forces is probably the graphical framework most used by business professors and MBAs, but while most can reproduce the textbook version, few are sure how to use it well to creatively analyse particular industries or strategy choices within an industry.

### Key Takeouts:
➜ Which forces have the biggest impact on your industry?
➜ What does it take to survive and thrive in this industry?

# Dell: A new pathway to market (*c.* 1990s)

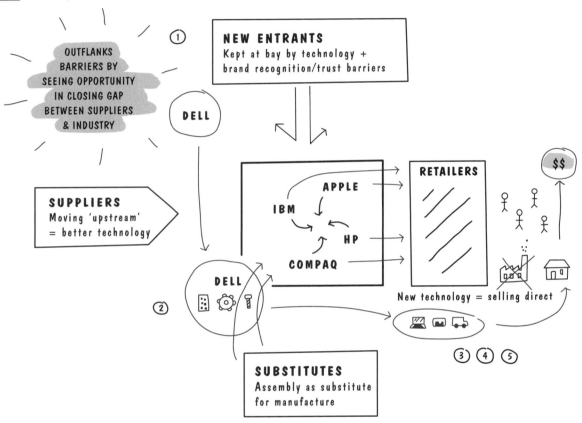

**OUTFLANKS BARRIERS BY SEEING OPPORTUNITY IN CLOSING GAP BETWEEN SUPPLIERS & INDUSTRY**

DELL

**NEW ENTRANTS**
Kept at bay by technology + brand recognition/trust barriers

**SUPPLIERS**
Moving 'upstream' = better technology

IBM  APPLE  HP  COMPAQ

DELL

**RETAILERS**

$$

New technology = selling direct

**SUBSTITUTES**
Assembly as substitute for manufacture

| ① | ② | ③ | ④ | ⑤ |
|---|---|---|---|---|
| Dell enters market outflanking trade barriers and harnessing the abilities of upskilling suppliers | It reduces cost by focusing on assembling what suppliers produce rather than investing in full-scale manufacturing | Cost to market reduced by using new technology, internet, credit card and transport developments to sell direct to the user | By focusing on domestic and small biz users, products can be simply modified to provide 'tailored' products | Dell also takes advantage of high growth in these two, relatively untapped at this time, segments |

**DRAW YOUR OWN HERE...**

1. Start on the horizontal. Depict key suppliers and their level of influence. Draw customers and their key behaviours on the other side.

2. List potential new entrants on the vertical. Draw barriers that discourage them from coming in and incumbents from leaving. Outline substitutes and draw the impact on industry.

3. In the rivalry box, depict industry growth rate. Insert main competitors, show the degree of competition and how it may change.

Creative ideas:
Draw how things might change over the next five years, or how a new entrant might enter and change dynamics. Or how things might look differently to one of your competitors.

**COMMON PITFALLS:** Don't confuse criteria: the five forces is about margins. Is using suppliers in developing countries with low factor costs good? Maybe not ethically, but in terms of margins (what the five forces is predicated on) it is.

Some suggest that the five forces places too much emphasis on competition and not enough on cooperation and alliances.

**GOOD IN COMBINATION WITH:** Other Porter frameworks such as the generic strategy matrix (no. 8), which can be used to analyse the nature of the rivalry box, or the value chain (no. 7), which can help to look at a firm's activities from suppliers on the left to buyers on the right in more detail. Using the value net (no. 11) can help show the role that alliances can play in an industry.

**MUTATION POTENTIAL:** You can add some of the most relevant categories of ESTEMPLE (no. 2) in the corners of the diagram to capture how macro factors might influence the forces. To bring out the role of cooperation, add 'complementors' from the value net (no. 11) to create a sixth force and/or draw connections to show the main alliances in the industry.

**INFO FOR FURTHER READING:**
- Grundy, T. (2006). Rethinking and reinventing Michael Porter's five forces model. *Strategic Change*, 15(5), 213–229.
- Porter, M.E. (1980). *Competitive Strategy: Techniques for Analyzing Industries and Competitors*. New York: Simon & Schuster.
- Porter, M.E. (2008). The five competitive forces that shape strategy. *Harvard Business Review*, January: 79–93.

**FIELD NOTES:**

## 6. Industry Life Cycle Curve

## AUTHOR: Raymond Vernon

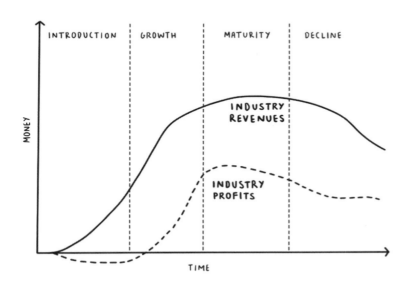

**WHEN TO USE:** To examine how an industry might change over time, to exhibit particular opportunities or threats, whether in an uncertain introductory period, high-growth early phase, increasing competition in maturity or falling sales during decline.

**COMPONENTS:** The vertical axis can be money or industry sales volume and the horizontal axis is time. The phases are introduction (start-up), growth, maturity, decline. Sometimes when relating the curve to particular products and portfolios, introduction is related to 'question marks'; growth to 'stars'; maturity to 'cash cows'; and decline to 'dogs'.

## DEVELOPMENT:

The industry life cycle describes the stages through which an industry passes from origination to ultimate demise. The framework suggests the industry starts with a slow increase in sales, whilst incurring losses through start-up. It then grows more rapidly and begins to make significant profits. In this phase there is growing competition but this is more than counterbalanced by market growth. In the mature phase, overall growth slows and plateaus, competition intensifies as competitors have to win from each other to maintain growth rate. Products and services become standardized, making competition through differentiation advantages increasingly difficult. Overall profits begin to decline. In the decline phase, sales fall and profits slowly tail off. In order to maintain growth and profitability, industries can innovate during growth and mature phases, which brings about rejuvenation.

The life cycle stages are not inevitable, but the model does provide a useful explanation for changes in competition patterns, profitability and innovation patterns. There is the possibility that innovation may halt or even reverse potential decline, so rejuvenating an industry. Links have also been made with changing importance of functions in business, with innovators being crucial at the outset, followed by engineers and sales for increased production and growing the market. Marketing then assumes importance in order to convince customers that products/services are different when differentiation advantages begin to recede. Financial controllers grow in importance when cost management becomes all-important.

## Key Takeouts:
➜ What stage of the life cycle is your organization located in?
➜ What opportunities and threats does this position present to you in terms of market?

# Apple: Reinventing the industry (*c.* 1980–2015)

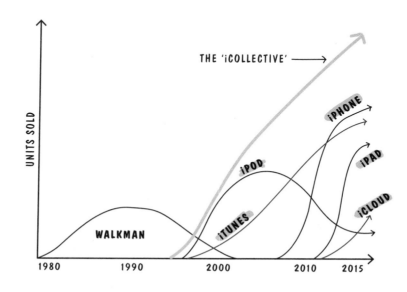

THE 'iCOLLECTIVE'

UNITS SOLD

iPHONE

iPOD

iPAD

iTUNES

iCLOUD

WALKMAN

1980    1990    2000    2010    2015

| ① | ② | ③ | ④ | ⑤ |
|---|---|---|---|---|
| The Sony Walkman kicked off a mobile music device industry but declined quickly in the 1990s | The portable CD prolonged the decline, but Apple rejuvenated the industry with the iPod | Apple then developed a portfolio that kept reinventing the industry as products matured: e.g. the iPhone and the iPad | But perhaps the cleverest strategy was to look behind the products to the transfer and storage of music with systems like iTunes and the iCloud | So while products may come & go, the 'iCollective' has mitigated the risk of industry decline |

**DRAW YOUR OWN HERE...**

1. Estimate the aggregate sales pattern of the industry over time. The current growth rate will determine which segment of the life cycle the industry is currently in.

2. When the current segment of the industry life cycle is determined, identify how this will affect: (1) competitive pressures; (2) industry profitability; (3) change in internal functional influence.

Creative ideas:

A. Consider the extent to which there is radical innovation in the industry in terms of (i) technology innovation and (ii) change in user experience (e.g. using Verganti's framework — consult the references at the end of this section for more details). This will suggest whether the industry is about to rejuvenate.

B. The life cycle can be perceived as the vertical dimension of some portfolio matrixes such as the BCG matrix, from which the terms question mark, star, cash cow and dog are taken, so you could use the curve to plot your multiple products/services across all industries in terms of these four characters.

**COMMON PITFALLS:** Accepting 'decline' as a fait accompli. Always be on the lookout for dolphin tail opportunities that can extend or rejuvenate an industry life cycle.

Assuming that good profits cannot be made in the decline phase – good strategic financial management can enable great cost savings in this phase.

Cognitive limits may cause managers to underestimate the opportunities for innovation in the maturity phase, as people are just happy to 'milk' cash cows.

**GOOD IN COMBINATION WITH:** The BCG or growth–share matrix – the life cycle can give an insight into one of the axes that is normally about industry attractiveness which can determine strategic options. The five forces framework to indicate the level of competition inside an industry – for instance, as industry shifts from growth to maturity, competition is likely to intensify and bargaining power will shift to customers, reducing overall profitability.

**MUTATION POTENTIAL:** Can be inserted into the categories of an ESTEMPLE analysis (no. 2) to consider what macro factors may influence the rate of change in the cycle. Can be placed into the rivalry box of a five forces analysis (no. 4) to indicate what stage the industry is at. This can focus thinking on rivalry behaviour (e.g. in the maturity phase, greater merger and acquisition activity is likely to occur as firms seek to achieve greater economies of scale to reduce their cost base).

**INFO FOR FURTHER READING:**
- Day, G.S. (1981). The product life cycle: analysis and application issues. *Journal of Marketing*, 45(4): 60–67.
- Morrison, A. and Wensley, R. (1991). Boxing up or boxed in?: A short history of the Boston Consulting Group share/growth matrix. *Journal of Marketing Management*, 7(2), 105–129.
- Verganti, R. (2009). *Design-driven Innovation: Changing the Rules of Competition by Radically Innovating what Things Mean*. Boston, MA: Harvard Business Press.
- Karniouchina, E.V., Carson, S.J., Short, J.C. and Ketchen, D.J. Jr. (2013). Extending the firm vs. Industry debate: does industry life cycle stage matter? *Strategic Management Journal*, 34(8), 1010–1018.

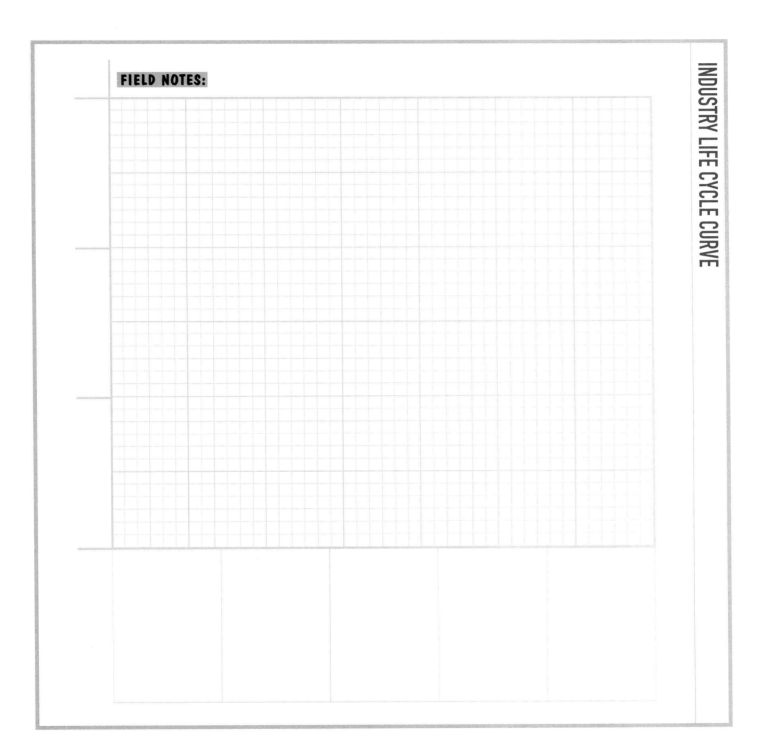

**FIELD NOTES:**

## The Best of the Environmental Frameworks Combined – First Foundation: The Environmental Ecosystem

### PURPOSE:

All of our five foundation frameworks are developed as a memory aid to help the user bring together aspects from each of the tools in a section of Strategy Builder. This should enable quicker strategic thinking and analysis 'on the run'. They are not, we believe, a substitute for deeper or more specific analysis afforded by the five tools covered in each section, but they can be a good way to engage in initial analysis or discussions and to summarize and bring together the findings from other frameworks. As such, the five have been designed to build on one another in a logical sequence to enable the development and presentation of a unified strategy (as we shall explain in more detail in Part 3 of the book). The purpose of the first foundation, the Environmental Ecosystem, is to combine key insights from environmental ecology frameworks to present the major opportunities and threats impacting on an organization's strategic development and enable fruitful discussion and debate.

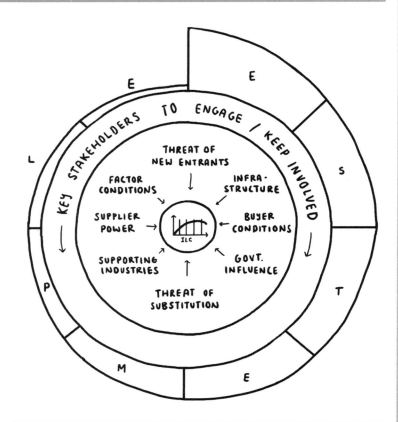

### COMPONENTS:

The Environmental Ecosystem (EE) is a series of concentric circles. Key ESTEMPLE impacts form the outermost ring. A ring for recording the key stakeholders who have the power and influence to impact on the strategy of the organization in question is next. The third ring provides space for depicting key industry and regional influences. The centre hub is where the life stage of the industry can be recorded.

## SpaceX's Environmental Ecosystem (c. 2012)

SpaceX (Space Exploration Technologies Corporation) was founded in 2002 by former PayPal and Tesla Motors CEO Elon Musk. In 10 years it has grown from nothing to being a key player in the future of space exploration by seizing on opportunities and recognizing how other organizations were withdrawing their services in the face of perceived threats in the space transportation industry. With NASA having become incredibly complex in its operations and the end of the Cold War reducing the funding imperative for the US government, the ecosystem drawing below represents the environmental drivers that enabled SpaceX's growth strategy to take off – a strategy of stepping in to bring together existing expertise in new ways to work with NASA on projects of national/global significance, combined with its own initiatives for developing new space delivery systems for satellites, other cargo and people.

## Key Takeout:

→ A single snapshot of the key macro, meso, regional and industry environmental impacts on an organization that can capture and prompt further discussion about the key opportunities and threats faced by that organization.

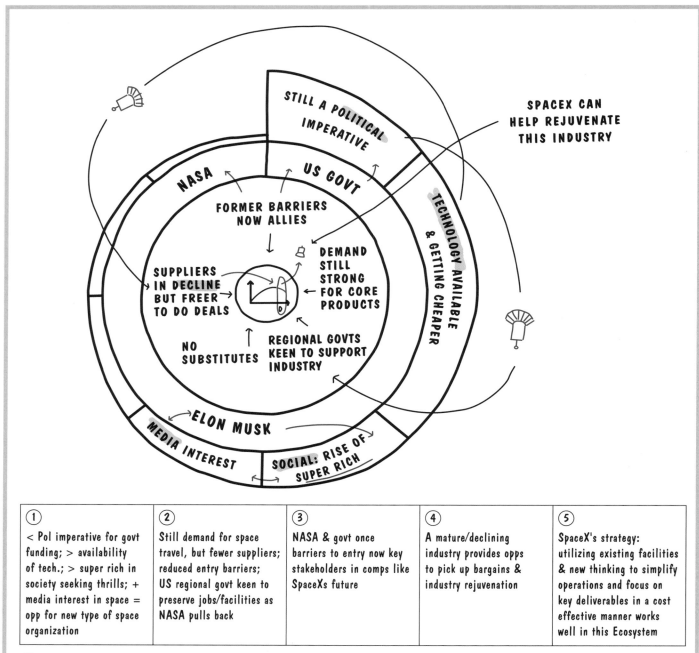

| ① | ② | ③ | ④ | ⑤ |
|---|---|---|---|---|
| < Pol imperative for govt funding; > availability of tech.; > super rich in society seeking thrills; + media interest in space = opp for new type of space organization | Still demand for space travel, but fewer suppliers; reduced entry barriers; US regional govt keen to preserve jobs/facilities as NASA pulls back | NASA & govt once barriers to entry now key stakeholders in comps like SpaceXs future | A mature/declining industry provides opps to pick up bargains & industry rejuvenation | SpaceX's strategy: utilizing existing facilities & new thinking to simplify operations and focus on key deliverables in a cost effective manner works well in this Ecosystem |

You can download templates of the Environmental Ecosystem to aid your drawing at www.wiley/go/strategybuilder.com or try out the app at www.strategicplan.com.

# COMPETITIVE POSITIONING

**Purpose:** Competitive positioning frameworks help to evaluate an organization's strengths and weaknesses, and make rational choices about the ways in which organizations might best differentiate themselves from other providers.

7. **The value chain** – A graphical depiction of a firm's key activities to see how they add value (and cost) to ensure that the total value created, or the price a customer is prepared to pay for the product of the activities, is higher than their total cost, thereby ensuring a margin.

8. **Generic strategy matrix (GSM)** – A simple outline that encourages strategic choice in strategic position between focusing on cost reduction or differentiating in other ways, and whether its competitive scope should be a broad target or a niche.

9. **Differentiation advantage categories** – More granulated ways of thinking through what particular form of strategic differentiation an organization should focus on developing.

10. **Blue ocean strategies** – A set of frameworks that promote strategies to take an organization away from what other firms are doing and how they are positioning themselves.

11. **Co-option/the value net** – A way of evaluating potential untapped or undervalued strengths that may lie in allying with other institutions for mutual strategic benefit. A useful complement to the five forces of industry.

## 7. The Value Chain

## AUTHOR: Michael Porter

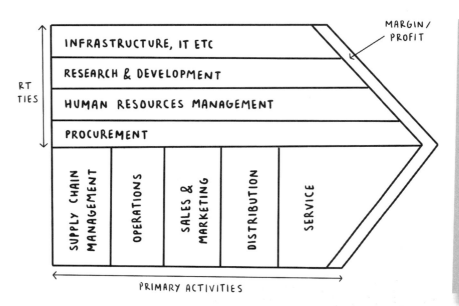

RT TIES

INFRASTRUCTURE, IT ETC

RESEARCH & DEVELOPMENT

HUMAN RESOURCES MANAGEMENT

PROCUREMENT

SUPPLY CHAIN MANAGEMENT | OPERATIONS | SALES & MARKETING | DISTRIBUTION | SERVICE

MARGIN/ PROFIT

PRIMARY ACTIVITIES

**RATINGS:** AIM's fourth most popular strategy tool and number one true strategy framework (> 40%). However, for manufacturing firms it rises to number three, with 51% usage. By contrast, it is used by less than 30% of public and not-for-profit companies. Like the five forces, having an MBA makes a manager almost 20% more likely to use it. Rated as the 14th most popular strategy tool by Aston. Eighth equal with balanced scorecard in China (37%).

**WHEN TO USE:** To analyse a firm's key activities to see how they add value (and cost) to ensure that the total value created, or the price a customer is prepared to pay for the product of the activities, is higher than their total cost, thereby ensuring the achievement of a margin.

**COMPONENTS:** Divided into two halves, with the top half incorporating support activities or what used to be called 'staff functions', such as human resource management (HRM) and information technology (IT), and the bottom primary activities or 'line functions' (e.g. operations, sales and service functions). The margin slice at the sharp end of the arrow is a reminder that you should sell what you produce for more than what it costs.

### DEVELOPMENT:

Perhaps the first graphical strategy frameworks that we can draw a clear line of origin to are those of Igor Ansoff, whose book *Business Strategy* (1965) is primary in the field. In it Ansoff outlined his growth options matrix (no. 18) and did much to define what strategy was about. Claiming that the current theory set included only a simple business policy approach where companies would have a number of set plays to respond to environmental changes, and a microeconomic theory of the firm that saw the organization as a 'black box' within which managers would seek to turn inputs into outputs more efficiently, Ansoff viewed strategic thinking as sitting above this chain making choices about how to configure and integrate operations differently from competitors.

Porter's value chain shines a light further inside the black box to illustrate the different activities that strategists could configure in order to reduce the costs of activities or increase the value that they added to the overall product or service. The direct 'line' functions are along the bottom half, 'staff' functions along the top. As with the five forces, the key objective is to maximize margins, but at the level of the firm: How can you best arrange things so as to make the gap between what people are prepared to pay for, or the value they attribute to the output, and the cost of producing it?

## Key Takeouts:
→ What are the key activities that really add value to the finished product, service or experience that you produce? How can they be enhanced?

→ Are you spending time and money doing things that don't add a lot of value?

# Amazon: Reconfiguring a value chain (*c.* 2005)

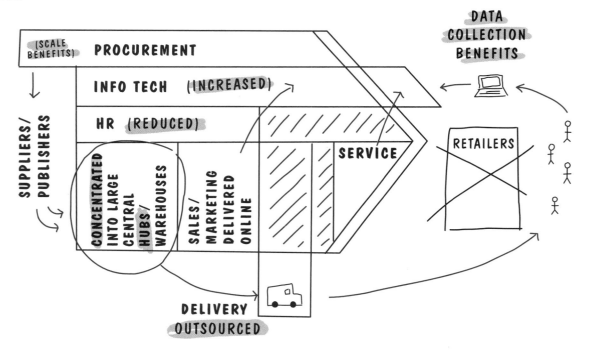

| ① | ② | ③ | ④ | ⑤ |
|---|---|---|---|---|
| Amazon's business model changes book retailing. The biro and highlighter over-writes show how | Instead of serving a large retail network, A concentrates into large warehouse/distribution hubs = procurement scale benefits | Trad sales/mktg functions deleted or moved online. HR costs decline, more emphasis on IT | Delivery outsourced to providers for whom parcel delivery is a core business | Knowledge gained from direct interface with book buyers provides info that informs focused expansion into related products/ services |

**DRAW YOUR OWN HERE...**

**1.** Start on the left-hand side and begin by thinking of (and drawing) what happens when supplies (including labour) arrive at your door at the start of the chain.

**2.** We find that the top of the chain (support activities) can be more difficult to draw, so just focus on the chain of primary activities to begin and add support activities later as you see fit.

Creative ideas:

**A.** Use metaphorical shapes to enhance memorability. If you produce cars, show the chain in the shape of a car; if you sell adventure holidays, show the chain as a series of steps up a mountain.

**B.** Think innovation. Think of new activities that add value and add them to your chain. Cut costs by taking things out. Can you increase volume? Show it by widening the chain. Can you relate differently to the market? Draw the link from the end of the chain to customers in a new way...

**COMMON PITFALLS:** Getting lost in the detail. You do not need to define every activity your organization performs or fill all the boxes and oblongs in the value chain to start building or communicating a strategy.

Sticking too much to script. You need not follow the mechanics of the chain too rigidly. An excellent article by Henry Mintzberg recommended drawing organigraphs that depicted what organizations actually do in pictures rather than text fitting into boxes.

**GOOD IN COMBINATION WITH:** It can be good to use the value chain, the generic strategy matrix (no. 7) and the five forces (no. 5) concurrently. Start with a value chain analysis, see if this aligns with where you see the organization in GSM terms (generic differentiation chains will probably be longer than cost-focused chains), then reflect on the industry pressures that can impact on this strategy using the five forces. Use the value chain together with blue ocean strategy (no. 10) to check if your alignment with industry standards is reflected in the amount of emphasis placed on each of your primary activities.

**MUTATION POTENTIAL:** One particularly useful approach is to draw value chains that represent organizations that provide a number of products by separating where activities are separate and joining then they are shared. We call these value chimera, after the creature with one body and three distinct heads.

**INFO FOR FURTHER READING:**
- Bilton, C. and Cummings, S. (2010). *Creative Strategy: Reconnecting Business and Innovation.* UK: Wiley – the 'six degrees of strategic innovation' framework from this book outlines six ways of innovating by drawing the value chain differently.
- Cummings, S. and Angwin, D. (2004). The future shape of strategy: Lemmings or chimeras? *The Academy of Management Executive*, 18(2), 21–36.
- Mintzberg, H. and Van der Heyden, L. (1999). Organigraphs: Drawing how companies really work. *Harvard Business Review*, 77, 87–95.

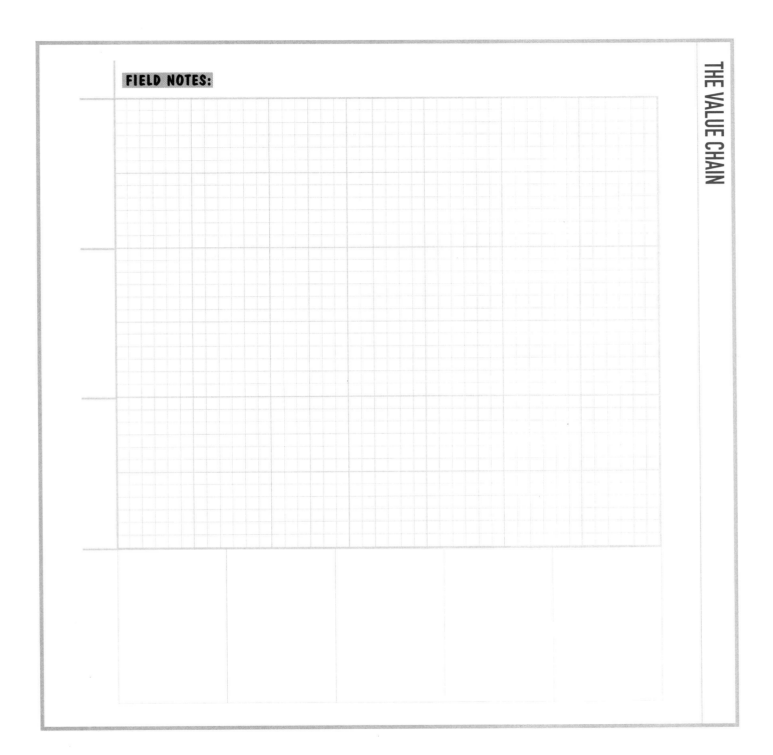

**FIELD NOTES:**

## 8. Generic Strategy Matrix (GSM)

## AUTHOR: Michael Porter

COMPETITIVE ADVANTAGE

| | LOWER COST | DIFFERENTIATION |
|---|---|---|
| BROAD TARGET | COST LEADERSHIP | DIFFERENTIATION |
| NARROW TARGET / NICHE | COST FOCUS | DIFFERENTIATION FOCUS |

COMPETITIVE SCOPE

**RATINGS:** AIM's 11th most popular strategy tool and fifth most popular framework (> 20%). Bowman's strategy clock, which is based on the GSM, rates 20th (and most likely to be dropped) and if the scores of these two frameworks were combined, the GSM would rate higher. The GSM is the 10th most popular framework in China according to He et al.'s (2012) study (34% usage).

**WHEN TO USE:** To encourage discussion about basic strategic choices between cost reduction or differentiating in other ways, and focusing on a broad target or a niche.

**COMPONENTS:** Early incarnations of the GSM arranged three generic strategies in relation to a vertical 'competitive scope' axis, stretching from narrow to broad, and a horizontal 'competitive advantage' axis divided in two: a focus on lower cost or differentiation (often, in contrast to low cost, seen as some form of higher quality). This became a 2 × 2 matrix by dividing the focus strategy into two: cost focus and differentiation focus.

### DEVELOPMENT:

In 1980's *Competitive Strategy*, Porter introduced the five forces of industry (no. 4) and the value chain (no. 7). 1985's *Competitive Strategy* introduced a framework for thinking about the generic strategic choices faced in this regard: 'cost leadership', 'differentiation' or a 'focus' on a particular niche. The GSM made a 2 × 2 matrix of these choices by crossing competitive advantage ('cost' or 'differentiation') and competitive scope ('broad' or 'narrow' target market) to create four generic strategies (focus dividing into 'differentiation focus' and 'cost focus'). The power of the framework is its simplicity, and students and executives enjoy being able to place rivals in an industry (e.g. cars – 1: Toyota, Ford, VW; 2: BMW, Volvo; 3a: Kia, Skoda; 3b: Land Rover, Mini, Ferrari) and discuss the implications.

All of the generic strategies can deliver good returns if executed well, proving Ansoff's idea that there is not one best approach to business policy (no. 19): it's a matter of strategic choice. Where you don't want to be, according to Porter, is stuck in the middle: caught between the alternatives and sub-optimizing. However, a later variation, Bowman's clock, provides an alternative arrangement whereby a well-executed 'hybrid' strategy (focused on both cost and differentiation, neither broad nor narrow, e.g. Honda) can be effective. And blue ocean strategy (no. 10) also promotes the simultaneous pursuit of cost reduction and value adding as it is a pre-competitive space.

## Key Takeouts:

➔ What generic strategic positions do you and your competitor occupy?

➔ What opportunities can you see for positioning change in the future?

# Komatsu: 'Encircle Caterpillar' (*c.* 1980s)

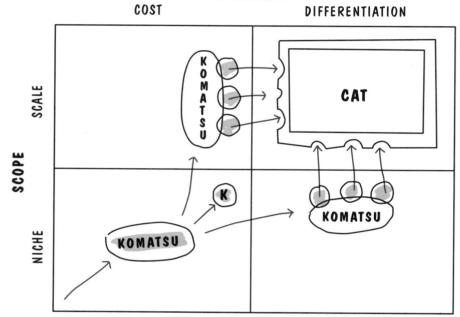

**ADVANTAGE**

COST       DIFFERENTIATION

**SCOPE**

SCALE

NICHE

KOMATSU

K

KOMATSU

CAT

KOMATSU

| ① | ② | ③ | ④ | ⑤ |
|---|---|---|---|---|
| Earthwork machinery company Komatsu's strategy a few decades ago was termed 'Maru-C' | But what this actually meant is a lot easier to understand when it's pictured using the GSM | Caterpillar was the dominant competitor with a high-quality rep and large market share | K moved from a cost-focused niche player investing on two fronts — R&D and mrkting — to build brand image and new prod dev to grow mkt share | These advancements then nibbled away at CATs advantage on both flanks (Maru means 'encircle' in Japanese) |

**DRAW YOUR OWN HERE...**

**1.** Start with your company (or that which you are focusing on) and place where you currently see them sitting in the matrix.

**2.** Think of this company's main competitors. Where would you place them?

**3.** If you placed your company in the middle, do you think this is for a good reason, e.g. a strategic gap or blue ocean (no. 10)? Companies like Honda or Samsung might be categorized this way. Or rather because you just lost focus over time (many accused Marks & Spencer and Hewlett-Packard of this in the 1990s)? You can represent this drift of purpose with symbols (a meandering line or a bullseye).

Creative ideas:

**A.** Rather than just placing your products/ services in one 'box', think in terms of the portfolio of things you do in more than one segment and share platforms where possible (e.g. the VW Group has brands in different segments: Seat, Skoda, VW, Audi, but with some shared platforms/componentry where strategically useful).

**B.** Think about how you might best develop/move your strategic position/s over time and draw this movement, the impact that this could have on your competitors, and how they might respond.

**COMMON PITFALLS:** The GSM's major strength (simplicity, which makes it easy to remember, draw and discuss) can also be a weakness. People can be driven to distraction arguing whether a strategy is narrow or broad. Does this distinction relate to geographical reach, product line variation or unit sales? It could be any of these things, so don't sweat the distinction too much – just use the framework to stimulate discussion.

Thinking there is 'one best way'. A firm can succeed (or achieve superior margins) in any box (or a portfolio of any combination); the key is executing your value chain components consistently and effectively (see hybrid potential discussion below).

**GOOD IN COMBINATION WITH:** As mentioned earlier, the GSM is an excellent way of drawing and discussing basic strategic positioning choices. But to look in more detail at what particular strengths, exactly, you want to focus on, a strategist would do well to lead on from such a discussion to a more fine-grained analysis of differentiation advantage categories (no. 9) or discuss how your positioning is above, below or completely different from current positioning norms using blue ocean strategy thinking (no. 10).

**MUTATION POTENTIAL:** Mutate the four GSM boxes into a 2 × 2 of four empty value chain arrow ▷ shapes – see framework no. 7. Think about how an effective value chain would be configured in each of the shells. Or you can meld a GSM with a value chimera (a variation of a value chain, see p. 000) to think through how a firm's different offerings might share platforms and be different on key attributes. In this hybrid you would have the Value Chimera's left-hand side on the left of the GSM and then separating into its different heads and entering into the boxes where each product/service offering of the portfolio was seen to sit.

**INFO FOR FURTHER READING:**
- Cummings, S. and Wilson, D. (2003). *Images of Strategy* (Chapter 1, p.1–31). London: John Wiley.
- Faulkner, D. and Bowman, C. (1995). *The Essence of Competitive Strategy.* Hemel Hempstead: Prentice Hall.
- Porter, M. (1985). *Competitive Advantage.* New York: The Free Press.

**FIELD NOTES:**

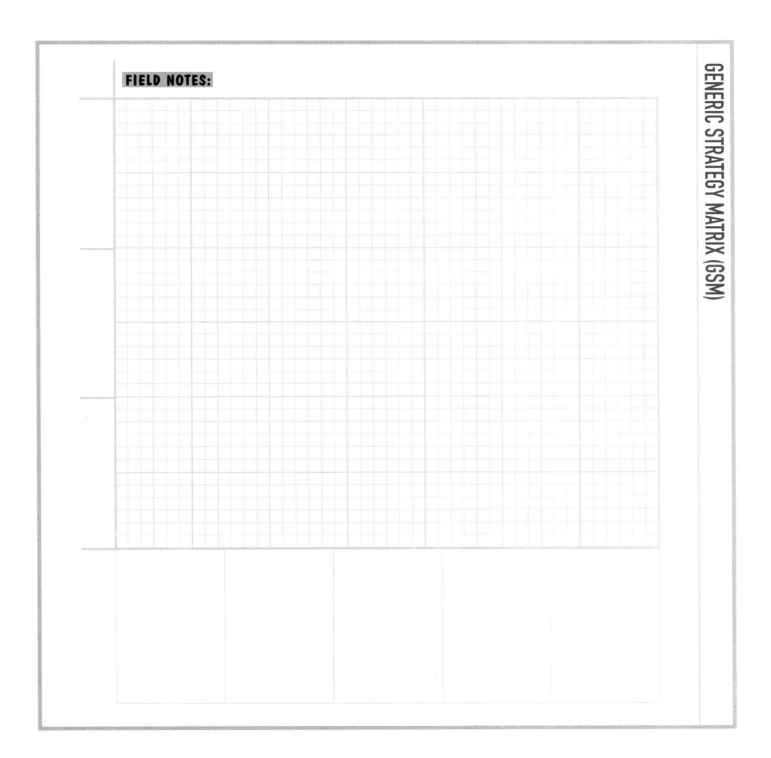

## 9. Differentiation Advantage Categories

## AUTHORS: Nigel Slack and Henry Mintzberg (and others)

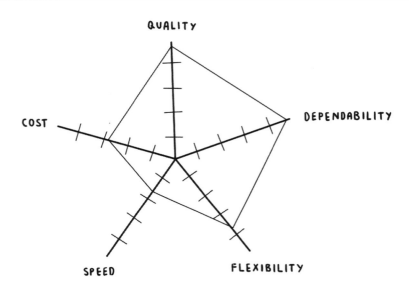

**WHEN TO USE:** To think through what particular strengths, and what form of strategic differentiation, an organization should focus on maintaining and developing.

**COMPONENTS:** In our experience, the ideas expressed here are best translated into graphics in the form of a 'spidergram', like the one above. The arms can consist of any activities or aspects that you believe are important in your industry (in the diagram here we have used Nigel Slack's 'five advantage categories').

**DIFFERENTIATION ADVANTAGE CATEGORIES**

## DEVELOPMENT:

Despite its ease-of-use value and appeal, there are two problems with the GSM's competitive advantage distinction between cost and differentiation. First, that focusing on cost reduction is a way of differentiating (thus the opposing axis points of cost and differentiation are flawed). Second, there are many other ways of differentiating than just these two options. Consequently, others have come up with different ways of exploring how a firm may position itself strategically through differentiation. Nigel Slack's five generic advantage categories (quality, speed, dependability, flexibility and cost advantage) are a useful starting point for strategic discussion, particularly if one makes a spidergram of them. Visualizing in this way helps with seeing that choices have to be made: a firm cannot excel in cost reduction without compromising a top score in flexibility or dependability. But choices need not be simple either/ors.

Another useful approach is to break up the GSM differentiation boxes into columns for different types of differentiation. For example, one might use Henry Mintzberg's differentiation advantage categories – image, support, quality – design for this purpose. As part of this elaboration Mintzberg also points out that 'undifferentiation' can be a useful strategy (e.g. for international car hire companies, it can be useful to comfort prospective customers by ensuring that the offering is very similar to other leading brands).

## Key Takeouts:

➔ What are the differentiating strengths that set you apart from the competition?

➔ What are the important deficits or weaknesses that customers may expect that you need to work on/ mitigate?

## Lamborghini: Orange is not the same as red (*c.* 1970s–2015)

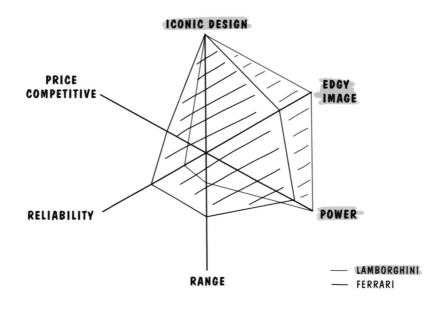

ICONIC DESIGN

PRICE COMPETITIVE

EDGY IMAGE

RELIABILITY

POWER

RANGE

—— LAMBORGHINI
—— FERRARI

| ① | ② | ③ | ④ | ⑤ |
|---|---|---|---|---|
| 1963 Lamborghini founded by spurned Ferrari customer. Contines trad of 'stuff you!' differentiation | Because of the cutting edginess Lambos are not most reliable | View is that customer is buying in to being part of innovation and prototyping (and hence maintenance) process | The models and options are very limited and they are staggeringly expensive. They are not for everyone! | But nothing growls as powerfully as a Lambo or has the edgy image and iconic design. And that's how they sustain competitive advantage |

**DRAW YOUR OWN HERE...**

1. Draw a centring dot in the middle of the page. Start with your biggest differentiating strength (a 4 or a 5 notch perhaps) as the first 'arm' and then work around the clock drawing in your other lesser attributes.

2. Don't be limited to the five 'arms' mentioned on the previous page. Replace them with more appropriate attributes in your industry or add in additional ones.

3. Don't just draw arms that relate to things your organization is good at. Also include the things that could be important to customers that you don't do so well.

Creative ideas:

A. On the same sketch, add in your main competitors. Connect your and their arm notches to create oblongs. Where are the main areas of difference?

B. Slack went on to promote an importance/performance matrix. Next to your spidergram draw a matrix with performance divided into low and high on one plane and importance (to customers) on the other. Place your high and low rating spidergram advantage categories into the matrix and discuss.

**COMMON PITFALLS:** A lack of honesty/reality. You can't be good at every possibility in strategy so be honest about what you are good at/different from relative to alternative providers. If you aren't, you'll undervalue the things you are really strong at and probably develop a strategy that lacks clarity of focus as a result.

If you are not going to use the generic differentiation factors proposed, then make sure you choose factors that have greatest resonance with winning in your marketplace.

**GOOD IN COMBINATION WITH:** Differentiation advantage categorizations and spidergrams are a good advance on an initial GSM analysis (no. 8). And having determined how you rate according to the arms of your spidergram, it can be good to combine this with a value chain (no. 7) analysis that looks specifically at what aspects your strategy should improve/maintain/develop and de-emphasize.

**MUTATION POTENTIAL:** As a form of strategic 'shorthand', it can be useful to graft some differentiation advantage categories on to the end of each of the eight ESTEMPLE columns (no. 2) to see how your strengths might enable you to take advantage of macro-environmental opportunities or mitigate threats; or how your weaknesses might make you unable to take advantage of opportunities/mitigate threats.

**INFO FOR FURTHER READING:**
- Mintzberg, H. (1988). Generic strategies: toward a comprehensive framework. *Advances in Strategic Management*, 5(1), 1–67.
- Slack, N. (1991). *The Manufacturing Advantage: Achieving Competitive Manufacturing Operations.* Mercury Books.
- Slack, N. (1994). The importance-performance matrix as a determinant of improvement priority. *International Journal of Operations & Production Management,* 14(5), 59–75.

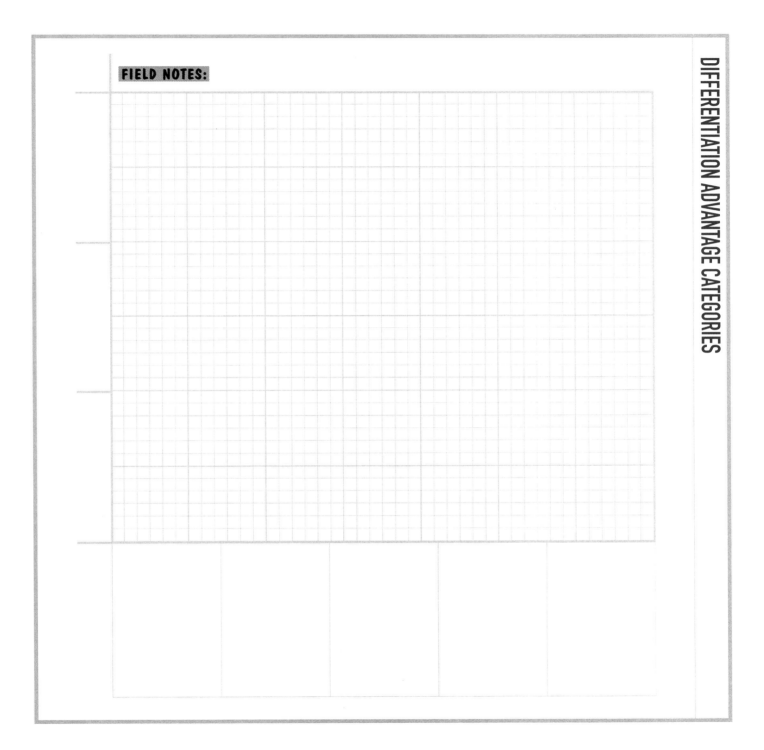

**FIELD NOTES:**

DIFFERENTIATION ADVANTAGE CATEGORIES

## 10. Blue Ocean Strategies

## AUTHORS: W. Chan Kim and Renée Mauborgne

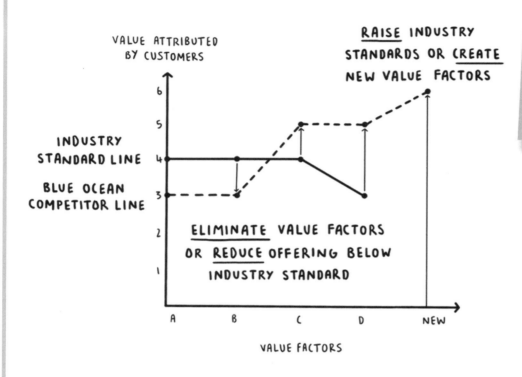

RAISE INDUSTRY STANDARDS OR CREATE NEW VALUE FACTORS

VALUE ATTRIBUTED BY CUSTOMERS

INDUSTRY STANDARD LINE

BLUE OCEAN COMPETITOR LINE

ELIMINATE VALUE FACTORS OR REDUCE OFFERING BELOW INDUSTRY STANDARD

VALUE FACTORS

**WHEN TO USE:** To challenge the boundaries of an industry (which are confines in earlier strategy frameworks) and promote strategies significantly different from those of other firms.

**COMPONENTS:** Blue ocean strategy (BOS) analysis is driven by a series of questions: (1) which key success factors (KSFs) that an industry takes for granted should be *eliminated*; (2) which KSFs should be *reduced* well below industry standards; (3) which KSFs should be *raised* well above industry standards; (4) which KSFs that an industry has never offered should be *created*?

## DEVELOPMENT:

Blue ocean strategy was developed by INSEAD professors W. Chan Kim and Renée Mauborgne. The underlying theme is differentiation. Red oceans are where similar competitors engage in close fighting, leaving blood in the water. Firms want to get to a blue ocean, where they are the only ones in their territory. Whereas the GSM (no. 8) warned against both reducing cost and differentiating on other characteristics, Kim and Mauborgne had for some time advocated adding real value by doing both. And while other differentiation advantage category approaches (no. 9) propose generic types of differentiation, BOS suggests instead a focus on the particular key success factors of value that a user gains from the particular product or service being focused upon. BOS develops and represents these ideas in two related frameworks: 'the four actions' and 'the strategy canvas'.

We have combined these into one picture on the previous page. The four actions suggest ways of differentiating from the norm: *reducing* standards or *eliminating* factors that some users may not want or need; *raising* an offering above the standard; or *creating* new value factors. The strategy canvas is where a firm can plot out its differentiation from other competitors, or where it separates itself from others in terms of key value factors. In the above canvas, the BOS competitor has reduced some factors (factors 1 and 2), raised others (factors 3 and 4), and created a new factor.

## Key Takeout:

→ Through really re-thinking the current KSFs for an industry, could a new competitive space be created which may enable you to achieve superior profitability?

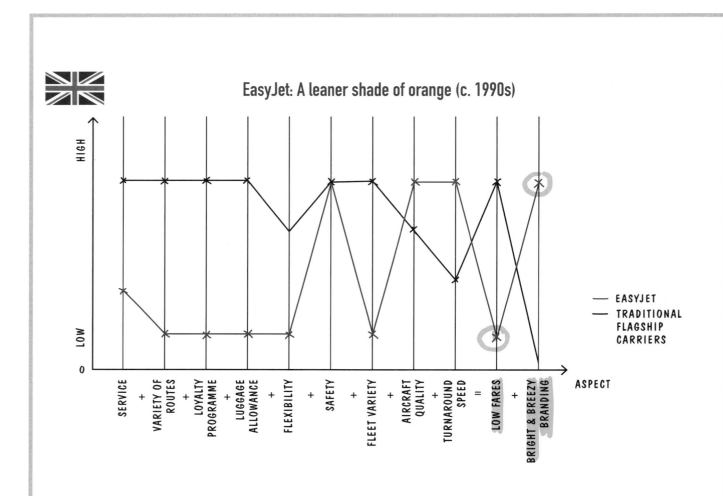

**EasyJet: A leaner shade of orange (c. 1990s)**

HIGH

LOW

0

ASPECT

SERVICE + VARIETY OF ROUTES + LOYALTY PROGRAMME + LUGGAGE ALLOWANCE + FLEXIBILITY + SAFETY + FLEET VARIETY + AIRCRAFT QUALITY + TURNAROUND SPEED = LOW FARES + BRIGHT & BREEZY BRANDING

—— EASYJET
—— TRADITIONAL FLAGSHIP CARRIERS

① EasyJet is now a leader in the airline industry. It got there by doing < than, > than, the same as & differently from the norm

② They ↓ costs by operating just one type of plane, diminishing freq flyer benefits, reducing onboard service, and using regional airports

③ They improved the time planes spend on the ground, and maintained safety standards

④ This all led to much lower fares & it grew the overall market for air travel, while comps found it hard to reduce/retool their systems

⑤ EasyJet also promoted a brand different from the traditional stuffy European airlines: bright, breezy, lean and orange

**DRAW YOUR OWN HERE...**

**1.** Draw a horizontal axis for value factors and label the vertical axis high and low for industry standards.

**2.** Along the horizontal axis, list key success factors for the industry and include those that are not currently KSFs but might become so.

**3.** Plot the industry standards for your factors and then map out your company's current standards.

**4.** Consider gaps that already exist and then think about which of the factors could be raised, lowered, eliminated or created.

Creative ideas:

**A.** Brainstorming is important for coming up with creative approaches to BOS and it may be beneficial to consider what may be eliminated or could be new, before focusing upon what are current industry KSFs and risk getting locked into existing industry logic.

**B.** Consider how your new value line may tap into or promote new customer demand.

**C.** Consider how easy it would be for competitors to copy your initiative.

**COMMON PITFALLS:** Being too conservative. Getting locked into an industry's logic and not being able to critically question current KSFs. BOS is about thinking outside of the square, so any potential new attribute, no matter how unusual, is worth considering.

Assuming that all blue oceans are good oceans. They may be too small to be worth bothering with or be very risky, even if offering high returns. They might also be transient as key success factors ebb and flow and competitors may also compete away the sources of differentiation – turning the blue ocean into a red ocean.

**GOOD IN COMBINATION WITH:** Blue ocean strategizing should be considered alongside other innovation frameworks such as the Verganti matrix, S-curves, and the next practice matrix (no. 21). There can also be value in considering BOS alongside the five forces of industry (no. 5) and other models taking a static view of industry boundaries, so that the assumptions about current industry boundaries can be tested.

**MUTATION POTENTIAL:** It can be very effective to place the blue ocean graph within the shell/ outline of a value chain (no. 7) and look across at the various primary activities performed to see if they are significant above standard/below cost/or additional to what competitors are providing. This can give real purpose to discussions about key strategic strengths that must be exploited and wasted resources.

**INFO FOR FURTHER READING:**

- Kim, W.C. and Mauborgne, R. (1997). Value innovation – the strategic logic of high growth. *Harvard Business Review*, 75, 103–112.
- Kim, W.C. and Mauborgne, R. (2004). Blue ocean strategy. *Harvard Business Review*, October, 76–85.
- Kim, W.C. and Mauborgne, R. (2005). *Blue Ocean Strategy: How to Create Uncontested Market Space and Make the Competition Irrelevant.* Boston: Harvard Business School Press.

**FIELD NOTES:**

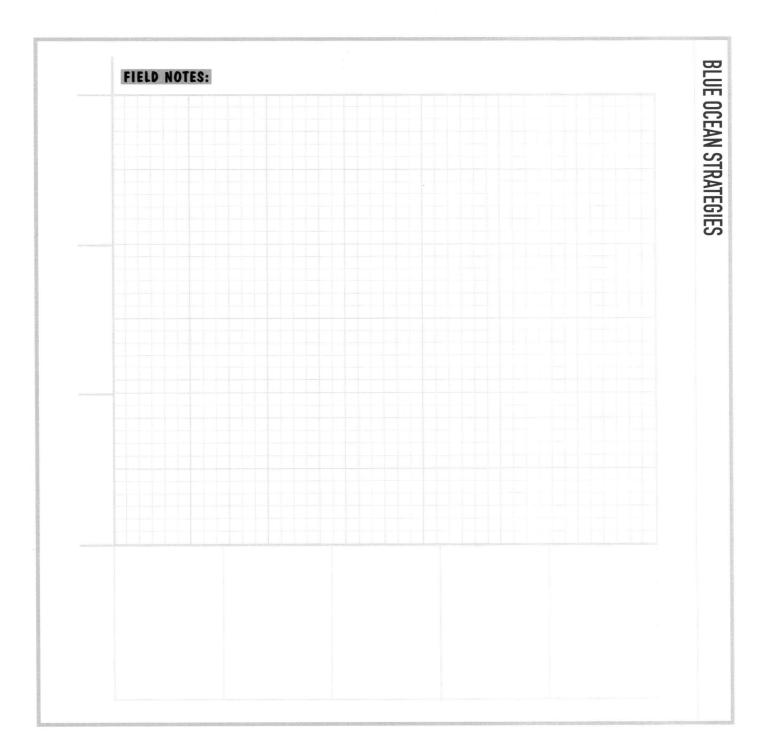

## 11. Co-option/The Value Net

## AUTHORS: Adam Brandenburger and Barry Nalebuff

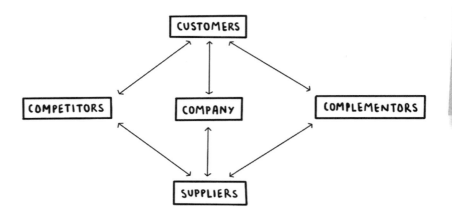

**WHEN TO USE:** To evaluate potential untapped or undervalued strengths that may lie in allying with other institutions for mutual strategic benefit.

**COMPONENTS:** The value net places the company or organization in focus at the centre of the picture, connects suppliers and customers either side of this on the vertical plane (which is unusual as most strategy frameworks follow the classic microeconomic theory of the firm and place these on the horizontal), and competitors and complementors (the framework's key point of difference) to the left and right, respectively.

## DEVELOPMENT:

Seen by many as an important extension to Porter's five forces (no. 5), the value net was developed by Adam Brandenburger and Barry Nalebuff of Yale School of Management in the mid-1990s. Using game theory, they added the concept of complementors. This is sometimes called 'the sixth force', an idea often credited to Andrew Grove, former CEO of Intel Corporation and a great advocate of the approach. The value net helps promote and understand the importance of strategic alliances (either formal alliances or informal or accidental ones).

While some have claimed that the notion of complementors overcomes an oversight on Porter's part, it is worth recalling that it is similar to the related and supporting industries element of his diamond of international competitiveness (no. 4), published in 1990. A further key difference between the value net and the five forces is that the value net examines a particular company as the unit of analysis or key focus, rather than a whole industry, which makes it more of a competitive advantage rather than an environmental ecosystem framework.

## Key Takeout:
→ What strengths can you gain and what weaknesses can you alleviate by aligning yourself strategically to benefit from mutually beneficial associations?

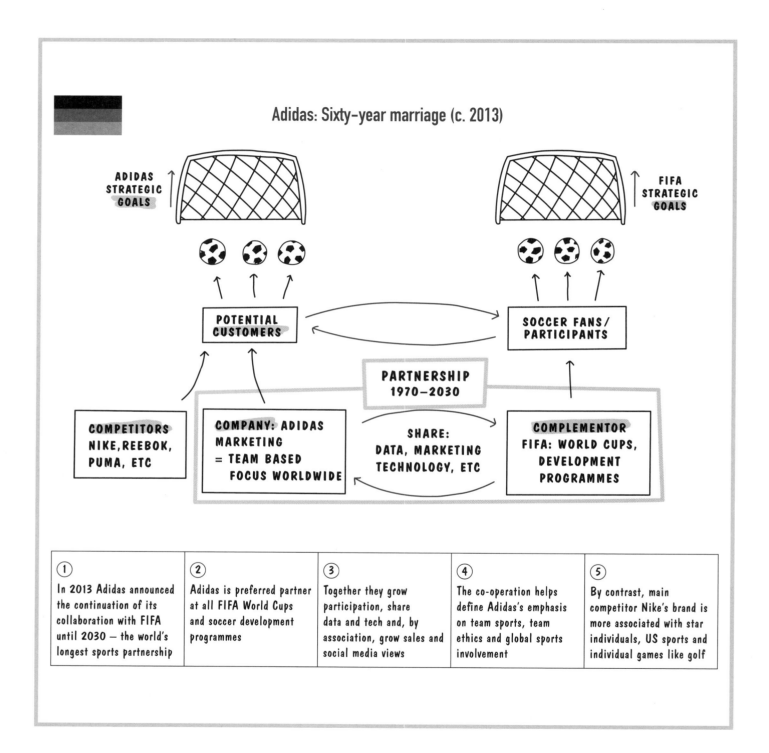

# Adidas: Sixty-year marriage (c. 2013)

**ADIDAS STRATEGIC GOALS**

**FIFA STRATEGIC GOALS**

**POTENTIAL CUSTOMERS**

**SOCCER FANS/ PARTICIPANTS**

**PARTNERSHIP 1970–2030**

**COMPETITORS** NIKE, REEBOK, PUMA, ETC

**COMPANY: ADIDAS MARKETING = TEAM BASED FOCUS WORLDWIDE**

**SHARE: DATA, MARKETING TECHNOLOGY, ETC**

**COMPLEMENTOR FIFA: WORLD CUPS, DEVELOPMENT PROGRAMMES**

① In 2013 Adidas announced the continuation of its collaboration with FIFA until 2030 — the world's longest sports partnership

② Adidas is preferred partner at all FIFA World Cups and soccer development programmes

③ Together they grow participation, share data and tech and, by association, grow sales and social media views

④ The co-operation helps define Adidas's emphasis on team sports, team ethics and global sports involvement

⑤ By contrast, main competitor Nike's brand is more associated with star individuals, US sports and individual games like golf

**DRAW YOUR OWN HERE...**

**1. Start** by drawing your organization in the middle of the page. Either as a logo, a symbol or perhaps as a simplified version of your value chain (no. 7).

**2. If you find** it difficult to think of suppliers and customers on the vertical plane, move the 'compass' around 90 degrees so that they sit to the left and right of your company.

**3. Use symbols** to aid meaning and memorization. If you're promoting soccer, use soccer balls in place of generic boxes; if you're promoting tourism services, use hotel and aeroplane shapes.

**Creative ideas:**

The key here is to advance beyond competitors by more effectively tapping into relationships with other institutions and associations, so actually draw yourself and your complementors rising up above competitors, the nature of the collaboration, how this will happen, and how it will enhance the value you provide to customers.

**COMMON PITFALLS:** Not being creative with the diagram. The value net is a pretty 'bare bones' framework. If all you do is put some words in the boxes, you are not likely to create much enthusiasm.

Getting hung up on doing the customers' and suppliers' boxes. If you've done a five forces analysis (no. 5) then you will have already covered these themes. Just take what you did there, plug that in here, and focus on the real added value of the net: how complementors will help you win against competitors.

**GOOD IN COMBINATION WITH:** A good addition to a five forces analysis (no 4.), the value net is also a good double-check when evaluating strategic development. For example, one can think about how allying with complementors may enable rising above industry standards (blue ocean strategy, no. 10), development and diversification (Ansoff's box, no. 19), or how the alliance may subsequently be best managed to achieve the desired result (post-acquisition matrix, no. 20), or indeed how social or environmental goals might be achieved (triple bottom line, no. 23).

**MUTATION POTENTIAL:** The most obvious, and probably the best, mutation of the value net is simply to graft it into a five forces, thereby creating a sixth force of industry – complementors – which can surround the competition box to mediate and enhance relations with suppliers and customers and/or act as barriers to substitutes and new entrants.

**INFO FOR FURTHER READING:**

- Garette, B. and Dussauge, P. (2000). Alliances versus acquisitions: choosing the right option. *European Management Journal*, 18(1), 63–69.
- Smith Ring, P. (2000). The three T's of alliance creation: task, team and time. *European Management Journal*, 18(2), 152–163.
- Child, J., Faulkner, D. and Tallman, S. (2005). *Cooperative Strategy: Managing Alliances, Networks, and Joint Ventures*. Oxford University Press.
- Brandenburger, A. M. and Nalebuff, B. J. (2011). *Co-opetition*. Random House.

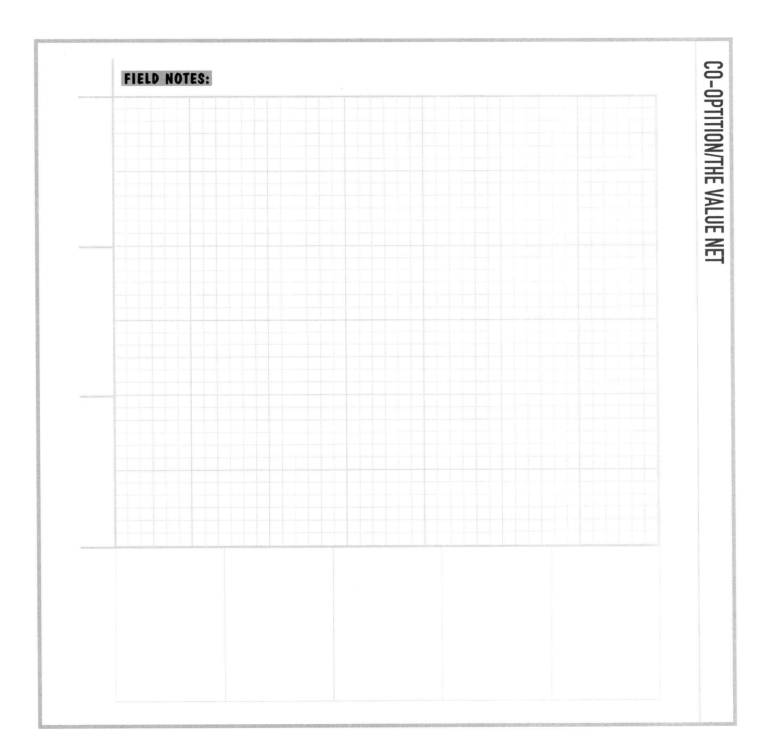

**FIELD NOTES:**

## The Best of the Competitive Positioning Frameworks Combined — Second Foundation: The Competitive Positioning Spidergram

### PURPOSE:

To bring together the key insights from a range of positioning frameworks and thus help present an organization's key competitive strengths and weaknesses graphically on one page to enable better strategic discussion and analysis.

### COMPONENTS:

The Competitive Positioning Spidergram (CPS) brings together key elements from the generic strategy matrix, differentiation categories and blue ocean strategy in two axes. The y-axis runs from a focus on a broad target at the top to a niche at the bottom. The x-axis runs from a cost reduction-focused strategy on the left to a focus on high quality on the right. Thinking about the position of the organization-in-focus relative to competitors can help in thinking about key aspects that should be focused upon the organization's value chain and who might be good collaborators.

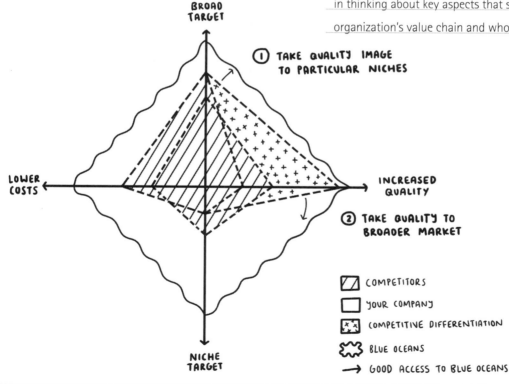

## Dyson's Competitive Positioning Spidergram (c. 1990–2010s)

Dyson will be well known to readers as the producers of the revolutionary vacuum cleaners. After thousands of prototypes developed by founder James Dyson, and years of struggling to get the funding to manufacture and launch on a commercial scale, the DC01 finally hit the market in 1994. The cleaner's revolutionary 'dual cyclone' technology, visible workings and unique design aesthetic made it significantly more expensive than other cleaners, but it became the biggest-selling vacuum cleaner in the UK within a period of just 18 months. The CPS below illustrates the initial Dyson's competitive positioning relative to other providers, its relation to competitive blue oceans and its subsequent strategic growth trajectory.

## Key Takeout:
→ A picture that helps determine what the key competitive strengths and weaknesses of an organization are and debate how this understanding should feed into the development of that organization's strategy.

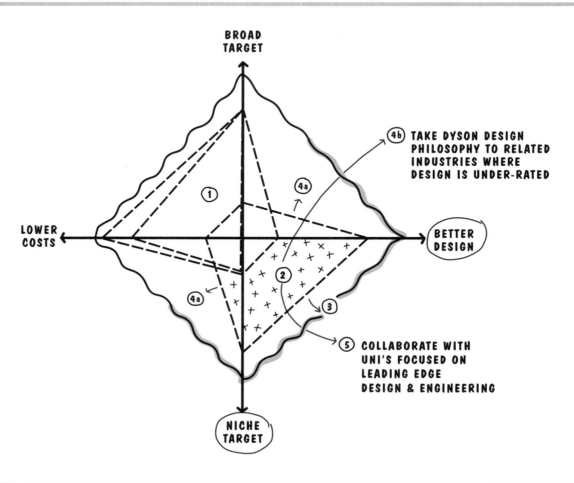

**BROAD TARGET**

**LOWER COSTS**

**BETTER DESIGN**

**NICHE TARGET**

4b TAKE DYSON DESIGN PHILOSOPHY TO RELATED INDUSTRIES WHERE DESIGN IS UNDER-RATED

4a

4a

1

2

3

5 COLLABORATE WITH UNI'S FOCUSED ON LEADING EDGE DESIGN & ENGINEERING

| ① | ② | ③ | ④ | ⑤ |
|---|---|---|---|---|
| Traditionally V cleaners were 'generic', targeted at broad segments with a focus on cost-consciousness & conservative prod development | D went for untapped blue ocean with relatively expensive 'designer' V cleaner | Dyson 'cleaned up' this segment, but not a lot of blue ocean left to exploit given original product was so extreme | Hence later moves to < reduce manufacturing costs, broaden appeal & goes into related industries with bottom-right gaps with D aesthetic: e.g. hand-dryers | Key aspect of D's val chain: hi-end design + mkting + difficult to imitate tech; good collaborators = unis focused on engineering/ design: Cambridge & Imperial |

You can download templates of the Competitive Spidergram to aid your drawing at www.wiley/go/strategybuilder.com or try out the app at www.strategicplan.com.

# RESOURCES AND CAPABILITIES

**Purpose:** Like the competitive advantage frameworks, those focused on resources and capability provide means by which internal strengths and weaknesses can be assessed. But here the focus is on strengths that emerge organically over time rather than positions that are designed or chosen by strategists in the present.

12. **VRIO** – Helps understand which of an organization's strengths could provide a sustained competitive advantage, and hence should be the primary basis of that organization's strategy.

13 **Resource strengths/importance matrix (RSIM)** – Identifies critical resources and capabilities that underpin an organization's competitive advantage.

14. **Dynamic capabilities** – Focuses the strategist on higher-order (and some would say most important) capabilities and strengths: those that enable a firm to learn, adapt and develop new capabilities for the future.

15. **Design thinking** – Encourages strategists and firms to develop the capability to think and act like good designers: thinking from the customer's experience, embracing constraints, prototyping and learning fast, and 'abductive logic'.

16. **7-S framework** – Evaluates how the elements that reflect an organization's culture might interact to enable or disable its strategic development. A good framework for examining how resources and capabilities can be aligned to reinforce one another.

## 12. VRIO

**AUTHORS: Birger Wernerfelt and Jay Barney**

IS THE STRENGTH, RESOURCE OR CAPABILITY...

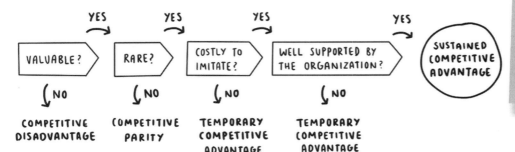

**WHEN TO USE:** When seeking to understand which of an organization's strengths could provide a sustained competitive advantage and hence should be the basis of that organization's strategy.

**COMPONENTS:** VRIO effectively consists of four questions: Is a particular strength, resource or capability *valuable* to customers? Is it *rare*? Is it costly, difficult or impossible for others to *imitate*? Are we supporting it in our *organization*?

## DEVELOPMENT:

The term 'resource-based view' of the firm (RBV) was coined by Birger Wernerfelt in 1984 and extended by Jay Barney, but others outlined similar ideas before this (Edith Penrose may have been the first in the 1950s). RBV-based frameworks, like VRIO, see an organization as a collection of firm-specific resources, routines, capabilities and competencies, and these are often intangible, organic, difficult to define and hard to replicate aspects that explain interfirm differences in competitiveness, as well the evolution of businesses and industries.

By focusing on active or emergent attributes or 'capabilities' as opposed to static strengths as sources of competitive advantage, the RBV (and Henry Mintzberg's work, which highlighted that good strategies tended to emerge organically over time rather than springing from managers' rational articulations of opportunities towards which strengths might be directed) encouraged a shift from seeking to articulate a SWOT in adjectives and nouns towards describing a firm's competitive attributes in active verbs. This perspective has gained greater currency as studies have shown that simply copying other organization's strategies, best-practice style, is generally not an effective approach. It is better to focus on developing a unique strategy, building on those attributes that really add *value*, are *rare* and *inimitable*, and then ensuring that these things are supported *organizationally*.

## Key Takeout:

→ Can you rank your strengths and capabilities in terms of the degree to which they might contribute to a competitive advantage that can be sustained over time?

## Underwater Cinema: Launching Underwater (*c.* 2008\*)

| | VALUABLE TO CUSTOMERS | | RARE | COSTLY TO IMITATE | SUPPORTED BY ORGANIZATION | |
|---|---|---|---|---|---|---|
| | GENERAL CINEMA-GOERS | SCUBA/DIVING ENTHUSIASTS | | | | |
| WORLD CLASS FILMING TECHNOLOGY → | ? | ✓ | ✓ | ✓ | ✓ | SUSTAINABLE ADVANTAGE |
| PATENTED LIGHTING OPTICS TECHNOLOGY → | ✗ | ✗ | ✓ | ✓ | ✓ | SUSTAINABLE ADVANTAGE |
| ENTREPRENEUR/ OWNER IS HIGHLY EXPERIENCED MOVIE CAMERA MAN → | ✗ | ? | ✗ | ✗ | ✓ | PARITY |
| EMPHASIS ON UNDERWATER FILMS IS DISTINCTIVE → | ? | ✓ | ✓ | ✓ | ✓ | SUSTAINABLE ADVANTAGE |

| ① | ② | ③ | ④ | ⑤ |
|---|---|---|---|---|
| UC has interesting set of capabilities and rare, hard to imitate, potentially valuable, tech for underwater film | Need to look at where product could be most valuable. May be little perceived value among general audiences | Concerns about whether this mkt wants full-length underwater feature + sound quality is problematic | But for niche mkt of dive enthusiasts there could be value in seeing such films | Launch strategy refocused upon developing specialist dive films + offering specialist content for other companies seeking particular underwater scenes |

\* The identity of this organization has been disguised.

**DRAW YOUR OWN HERE...**

**1.** Start by noting all of the strengths that a SWOT analysis (no. 1) might highlight about the organization in focus in a vertical list on the left side of the page.

**2.** List the four categories/boxes from the diagram on the previous page as headings along the top of the page to create a table.

**3.** Draw arrows next to each strength and continue each arrow rightwards until the answer to the question posed by the next column is 'no'. Those arrows that make it to the end are your VRIO capabilities or strengths.

Creative ideas:

Take the outlines of a few of your favourite frameworks from previous sections (e.g. think about the stakeholders that need to work to ensure that a VRIO capability is maintained and where these stakeholders are placed on your PI matrix; if you say a capability is supported organizationally, draw it in the centre of a 7-S framework and list how each of the seven nodes supports it).

**COMMON PITFALLS:** Underestimating the competition. You might think it would be difficult to replicate your unique culture or amazing technology, but many strategic failures are based upon not thinking seriously enough about how determined the competition might be to catch and surpass you. Really think through how a desperate competitor or new entrant could copy, mitigate or best your capabilities.

**GOOD IN COMBINATION WITH:** VRIO is a great filter for developing your findings from an initial SWOT analysis (no. 1). It can also be very useful to take the findings from your VRIO back to an ESTEMPLE analysis (no. 2) as you think through how (or whether) your VRIO capabilities will enable you to take advantage of emerging opportunities or mitigate emerging threats in the macro-environment. You can do similar with industry Os and Ts, reflecting back on the five forces (no. 5).

**MUTATION POTENTIAL:** Merge your VRIO capabilities into the centre of a 7-S analysis (no. 16) to look at what should be 'shared capabilities' rather than shared values. Then go around the other six nodes of the 7-Ss and draw or write how they contribute organizational support to these capabilities.

**INFO FOR FURTHER READING:**
- Barney, J.B. and Hesterly, W.S. (2009). 'Evaluating a firm's internal capabilities', chapter 3. In: *Strategic Management and Competitive Advantage*. Pearson Education.
- Collis, D.J. and Montgomery, C.A. (1995). Competing on resources: strategy in the 1990s. *Harvard Business Review,* 73 (July–August), 118–129.
- Wernerfelt, B. (1984). A resource-based view of the firm. *Strategic Management Journal,* 5(April–June), 171–180.

**FIELD NOTES:**

VRIO

## 13. Resource Strengths/Importance Matrix (RSIM)

### AUTHOR: Unknown

|  | SAME AS COMPETITORS OR EASY TO IMITATE | BETTER THAN COMPETITORS & DIFFICULT TO IMITATE |
|---|---|---|
| **RESOURCES** | THRESHOLD RESOURCES | UNIQUE RESOURCES |
| **CAPABILITIES** | THRESHOLD CAPABILITIES | CORE CAPABILITIES / COMPETENCIES |

**RATINGS:** AIM rates 'resource-based analysis' number seven in most popular strategy tools and part of their core toolkit. Top five for strategy choice and number two for strategy implementation, as it may often be employed to summarize findings and create action points from other tools. Resource-based planning is rated number 15 by Aston study. He et al.'s (2012) study rates resource analysis fourth most popular strategy tool in Chinese companies (51%).

**WHEN TO USE:** To distinguish between the resources and capabilities necessary to compete and those that are unique to the company and which can enable superior performance in the market (although a core competence does not automatically confer competitive advantage).

**COMPONENTS:** Threshold resources include tangible and intangible resources (such as financial, physical, human and intellectual). Threshold capabilities (processes, activities or routines applied to resources) are those required to meet customers' minimum requirements. Unique resources critically underpin competitive advantage and cannot be imitated or obtained. Core competencies are the capabilities needed to achieve competitive advantage.

## DEVELOPMENT:

The RSIM emerged with a range of new frameworks, including VRIO (no. 12) in the wake of the resource-based view of the firm in the 1990s. In particular, the RSIM encourages strategists to separate out static resources from the more dynamic and difficult to acquire, imitate or replicate capabilities that were recognized as being key sources of sustained competitive advantage during this period. The framework is useful in sifting aspects crucial to an organization's competitive advantage from those which are only 'hygiene factors' in competitive markets – things that are necessary to keep a company 'in the game'.

Companies can make errors in thinking those aspects in which they have put effort and investment are therefore crucial to competitive advantage when they may be just hygiene factors. The crucial aspects, which might be 'game changers', may be elements that we focus 20% of our energy on, but they may make 80% of the difference. In this way, the RSIM is a good addition to, and link between, the VRIO framework described earlier and the notion of dynamic capabilities, which looks at how some particular capabilities not only can sustain competitive advantage but also refresh and evolve that advantage over time.

## Key Takeout:

→ Have you isolated those critical resources and capabilities – active properties that are better than your competitors and difficult for them to replicate – that can really drive a sustained competitive advantage?

# Lush: Smells like a strategy (*c.* 2010)

|  | SAME AS COMPETITORS OR EASY TO IMITATE | BETTER THAN COMPETITORS & DIFFICULT TO IMITATE |
|---|---|---|
| **RESOURCES** | SHOP LOCATIONS & FIT OUT<br>RETAIL EMPLOYEES<br>NATURAL INGREDIENTS<br>BRIGHT LIGHTING<br>FREE SAMPLE | UNIQUE PRODUCTS DISPLAYED WITHOUT PACKAGING<br><br>COCKTAIL OF EXCITING, INNOVATIVE PRODUCTS<br><br>BIG BASINS + MIRRORS CREATE FEEL OF LUXURIOUS BATHROOM |
| **CAPABILITIES** | PRODUCT DEVELOPMENT OF ITEMS IN RANGE OF COLOURS, TEXTURES, SMELLS<br><br>HELPFUL, FRIENDLY STAFF WHO ENCOURAGE TRYING PRODUCTS | VIVID SENSORY EXPERIENCE<br>ENGAGING, LUXURIOUS<br>+ FUN AMBIENCE<br>COOL MAGAZINE<br>+ ONLINE PRESENCE<br>PASSIONATE STAFF BOUGHT INTO THE BRAND<br>A SENSORY OVERLOAD YOU WANT TO SHARE / GIFT |

**THE CORE OF LUSH**

| ① | ② | ③ | ④ | ⑤ |
|---|---|---|---|---|
| Lush has amped up retailing with colourful, aromatic and organic-looking products that excite senses | Removal of packaging enables shoppers to actively experience product sensually: sight, smell, touch... | Bright colours, vivid aromas + other related promos attract passers-by into the store | Shopping becomes process of trying out, taking away samples, rather than a transaction — 'experiencing' this encourages sales | In combination, these elements create an exotic and memorable experience that keeps Lush 'top-of-mind' |

**DRAW YOUR OWN HERE...**

**1.** The RSIM works better graphically if you reverse the Rs and Cs on the y-axis. Once you've redrawn the matrix this way, start by noting all the things that are necessary to compete in your market in the bottom left box (threshold Rs).

**2.** Think about whether these things are a stock or supply of assets (Rs) or things we do (processes/ activities) (Cs). Move the Cs upwards (threshold Cs).

**3.** Think about which Rs and Cs are unique to your firm and difficult for competitors to imitate. Move them into the appropriate box in the right column.

Creative ideas:

**A.** Look at the system within the matrix. Once you've noted all your main Rs and Cs, draw links between them with arrows to illustrate how interconnected (and thus even more difficult to replicate by competitors) your capability system is.

**B.** Make the RSIM into a value chain shape that depicts how your Rs and Cs combine to create value for users/customers/stakeholders.

**COMMON PITFALLS:** Struggling to distinguish Cs from Rs. While capabilities may be regarded as resources for, or assets of, an organization, resources cannot be capabilities. A good way to distinguish the two is to remember that Cs have some active component; they are verbs. Resources are static and generally described by nouns.

While it is fairly easy to ascertain whether an R or a C is unique in an industry, people often overestimate the difficulty others may have in imitating such things. Really think through how an R or C might be copied, rather than assuming that it can't.

**GOOD IN COMBINATION WITH:** Together with VRIO (no. 12) and dynamic capabilities (no. 14) the RSIM enables the strategist to develop a good appreciation for and handle on the distinctive capabilities that, if harnessed well, can drive an organization's strategic development.

**MUTATION POTENTIAL:** As mentioned in the 'creative ideas' section, crossing the RSIM with a value chain can help to give real point to a discussion about how an organization's resources and capabilities work together to process inputs into outputs in ways that create superior value. In addition, it can be useful to use the O (for 'organizationally supported') piece from VRIO and circle those Rs and Cs that are promoted and rewarded by the organization.

**INFO FOR FURTHER READING:**
- Barney, J. (1991). Firm resources and sustained competitive advantage. *Journal of Management*, 19(1), 99–120.
- Barney, J. and Clark, D. (2007). *Resource Based Theory*. Oxford: Oxford University Press.
- Evans, V. (2013). Key *Strategy Tools: The 80+ Tools for Every Manager to Build a Winning Strategy*. UK: Pearson.

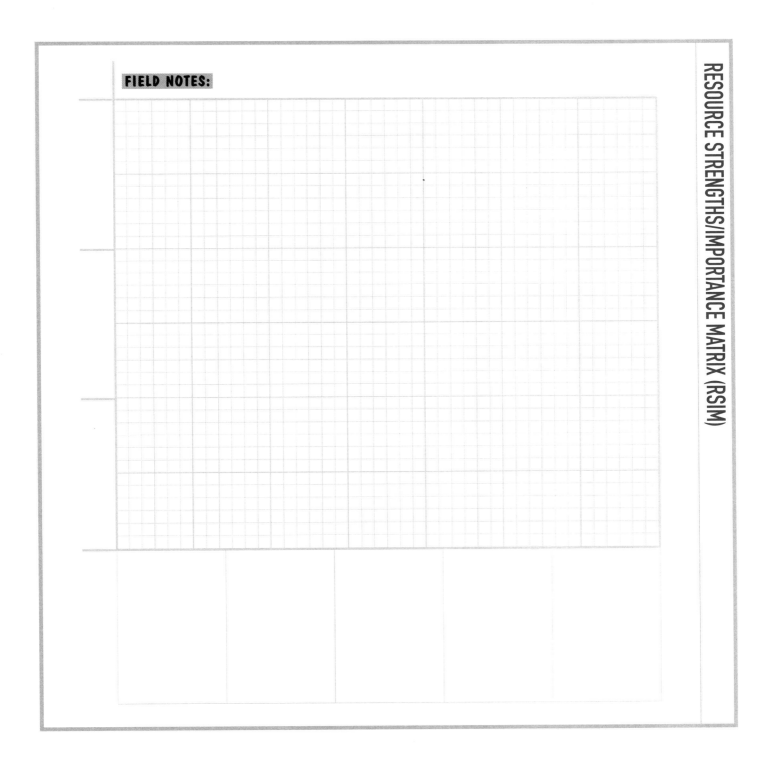

**FIELD NOTES:**

RESOURCE STRENGTHS/IMPORTANCE MATRIX (RSIM)

## 14. Dynamic Capabilities

## AUTHOR: David Teece (and others)

**SENSING CAPABILITIES –** CAPABILITIES THAT ENABLE THE EFFECTIVE EXPLORATION OF OPPORTUNITIES FOR DEVELOPMENT & GROWTH

**SEIZING CAPABILITIES –** CAPABILITIES THAT ENABLE OPPORTUNITIES TO BE EFFECTIVELY CAPTURED & EXPLOITED

**THREATS MANAGEMENT & TRANSFORMATION CAPABILITIES –** WHICH MITIGATE THREATS, INTEGRATE NEW ACTIVITIES & IMPLEMENT SUBSTANTIAL CHANGE

**RATINGS:** A new concept not known to many managers, nevertheless, dynamic capabilities (DC) analysis is already AIM's 16th most popular strategy tool, while capabilities are seen as the fourth most popular strategy tool in the Aston study.

**WHEN TO USE:** When seeking to ascertain what elements of an organization should be focused on that will enable it not only to succeed in the present, but also to learn and adapt, so as to develop new ways to succeed in the future.

**COMPONENTS:** There are a number of different manifestations of DC analysis. Most are complex. Even David Teece's framework (on which the diagram is based) has 15 elements. But we just isolate the main or fundamental DCs here: sensing capabilities, seizing capabilities and transforming capabilities.

## DEVELOPMENT:

As the relationship between difficult to replicate capabilities, the importance of learning and adaptation in complex environments, and effective strategy development was examined further in the 2000s, the concept of DCs emerged. DCs are essentially second- or higher-order capabilities: those that enable adaptation through the development of new strengths and capabilities and the refreshing of existing ones as an organization evolves. Such capabilities are fewer in number in an organization than the list of strengths that might have traditionally been drawn up in a strategic planning exercise, so a focus on DCs can enable a greater degree of emphasis on the things that really maintain value in the long term.

The most useful framework for thinking about DCs in relation to a particular firm may be David Teece's sequence of 'sensing → seizing → transforming', where an organization's DCs are divided into a series that follows the generally accepted 'explore → exploit' pattern of successful strategic growth. Organizing an organization's value-adding capabilities in this way and discussing their relationship can be particularly useful for organizations seeking to grow through acquisition, where the aim is to acquire good targets and add value to these acquisitions, or organically, by building on existing capabilities and growing new ones.

**Key Takeout:**

→ What can you do that will enable us to create the capabilities that will ensure your survival in the future?

## Toyota: The evolutionary hub (*c.* 1950–2015)

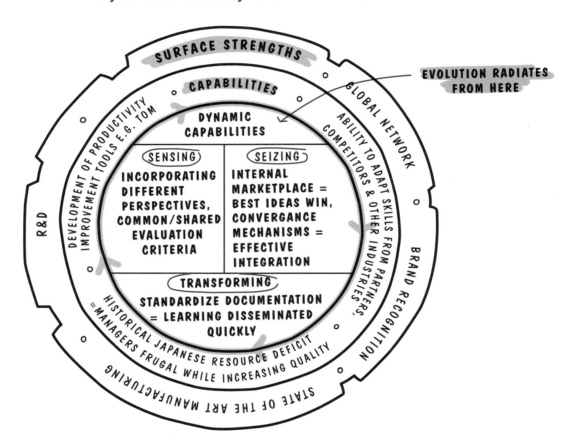

**SURFACE STRENGTHS**

**CAPABILITIES**

EVOLUTION RADIATES FROM HERE

DEVELOPMENT OF PRODUCTIVITY IMPROVEMENT TOOLS E.G. TQM

GLOBAL NETWORK

ABILITY TO ADAPT SKILLS FROM PARTNERS, COMPETITORS & OTHER INDUSTRIES

BRAND RECOGNITION

R&D

STATE OF THE ART MANUFACTURING

HISTORICAL JAPANESE RESOURCE DEFICIT = MANAGERS FRUGAL WHILE INCREASING QUALITY

**DYNAMIC CAPABILITIES**

SENSING
INCORPORATING DIFFERENT PERSPECTIVES, COMMON/SHARED EVALUATION CRITERIA

SEIZING
INTERNAL MARKETPLACE = BEST IDEAS WIN, CONVERGANCE MECHANISMS = EFFECTIVE INTEGRATION

TRANSFORMING
STANDARDIZE DOCUMENTATION = LEARNING DISSEMINATED QUICKLY

| ① | ② | ③ | ④ | ⑤ |
|---|---|---|---|---|
| It's easy to recognize Toyota's surface strengths: brand, global network, product range, etc. But it pays to look deeper | Behind these strengths are deeper capabilities and dynamic capabilities that drive Toyota's evolution | Incorporating diverse perspectives combined with common eval criteria helps the continued <u>sensing</u> of ops | An internal marketplace & excellent convergence/ integration mechanisms ensure ops are <u>seized</u> well | Standardized documentation systems mean learning is circulated quickly to enable the whole org to <u>transform</u> itself |

**DRAW YOUR OWN HERE...**

**1.** Start by jotting down your VRI strengths in any of the three sensing, seizing and transforming boxes, depending on how you think they would be best categorized.

**2.** If you are left with gaps in any of the three boxes, look back at your VRIO table and see if there are other capabilities that could be made more inimitable.

**3.** Articulate these and draw them into the appropriate boxes in a different coloured pen as capabilities that your strategy should aim to enhance.

**Creative ideas:**

DCs are almost always systems of multiple parts and relations (one of the main reasons why they are dynamic, self-perpetuating and difficult for others to replicate). Instead of listing them as text in the boxes, draw each of them as a system of components and show how the sensing system links to the seizing system and so on in a cycle rather than just a linear arrangement.

**COMMON PITFALLS:** An inability to think of strategic processes and practices rather than static strengths and strategic 'contents'. Think about how a strategic behaviour actually helps you not just to be, but to adapt and become something different.

An inability to really think into the future. Not so much an inability really as something that is difficult to do and which DC thinking can really encourage if you let it. While 'curiosity about other industries' may not seem anything tangible to add to the bottom line right now, it might be what saves your company in the future.

**GOOD IN COMBINATION WITH:** SWOT (no. 1), VRIO (no. 12) and DCs make a good team. SWOT starts you out broad, a good way of brainstorming (or brain-dumping) a raft of strengths. VRIO helps narrow in on those few things that can sustain a competitive advantage. DCs promote far-sightedness into how this competitive advantage might be adapted in the future. DCs are also a good bridge to Strategy Builder block 4's focus on growth options. Hence, one of the newest strategy frameworks might be fruitfully followed up with a discussion using something like Ansoff's diversification matrix (no. 19).

**MUTATION POTENTIAL:** Place your DCs in a cycle into the top right square of a PI matrix. Ask yourself if your key stakeholders that drive your key DCs are all in that crucial top right square. Additionally, melding sensing, seizing and transforming DCs into the middle of Ansoff's box can help you think through the best way/s to utilize these DCs to grow the business.

**INFO FOR FURTHER READING:**
- Teece, D. and Pisano, G. (1994). The dynamic capabilities of firms: an introduction. *Industrial and Corporate Change*, 3(3), 537–556.
- Teece, D.J. (2007). Explicating dynamic capabilities: the nature and microfoundations of (sustainable) enterprise performance. *Strategic Management Journal*, 28(13), 1319–1350.
- Helfat, C.E., Finkelstein, S., Mitchell, W., Peteraf, M., Singh, H., Teece, D. and Winter, S.G. (2009). *Dynamic Capabilities: Understanding Strategic Change in Organizations.* John Wiley.

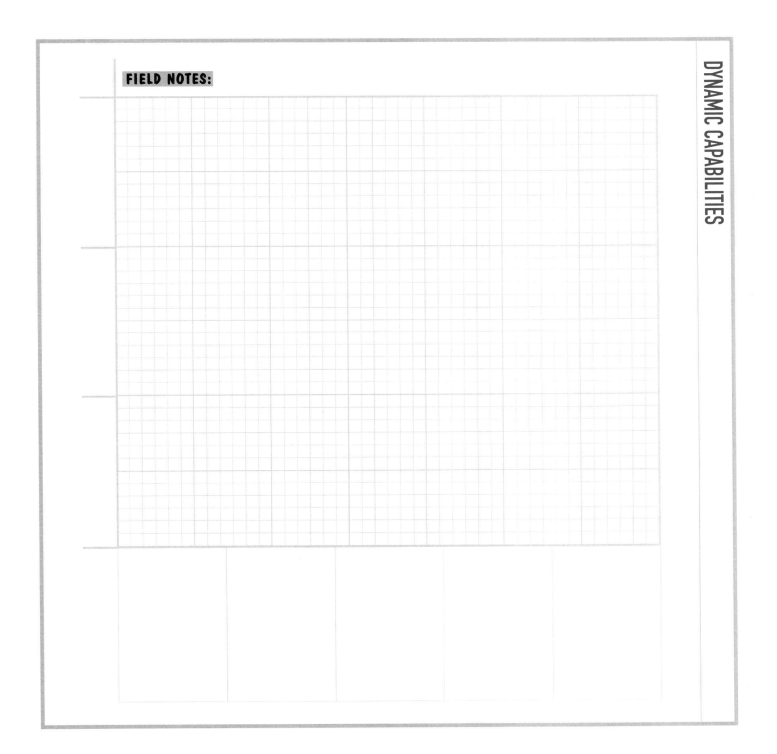

**FIELD NOTES:**

## 15. Design Thinking

## AUTHOR: Roger Martin (and others)

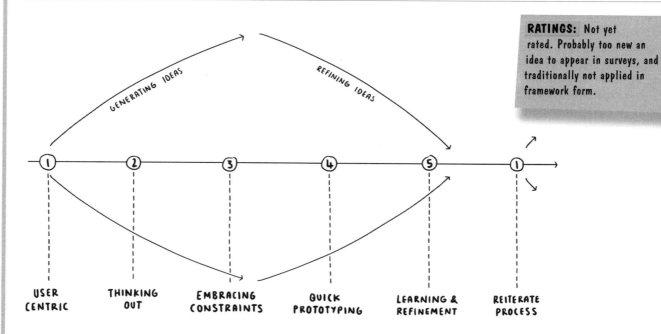

**RATINGS:** Not yet rated. Probably too new an idea to appear in surveys, and traditionally not applied in framework form.

Diagram labels:

GENERATING IDEAS — REFINING IDEAS

① USER CENTRIC   ② THINKING OUT   ③ EMBRACING CONSTRAINTS   ④ QUICK PROTOTYPING   ⑤ LEARNING & REFINEMENT   ① REITERATE PROCESS

**WHEN TO USE:** To encourage innovative strategies by promoting thinking like a good designer: thinking from the customer's experience, embracing constraints, prototyping and learning fast, and utilizing 'abductive' logic.

**COMPONENTS:** Many and varied, but we have narrowed this down to five: being user-centric in your strategic thinking; thinking out beyond traditional planning periods; recognizing and embracing constraints; quick prototyping of ideas; and fast failing and refinement.

## DEVELOPMENT:

The most influential new trend in business thinking in the recent past has been the promotion of 'design thinking'. Design thinking as a new way for considering business or strategy development may be traced to Silicon Valley's IDEO, formed in 1991. They were perhaps the first design company to actively promote their process to a wider audience. IDEO drew heavily on the Stanford University design curriculum, and IDEO's David Kelley was one of the first to explicitly articulate the idea that business people should think like designers. The academic most associated with promoting design thinking is Roger Martin, whose 2009 book, *Design of Business*, popularized the notion.

What thinking like a designer might mean varies depending on who is doing the telling, and there is a lack of a clear diagram which simply articulates key elements, but the framework above outlines the importance of 'thinking out' through 'abductive logic'. This means that, rather than using inductive or deductive logic to make decisions based on past or present conditions and possibilities, you imagine something that might be and reach out to understand and develop it (Steve Jobs, Martin Luther King and JFK are held up as visionaries in this regard). User-centricism (or thinking from the perspective of the user rather than the producer), embracing constraints as interesting parts of the design brief rather than being frustrated by them, and looking for opportunities to fail fast, learn and quickly improve the offering through quick prototyping, learning quickly through failing, and refinement.

**Key Takeouts:**

➔ How do users of your product or service really experience it?

➔ How can we think differently to make this experience better?

# Swatch: The Second Watch (*c.* 1980)

③ **EMBRACE CONSTRAINTS / QUICK PROTOTYPING**
MAKE HIGH QUALITY FASHIONABLE WATCH CHEAPER
-NEW MATERIALS
-MASS-PRODUCTION FRIENDLY CONSTRUCTION

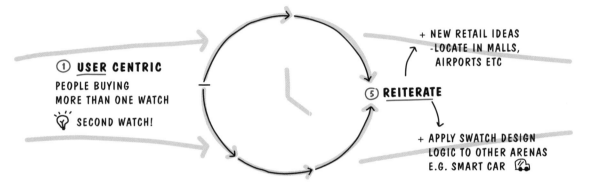

① **USER CENTRIC**
PEOPLE BUYING
MORE THAN ONE WATCH

💡 SECOND WATCH!

+ NEW RETAIL IDEAS
-LOCATE IN MALLS,
 AIRPORTS ETC

⑤ **REITERATE**

+ APPLY SWATCH DESIGN
LOGIC TO OTHER ARENAS
E.G. SMART CAR

② **THINKING OUT**
WHAT IF A SWISS WATCH WAS
- A FASHION STATEMENT
- WORLD'S SMALLEST CANVAS

④ **REFINE EXISTING IDEAS**
- SWISS ENGINEERED
  SUPER-THIN WATCH
- PREVIOUS ATTEMPTS AT
  PLASTIC WATCH CONSTRUCTION

| ① | ② | ③ | ④ | ⑤ |
|---|---|---|---|---|
| Swiss watchmakers worried about Asian competition. But N.G. Hayek observes an opportunity... | Looking at how this has changed user behaviour, encouraging multi-buying, he conceives the '2nd watch' concept | Swatch seeks to rethink what a Swiss watch can be, seeing trad constraints as challenges to be overcome | Innovations that missed the market (Tissots' plastic, Concord superthin) are learnt from/refined | Continued user-centric thinking out leads to new retail ideas and projects like the SMART (Swatch Mercedes Art) car |

**DRAW YOUR OWN HERE...**

1. Begin by isolating a particular customer and draw him/her in the middle of the page.

2. Work through the design thinking phases asking how the customer is experiencing your company and draw the results. Then 'think out' to consider how this could be improved; draw the constraints and design with and around them; how can you prototype this thinking fast; and how will you learn and adapt as you see the impact of these developments on the user experience?

Creative ideas:

Don't just imagine how customers experience your products, pick up a phone or step into a showroom and ask them to describe or draw this. Or search social media for what people are saying about your company and the use quotations from this as basis of your drawing/design thinking.

**COMMON PITFALLS:** Getting carried away with design thinking at the expense of a solid strategic underpinning for it. Developing design thinking is good, but it should be aimed at particular opportunities, customer needs or aspirations, and seek to build on current strategic strengths and capabilities, otherwise it may be an expensive exercise in missing the mark. Recent research shows, for example, that just winning design awards has no significant effect on an organization's financial performance.

**GOOD IN COMBINATION WITH:** Design thinking is future-focused but draws on past and present experiences, so it is good to use in combination with a summary of the key Os and Ts identified in an environmental ecosystem analysis (block 1) and Ss and Ws from applying competitive advantage and resources and capabilities frameworks (block 2). Think about how design thinking can help you develop strategies that take advantage of satisfying opportunities for new customer experiences while building on traditional and emerging strengths and capabilities.

**MUTATION POTENTIAL:** A good way of keeping design thinking grounded is to place a mirror image of the 'design fish' into a value chain so that it ends on the right-hand side of the value chain with user experience. Explore how customer experiences of your products/services represent value, then work backwards through the chain to explore new ways of prototyping and developing new offerings that add greater value in the future, and what this will require of various primary and support activities, supplier relationships and so on.

**INFO FOR FURTHER READING:**

- Brown, T. (2008). Design thinking. *Harvard Business Review*, 86(6), 84.
- Cummings, S., Petty, M.M. and Walker, B. (2014). 'Innovation is not the only thing'. In: *Handbook of Management and Creativity*. Edward Elgar: London.
- Martin, R.L. (2009). *The Design of Business: Why Design Thinking is the Next Competitive Advantage*. Harvard Business Press.

**FIELD NOTES:**

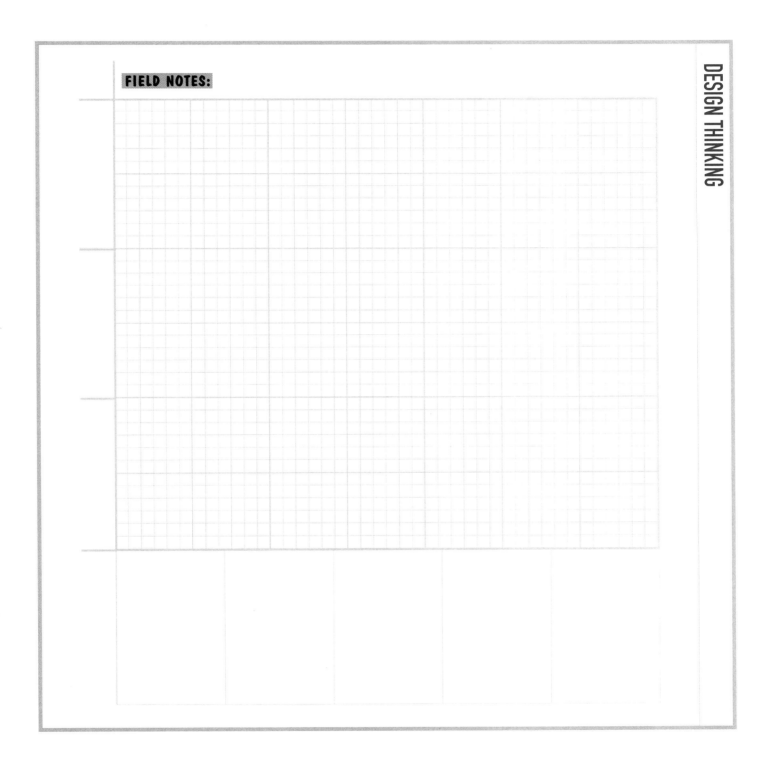

DESIGN THINKING

RESOURCES AND CAPABILITIES  **129**

## 16. 7-S Framework

**AUTHORS: Tony Athos, Richard Pascale, Tom Peters and Robert Waterman**

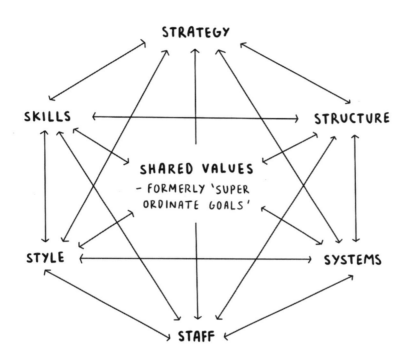

**WHEN TO USE:** To evaluate how the elements that reflect an organization's culture may interact to enable or disable its success and strategic development.

**COMPONENTS:** Seven interconnected nodes that are seen to reflect the elements of an organization's culture that can influence its strategic development. All seven start with the letter S, more as a memory aid than for any other reason (earlier versions used different terms – see the following page).

## DEVELOPMENT:

Management went 'Pop' around 1980 as a growing managerial class turned *Theory Z, The Art of Japanese Management* and *In Search of Excellence* into bestsellers. The first two titles tapped into an anxiety that Japan was outperforming the West. They found the reason to be something previously avoided by business strategists: intangibles like culture and values (remember the Stanford team behind SWOT (no. 1) chose to park 'values' to focus on 'appraisal'). The latter two books shared a framework for making these intangibles more tangible: the 7-S framework. A key driver behind its development was the growth of the Boston Consulting Group (who had just developed the Boston Consulting Group (BCG) matrix – see no. 6). This provoked McKinsey & Co. to develop competing products via link-ups with professors such as Harvard's Athos. In 1980, Waterman claimed that they spent 'a little over a year and a half pondering' the right framework, but how it emerged is unclear. Peters has recently said that the key to success was Athos's helping to turn their ideas into a snappy framework they termed 'a new view of organization'. However, the 7-S framework is also very similar to a seven-node model of 'effective organizational dynamics' published in 1978 by Athos's Harvard colleague John Kotter. Kotter's model lacked the snappy alliteration (e.g. he had 'formal organizational arrangements' rather than 'systems') and it never caught on. Inspired by the interest in the softer aspects of strategy that the 7-S framework helped foster, the stern sounding 'super-ordinate goals' later became 'shared values'. In recent years, a similar framework called 'the cultural web' (by Gerry Johnson and Kevan Scholes) has been widely used to similar effect in Europe.

**Key Takeout:**

➔ Are the elements of your culture consistently reinforcing one another and your strategy, or are they inconsistent, leading to confusion, inefficiencies and wasted effort?

# Barcelona FC: La Familia (*c.* 1930s–2015)

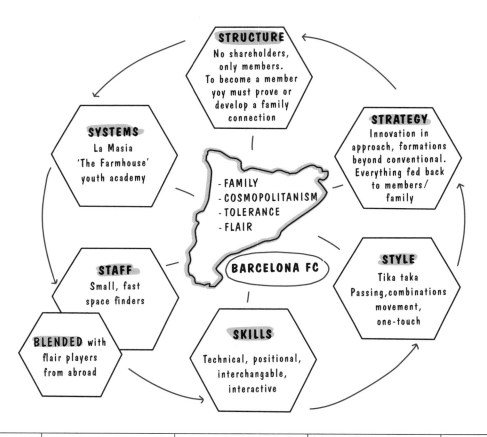

**STRUCTURE**
No shareholders, only members. To become a member yoy must prove or develop a family connection

**SYSTEMS**
La Masia 'The Farmhouse' youth academy

**STRATEGY**
Innovation in approach, formations beyond conventional. Everything fed back to members/ family

- FAMILY
- COSMOPOLITANISM
- TOLERANCE
- FLAIR

**BARCELONA FC**

**STAFF**
Small, fast space finders

**STYLE**
Tika taka Passing,combinations movement, one-touch

**BLENDED** with flair players from abroad

**SKILLS**
Technical, positional, interchangable, interactive

| ① | ② | ③ | ④ | ⑤ |
|---|---|---|---|---|
| Barca is one of the world's great teams: the elements of their culture reinforce each other & drive strategy | The club is shaped by Catalan values: tolerance, cosmopolitanism, innovation, flair & above all family. All understand what Barca is about | The values inform the academy, the ownership structure, the Barca style, players sought & strategy | In the words of Pep Segura, Barca's system 'is about creating one philosophy from the bottom of the club to the top' | This clarity + tolerance & the appreciation of diversity enable ideas and players from abroad to be effectively blended with the Barca way |

**DRAW YOUR OWN HERE...**

**1. Pencil** in all the seven circles and leave them blank. Get started by jotting notes in one circle in which you think the organization has real strength.

**2. Fill in** the other circles as you see fit. There is no order you need to follow, and apart from shared values in the middle, you can move the other nodes around to suit the connections and links you see.

**3. Show strength** of the connections or reinforcement between nodes through the width of the connecting lines. A lack of connection could be drawn as a dashed line. No connection or inconsistency could be indicated by no line.

Creative ideas:

A. Alter the size of the circles to indicate their importance/contribution to your strategy.

B. Draw the present situation. Then, next to that, draw the ideal that you think the organization should move towards.

C. If you find it hard to articulate the organization's shared values, think of the personality or even the car brand that is most analogous to the company and draw them or it in the middle (e.g. an earlier book of ours contained a case that looked at how HSBC staff found it useful to relate the company to actor and travel show host Michael Palin). Are the other six nodes consistent with this character/brand or not?

**COMMON PITFALLS:** Trying to start in the middle, which seems logical given the shape of the diagram, can lead to getting bogged down and frustrated. Just like a jigsaw, deal with the most tangible and least ambiguous pieces like structure and staff first, then work your way in.

Thinking it all has to be filled in before you can start thinking strategically. Can't agree on what your shared values of stories are? Don't let that stop you. Perhaps recognizing a need to develop a clearer understanding of these things should be an important strategic objective and outcome of your analysis.

**GOOD IN COMBINATION WITH:** Any other framework that helps you to articulate strengths and weaknesses – SWOT (no. 1), value chain (no. 7), blue ocean (no. 10), VRIO (no. 12), dynamic capabilities (no. 14) – can benefit from having the 7-S diagram sketched alongside. Because of its shape and systemic nature, the 7-Ss can be a useful way of seeing how your key strengths relate to/reinforce one another and where your weaknesses lie in the organization.

**MUTATION POTENTIAL:** As mentioned in 'creative ideas' on the previous page, it can be useful to aid visualization of the ideas conveyed in the 7-Ss by relating shared values to brand or corporate personality. You can similarly meld the 7-Ss with your own branding by putting your corporate logo, or latest ad campaign, and what it seeks to symbolize in the centre and thinking through its consistency with the reality of your structure, staff, stories, etc.

**INFO FOR FURTHER READING:**
- Angwin, D., Cummings, S. and Smith, C. (2011). *The Strategy Pathfinder: Core Concepts and Live Cases.* John Wiley & Sons (chapter 6).
- Johnson, G., Whittington, R., Scholes, K., Angwin, D.N. and Regner, P. (2014). *Exploring Strategy: Text & Cases,* 10th edition. Harlow: Financial Times Prentice Hall – outlines a useful alternative framework, 'the cultural web'.
- Pascale, R.T. and Athos, A.G. (1981). *The Art of Japanese Management: Applications for American Executives.* New York: Simon and Schuster.
- Waterman, R.H., Jr, Peters, T.J. and Phillips, J.R. (1980). Structure is not organization. *Business Horizons,* 23(3), 14–26.

**FIELD NOTES:**

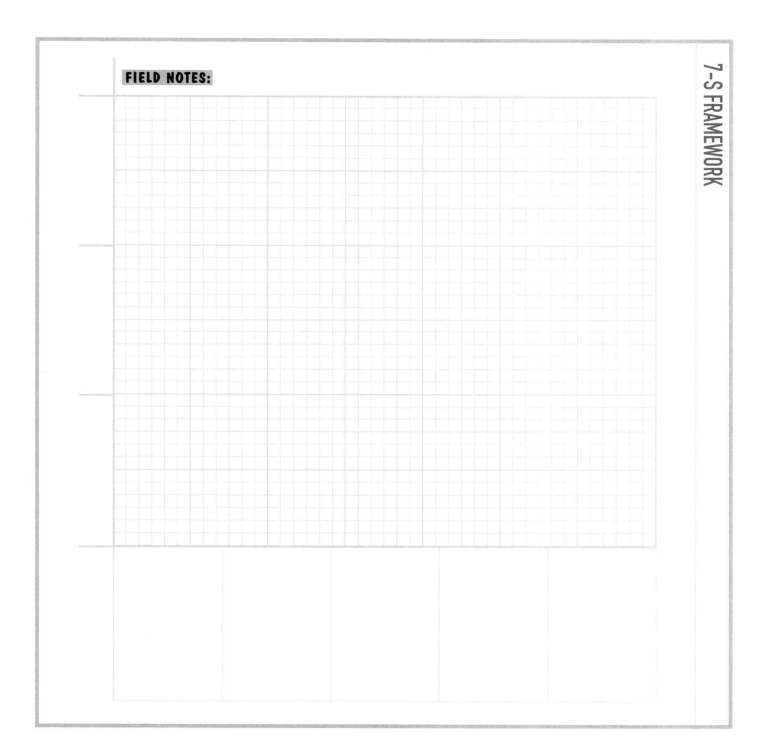

# The Best of the Resources and Capabilities Frameworks Combined — Third Foundation: The Capability Radar

## PURPOSE:

To bring together the key insights from a range of capability frameworks to help present key capabilities in combination with the competitive spidergram's assessment of strengths and weaknesses to enable more focused strategic analysis and decision-making.

## COMPONENTS:

The Capability Radar (CR) multiplies many of the important dimensions of the capability frameworks outlined in this section to identify an organization's most strategically important strengths and weaknesses and frames this with 'design thinking'. Valuable capabilities in an industry are listed in the top left column. Below these are listed potentially valuable capabilities unique to the organization in focus. The organization is then assessed in terms of whether their capability in each category is rare, organizationally supported, inimitable and dynamic. The right-hand column allows space for considering how particular users may experience these capabilities. The top-scoring capabilities are then presenting in a radar chart, with the strongest scoring capabilities being key strengths and the lowest weaknesses.

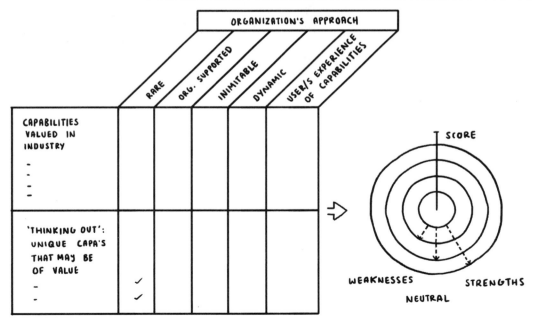

## McLaren Advanced Technologies' Capability Radar (c. 2015)

Founded in 1963 by New Zealand racer, engineer and inventor Bruce McLaren, McLaren started life, and is still best known as, a Formula 1 racing team. The McLaren Group now has a range of automotive interests directed from its state-of-the-art technology centre in England's 'Motorsport Valley'. While McLaren Advanced Technology (MAT), one of its newer subsidiaries, has recently moved into management consultancy, and this may seem an unusual step, seen through the lens of the Capability Radar it makes a lot of sense. McLaren's traditional focus on generating better performance by understanding the human/technology interface could exploit a gap between traditional consultancies and IT providers who have moved in more recently. Perhaps MAT can apply the values that date back to 1963: being technically driven but understated and completed focused on problem-solving to enhance performance, to shake up the maturing market of management consultancy?

## Key Takeout:

➜ A radar-like picture isolating an organization's key capabilities and weaknesses to be considered in strategic growth option development.

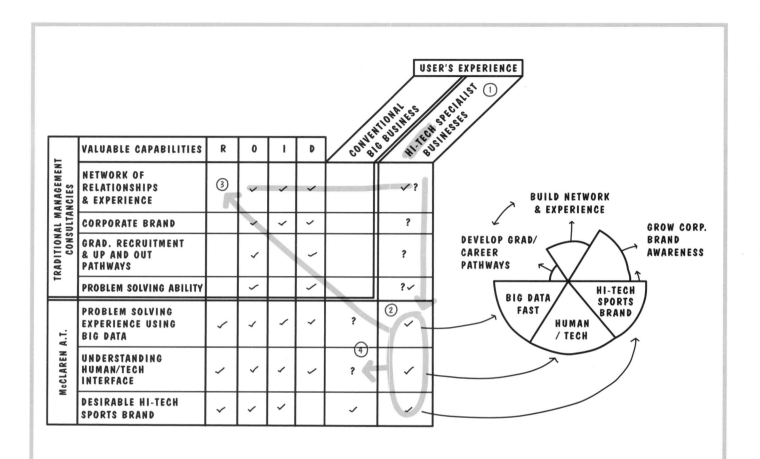

| | VALUABLE CAPABILITIES | R | O | I | D | CONVENTIONAL BIG BUSINESS | HI-TECH SPECIALIST BUSINESSES |
|---|---|---|---|---|---|---|---|
| **TRADITIONAL MANAGEMENT CONSULTANCIES** | NETWORK OF RELATIONSHIPS & EXPERIENCE | ③ ✓ | ✓ | ✓ | | | ✓ ? |
| | CORPORATE BRAND | | ✓ | ✓ | ✓ | | ? |
| | GRAD. RECRUITMENT & UP AND OUT PATHWAYS | | | ✓ | ✓ | | ? |
| | PROBLEM SOLVING ABILITY | | | ✓ | | ✓ | ? ✓ |
| **McLAREN A.T.** | PROBLEM SOLVING EXPERIENCE USING BIG DATA | ✓ | ✓ | ✓ | ✓ | ? ② | ✓ |
| | UNDERSTANDING HUMAN/TECH INTERFACE | ✓ | ✓ | ✓ | ✓ | ? ④ | ✓ |
| | DESIRABLE HI-TECH SPORTS BRAND | ✓ | ✓ | ✓ | | | ✓ |

Radar diagram labels: USER'S EXPERIENCE ①, BUILD NETWORK & EXPERIENCE, DEVELOP GRAD/CAREER PATHWAYS, GROW CORP. BRAND AWARENESS, BIG DATA FAST, HUMAN/TECH, HI-TECH SPORTS BRAND

| ① | ② | ③ | ④ | ⑤ |
|---|---|---|---|---|
| MAT has some of the trad important capa's but can also tap into: hi-perf sports-tech brand, engineering related to human/tech interface, hi-speed prob-solving culture | These 'out of the box' capa's are rare, org supported & hard to imitate. The culture & human/tech focus are dynamic capabilities | These capa's may be esp. appealing to specialist hi-tech or engineering focused firms whose cultures may jar with trad consult. firms | Once they are established here, MAT may broaden focus while building their networking & biz acumen capa's | MAT must keep key strengths/systems/staff etc. networked to each other & to shared values as they grow |

You can download templates of the Capability Radar to aid your drawing at www.wiley/go/strategybuilder.com or try out the app at www.strategicplan.com.

# STRATEGIC GROWTH OPTIONS

**Purpose:** Growth Options frameworks provide means by which insights gleaned from wider environmental analysis and competition and capability frameworks can be taken forward to provide options and pathways for strategic development.

17. **Confrontation matrix** – Sets strengths and weaknesses against opportunities and threats to help determine which combinations provide the best pathways for strategic development.

18. **General Electric/McKinsey screen** – Enables seeing the 'bigger picture' in a multi-activity operation so that decisions can be made about whether to invest further or divest particular parts of the organizations portfolio.

19. **Ansoff's box** – Breaks growth options down to four simple to understand generic categories that have held true for 60 years.

20. **Post-acquisition matrix** – Helps focus minds on the all-important post-acquisition phase of growth through adding value by buying another entity, so that this can be part of the strategic decision-making process relating to the acquisition.

21. **Next practice matrix** – A structured way of encouraging developing strategic initiatives other than simply following the current leader's best practices.

## 17. Confrontation Matrix

**AUTHOR: Unknown**

| | OPPORTUNITIES | | | | THREATS | | | |
|---|---|---|---|---|---|---|---|---|
| | O1 ↓ | O2 ↓ | O3 ↓ | O4 ↓ | T1 ↓ | T2 ↓ | T3 ↓ | T4 ↓ |
| **STRENGTHS** S1 → | | | | | | | | |
| S2 → | | | | | | | | |
| S3 → | | | | | | | | |
| S4 → | | | | | | | | |
| **WEAKNESSES** W1 → | | | | | | | | |
| W2 → | | | | | | | | |
| W3 → | | | | | | | | |
| W4 → | | | | | | | | |

**RATINGS:** Not rated, but the Confrontation Matrix can be seen as a graphical development of number on ranked SWOT analysis that seeks to overcome many of its traditional weaknesses.

**WHEN TO USE:** An effective way to bring together the results of external and internal strategic analyses, to assess the fit of the company with its context. The assumption is that a good fit means a more profitable and sustainable strategic position.

**COMPONENTS:** Strengths (organizational strengths better than industry standard); weaknesses (organizational weaknesses below industry standard); threats (negative pressures from external environments); opportunities (positive pressures from external environments).

## DEVELOPMENT:

This is an extension of SWOT, with which we began our review of strategy frameworks. There we saw how SWOT analysis could be improved by portraying it as a matrix so that relationships between Os and Ts and Ss and Ws could be more easily observed and charted. The confrontation matrix (CM) takes this to the next level, placing the main factors gleaned from a SWOT analysis on an organization outside of the matrix as column and row headings and forcing the user to explicitly set, or collide, internal factors of the organization against external factors. It is a deceptively simple framework, but the confrontation exercise can be more difficult in practice than it appears. However, it should result in a clearer picture of real opportunities – those that the organization can seize with its strengths; real threats – those that the company's strengths cannot mitigate; potential opportunities – those opportunities that are currently hindered by company weaknesses; and potential threats – those that the company's strengths may help to reduce. This analysis can serve to provide the best pathways for strategic development. The framework may also provide an insight into organizational barriers for change to the organization. The example given on the previous page is a numeric scoring version, but the framework can also be used in a more conceptual or developmental way as an aid to stimulate debate and discussion about where the emphasis would be placed in an organization's strategic development plan.

## Key Takeout:
➔ What are the key external forces and internal elements from which you should develop your strategic priorities and objectives for the future?

# Morgan: Avoiding a high-impact collusion (*c.* 2010)

**Opportunities (O):**
- LONG ORDER BOOK
- CUSTOMER LOYALTY
- SECONDARY MARKET FOR PLACES ON LIST
- RISING ASIAN/MIDDLE EAST DEMAND

**Threats (T):**
- INCREASING SAFETY REGS
- WELL-RESOURCED COMPETITORS
- COMPETITORS' SUPERIOR TECHNOLOGY
- RISING LABOUR COSTS

**Strengths (S):**
- ICONIC BRAND
- DESIGN
- 'HAND BUILT'
- MORGAN-CLUB CULTURE

**Weaknesses (W):**
- INEFFICIENT MANUFACTURING
- LIMITED CAPACITY
- HIGH % OUTSOURCED COMPONENTS
- HIGHLY CHANGE-RESISTANT CULTURE

|  | Opportunities | Threats |
|---|---|---|
| **Strengths** | **REAL OPPORTUNITY**<br>-DEMAND TO BE TAPPED<br>-GROWTH POTENTIAL, INCREASED PRICES, PROFITS POSSIBLE<br>-AND/OR INCREASE OUTPUT | **POTENTIAL THREATS**<br>-WHILE BRAND IS STRONG M COULD PRICE THEMSELVES OUT OF MARKET<br>-TECHNOLOGY GAP BETWEEN MORGAN & COMPETITORS COULD GROW TOO LARGE |
| **Weaknesses** | **POTENTIAL OPPORTUNITIES**<br>-LIMITED CAPACITY/ INEFFICIENCY PREVENTS GROWTH<br>-CULTURE PREVENTS CHANGE TO REALIZE OPPORTUNITIES | **REAL THREATS**<br>-RISING CUTS & INEFFICIENCY & LACK OF INVESTMENT UNDERMINING BRAND<br>-COMPETITORS MOVING AHEAD<br>-CONSERVATIVE CULTURE IGNORING THREATS & NEED FOR CHANGE |

*MUST ADDRESS THIS NOW/FIRST*

| ① | ② | ③ | ④ | ⑤ |
|---|---|---|---|---|
| Morgan cars are distinctive. Their advantage traditionally enabled by history, values and affection for the brand | Intensifying external factors present rising challenges, threatening M's traditional business model | Others increasingly able to offer tech superior cars to customers at lower prices | Strong M culture enables brand image but has become barrier to change that is increasingly necessary | High % of parts bought in, no scale economies, no investment = big problems. Big collusion in T/W square means culture change strategy must be priority |

**DRAW YOUR OWN HERE...**

**1.** Start with opportunities and threats as row or column headings first. Then insert key strengths and weaknesses as headings on the other axis so that they 'collide' into the Os and Ts.

**2.** Edit! Just list what your previous analysis has indicated are the key Os and Ss etc.

**3.** As ideas for strategic priorities and objectives emerge from your drawing, analysis and discussion, note them down underneath your matrix, linking them back to the collisions from where they emerged with arrows.

Creative ideas:

**A.** Rather than get bogged down looking at each individual collision, look more holistically as groups, e.g. all Ts versus all Ss, and note your general insights across the wider Ts versus Ss box of the matrix.

**B.** A good shorthand version of the CM can be just to look at colliding Os and Ss.

**C.** Look at the priorities/objectives you've noted down and categorize them as economic, social or environmental (using the triple bottom line – no. 23) or short-term or long-term and profit- or people-oriented (using balanced scorecard thinking – no. 24).

**COMMON PITFALLS:** The common pitfalls of CM are similar to those of its 'parent', SWOT, namely that:

1. the framework can be used as just a dumping ground of ideas from a superficial brainstorming exercise rather than a carefully crafted summary of prior analysis from other frameworks;

2. the aforementioned problem or an inability to edit down to just the key Ss, Os etc. can result in data overload as an unwieldy collection of ideas are collided against one another;

3. the lack of firm basis on which the CM is developed can lead to a lack of precision and ambiguity in discussion, which can make the resulting analysis subject to political manipulation that may result in necessary change being resisted or not recognized.

**GOOD IN COMBINATION WITH:** The CM is best used as something of a linchpin. It is an excellent way of summarizing and pulling together the results of other frameworks – e.g. external analysis findings from frameworks, such as ESTEMPLE (no. 2), the PI matrix (no. 3), Porter's diamond (no. 4) and five forces of industry (no. 5), and internal analysis results from frameworks such as the value chain (no. 7), differentiation categories (no. 9), VRIO (no. 12) and the RSIM (no. 13). The results from the CM can then be used to inform discussion on strategic growth options.

**MUTATION POTENTIAL:** It is possible to make the framework technically more sophisticated by blending it with heat map imagery and risk profiles. It can also be broken down with each box breaking into sub-boxes using a further company-specific dimension and these can then spawn particular goals that can be directly linked in to frameworks such as the triple bottom line and the balanced scorecard (nos 23 and 24) to show how the collision of Ss and Ws with Os and Ts has led to a set of balanced strategic objectives.

**INFO FOR FURTHER READING:**
- Piercy, N. and Giles, W. (1989). Making SWOT analysis work. *Marketing Intelligence & Planning*, 7(5/6), 5–7.
- Weihrich, H. (1982). The TOWS matrix – a tool for situational analysis. *Long Range Planning*, 15(2), 54–66.

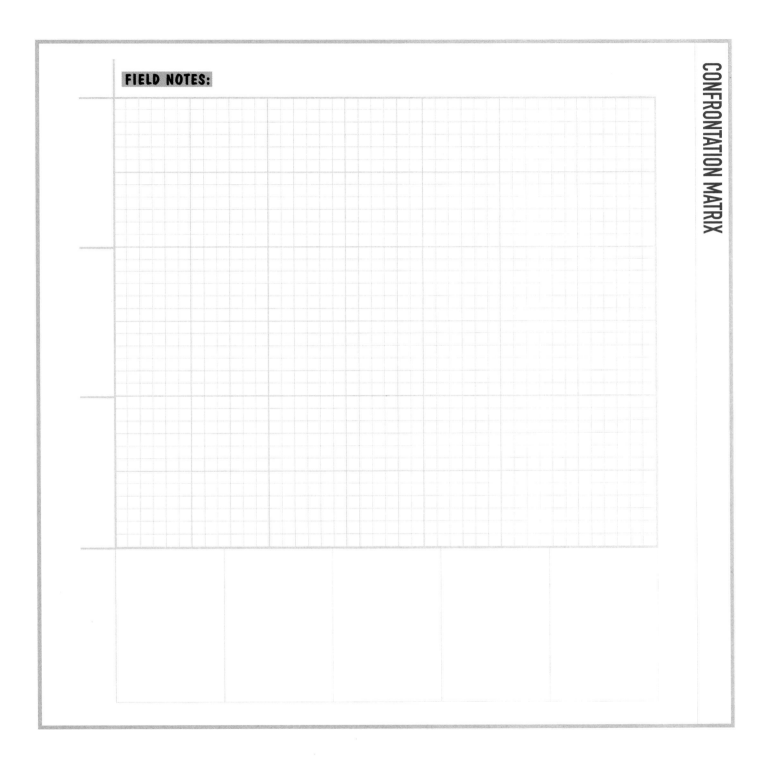

**FIELD NOTES:**

## 18. General Electric/McKinsey Screen

## AUTHOR: McKinsey & Co.

BUSINESS POSITION

|  | HIGH | MEDIUM | LOW |
|---|---|---|---|
| **HIGH** | INVEST HEAVILY FOR GROWTH | INVEST SELECTIVELY & BUILD | DEVELOP FOR INCOME |
| **MEDIUM** | INVEST SELECTIVELY & BUILD | DEVELOP SELECTIVELY FOR INCOME | HARVEST OR DIVEST |
| **LOW** | DEVELOP SELECTIVELY & BUILD ON STRENGTHS | HARVEST | DIVEST |

MARKET ATTRACTIVENESS

**WHEN TO USE:** To better see the 'bigger picture' in a multi-activity operation, so that decisions can be made about whether to invest further in, or divest, particular parts of an organization's portfolio.

**COMPONENTS:** A matrix built on two axes: (1) strength of the business unit or investment in terms of profitability and strength in the market relative to competitors; (2) attractiveness of the market for that offering in terms of size, anticipated growth rate, competitive intensity, profitability and risk. Within this matrix, business units are generally represented by circles showing the market size, market share or contribution to group revenues or profits.

## DEVELOPMENT:

The GE matrix (GEM) was developed in the 1970s by the consulting firm McKinsey & Co. for helping what was at that point in time probably the world's largest multi-business firm. Because of this history, it is sometimes called the GE/McKinsey matrix. It proved extremely useful for analysing GE's various activities and discussing future strategic growth and divestment options and was quickly adopted by other multi-business operations and in MBA classrooms where it can provide an excellent template upon which activities and choices can be plotted when discussing a particular case.

While it is not necessary to plot the activities as circles, this can be a useful way of depicting additional important information graphically. Most often the size of the circle represents the size of the market and the pie slice the company in focus's share of the market. But other information such as relative contribution to the group's revenues and net profits can also be useful to plot and discuss as part of an analysis into the state of the organization's portfolio and strategies for future development. Arrows leading from the circles depicting the projected movement of these activities/units inside the GEM over time can also be useful.

**Key Takeouts:**
→ Which businesses should you invest in further?
→ Which businesses might you be best to move out of?
→ Could your portfolio be better balanced?

# Virgin: Portfolio of Possibilities

## RELATIVE BUSINESS STRENGTH

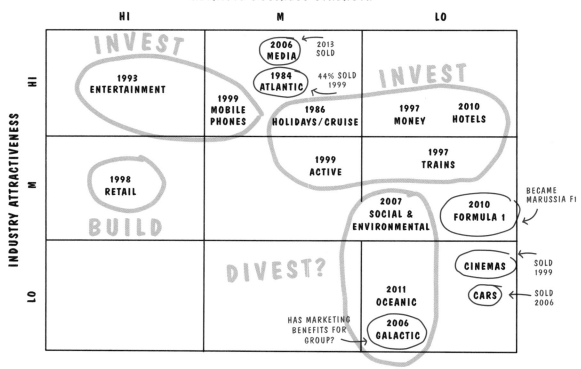

|  | ① | ② | ③ | ④ | ⑤ |
|---|---|---|---|---|---|
|  | Richard Branson's Virgin Group has grown from a small recording label to a multi-business giant through investment and divestment | Some investments have been consistently solid: retail, entertainment and phones | Others have been sold or part-sold because they weren't performing or when the timing was right to free up cash for new investments | Others could grow stronger and more attractive with further investment | A few are performing poorly but provide other benefits: e.g. Galactic keeps Branson in the public eye & feeds Virgin brand image |

These depictions are only approximations based on publicly reported information.

**DRAW YOUR OWN HERE...**

**1.** Start by listing your business units, investments or key activities.

**2.** Estimating their size as a contribution to revenue and the percentage of this revenue that is net profit for the business.

**3.** Determine the strength of the business unit(s) in question in terms of profitability and strength relating to their cost-effectiveness and differentiation from competitors' offerings.

**4.** Determine the attractiveness of the market(s) in terms of size, anticipated growth rate, competitive intensity, profitability and risk, and plot your business units accordingly.

Creative ideas:

**A.** You only need estimate these things broadly — don't get bogged down or paralysed if you do not have the exact figures and percentages. Broad estimates will enable you to get a debate going about your situation. You can always seek further details at a later stage.

**B.** For a third dimension, draw an industry life cycle (no. 6) alongside your GEM and plot your business units in terms of where the industries they serve are on the industry life cycle.

**COMMON PITFALLS:** Sticking to analysing business units as a whole, which may contain products that have different levels of attractiveness. It is more useful to split these units up for the purposes of a GEM analysis.

While it may be necessary to estimate relative attractiveness and business positions, it is important that these estimates are checked and eventually grounded in sound analysis to avoid the GEM being used subjectively.

The matrix is prescriptive in suggesting that low business and industry strength should result in the disposal of business units. However, there may be good reasons to override this. For example, if those business units provide essential services or support to other businesses in the portfolio.

**GOOD IN COMBINATION WITH:** As mentioned in the previous pages, the GEM can be usefully used in combination with the industry life cycle (no. 6). This can give a better or more holistic indication of the balance of an organization's businesses across the life cycle. The matrix can also be used in combination with frameworks that assess levels of competition in an industry. Using the five forces (no. 5) and the value net (no. 11) can also enrich your understanding of the strategic context and potential.

**MUTATION POTENTIAL:** Because there is quite a lot going on inside the matrix already, it can be difficult and confusing to graft it onto other frameworks. However, we have seen it used effectively in the middle box of a five forces analysis (no. 5) where it takes the place of competitors and can be used to graphically display and think through how an organization's portfolio is fed by suppliers, is passed on to a range of customers, and can work together to rebut new entrants and substitutes.

**INFO FOR FURTHER READING:**

- Ghemawat, P. (2002). Competition and business strategy in historical perspective. *Business History Review*, 76(01), 37–74.
- Coyne, K. (2008). Enduring ideas: The GE–McKinsey nine-box matrix. *McKinsey Quarterly*, September. Available at: www.mckinseyquarterly.com/Enduring_ideas_The_GE-McKinsey_nine-box_matrix_2198.
- Proctor, R.A. and Hassard, J.S. (1990). Towards a new model for product portfolio analysis. *Management Decision*, 28(3): 14–17.

**FIELD NOTES:**

## 19. Ansoff's Box

## AUTHOR: Igor Ansoff

|  | EXISTING PRODUCTS | NEW PRODUCTS |
|---|---|---|
| **EXISTING MARKET** | MARKET PENETRATION | PRODUCT DEVELOPMENT |
| **NEW MARKET** | MARKET DEVELOPMENT | DIVERSIFICATION |

**RATINGS:** The box is rated as the number 13 most popular strategy tool by AIM (17%) — the oldest true strategy framework on their list. At 60 years old this framework has certainly stood the test of time!

**WHEN TO USE:** An excellent way to stimulate strategic thinking and discussion about general growth options for an organization.

**COMPONENTS:** Breaks strategic growth options down to four generic categories – market penetration, product development, new market development and diversification into new arena – and arranges these in a 2 × 2 matrix with existing market–new market on the vertical axis and existing product/service–new product/service on the horizontal.

## DEVELOPMENT:

First published in 1957, Igor Ansoff's product–market growth matrix (aka the Ansoff growth matrix or simply Ansoff's box or AGM) may be the first graphical strategy framework. Ansoff emigrated from Russia to the US and gained degrees in general engineering, a masters in dynamics and a PhD in mathematics. He worked as an applied mathematician, but shifted emphasis to planning while with the Rand Corporation and was hired as a planning specialist for Lockheed where he became vice president of planning and director of diversification. The box was inspired by this broad academic and practical experience. It outlines the four generic strategic growth options that a firm may select or combine, and presenting these graphically can be a useful way of seeing and discussing opportunities and risks.

Market penetration is low-risk but will probably offer poor returns in mature and declining markets (see the industry life cycle, no. 6); choosing product or market development might be encouraged if the firm has the capabilities to do this effectively. Diversification is the most risky of the four growth strategies as it takes the firm furthest from what it knows. Three 'tests' are often applied to determine whether this kind of unrelated diversification is worth the risk: the attractiveness of the targeted industry; the expensiveness of cost of entry; and the better-offness test – would the new development be better off for its link with the existing firm and would the firm be better off from the expansion too?

## Key Takeout:

→ Do you understand the best options for our continued growth and strategic development?

## Tesco: Every little (type of growth) helps (*c.* 1990–2015)

|  | EXISTING PRODUCTS | NEW PRODUCTS |
|---|---|---|
| **EXISTING MARKET** | **1950s** – START BUYING UP SMALL COMPETITORS<br>**1987** – TAKEOVER OF HILLARDS<br>**1990** – ATTEMPTED TAKEOVER OF SAINSBURYS<br>↳ MARKET HEATING UP<br><br>**CONSOLIDATION / PENETRATION** | **1974** – PETROL STATIONS<br>**1995** – LAUNCH 'CLUB' CARD<br>**2000** – TESCO.COM & MAJOR PUSH INTO DURABLES: CLOTHING, ELECTRONICS<br>**2006** – CATALOGUES<br>↳ FEWER OPPORTUNITIES<br><br>**PRODUCT DEVELOPMENT** |
| **NEW MARKET** | **1996** – CZECH REPUBLIC<br>**1998** – THAILAND<br>**2002** – MALAYSIA<br>**2003** – TURKEY<br>**2004** – CHINA<br>**2007** – USA (SOLD 2013)<br>**2008** – SOUTH KOREA<br>**2014** – JOINT VENTURE IN INDIA<br>GLOBAL MARKET HEATING UP ↳<br><br>**MARKET DEVELOPMENT** | **1999** – MOBILE PHONES<br>**2009** – TESCO'S BANK<br>**2013** – 'HUDL' TABLET<br><u>RISKIER.</u> BUT HIGHER RETURNS NOW THAN OTHER OPTIONS<br><br>**DIVERSIFICATION** |

| ① | ② | ③ | ④ | ⑤ |
|---|---|---|---|---|
| Tesco was born in 1919. But the past 60 years have seen it become a giant by working many kinds of growth options | After many years of penetrating its trad market, since the 1990s it has branched out developing new products | In the 2000s growth primarily came from international expansion | This combo of mkt and prod development has been largely successful but as these ops diminish new growth is needed | More risky diversifications are being developed as comp in trad mkts gets tougher and portfolio approach sees some less profitable parts being divested |

**DRAW YOUR OWN HERE...**

**1.** If the organization you are focusing on is involved in more than one business or has more than one business unit, it will probably be better to separate those units out and analyse each with a separate AGM.

**2.** Having done this, you can bring these different analyses together into this one unified frame.

**3.** Mark out what directions the firm is going to take (colour-code business units if you have more than one), by having them drop in from the top left corner and draw an arrow to show the square in which they should develop.

**Creative ideas:**

**A.** The matrix can be rotated. If it makes more sense to you to show the unit's development coming in from the bottom left corner and growing rightwards and/or upwards then reverse the 'new market' and 'existing market' rows.

**B.** Once you've developed a sense for where things need to go, it can be useful to think about and draw how the required change should be managed. Underneath the matrix, make some notes using a basic change framework like unfreeze—move—refreeze about what will need to be done to lead the organization toward this growth.

**COMMON PITFALLS:** Trying to perform a single AGM analysis and believing that you have to choose a single path for a multi-business firm. An organization may benefit from choosing to follow multiple pathways.

**GOOD IN COMBINATION WITH:** It can be good to use the AGM after using the industry life cycle and the related BCG matrix (no. 6) and portfolio matrices such as the GE Matrix (no. 18) to analyse where various parts of the business are in terms of industry maturity and attractiveness and market prominence. This can help to determine the urgency for development and give real purpose to an ensuing AGM discussion.

**MUTATION POTENTIAL:** Elements of the AGM can be fruitfully grafted onto a confrontation matrix (no. 17) to present growth options. Where diversification is intended, then matrices such as the five forces (no. 5) and the diamond of international competitiveness (no. 4) can provide insights into good industry and geographic location opportunities.

**INFO FOR FURTHER READING:**
- Ansoff, I. (1957). Strategies for diversification. *Harvard Business Review*, 35(5), 113–124.
- Porter, M. (1987). From competitive advantage to corporate strategy. *Harvard Business Review*, May–June(3): 43–59.

**FIELD NOTES:**

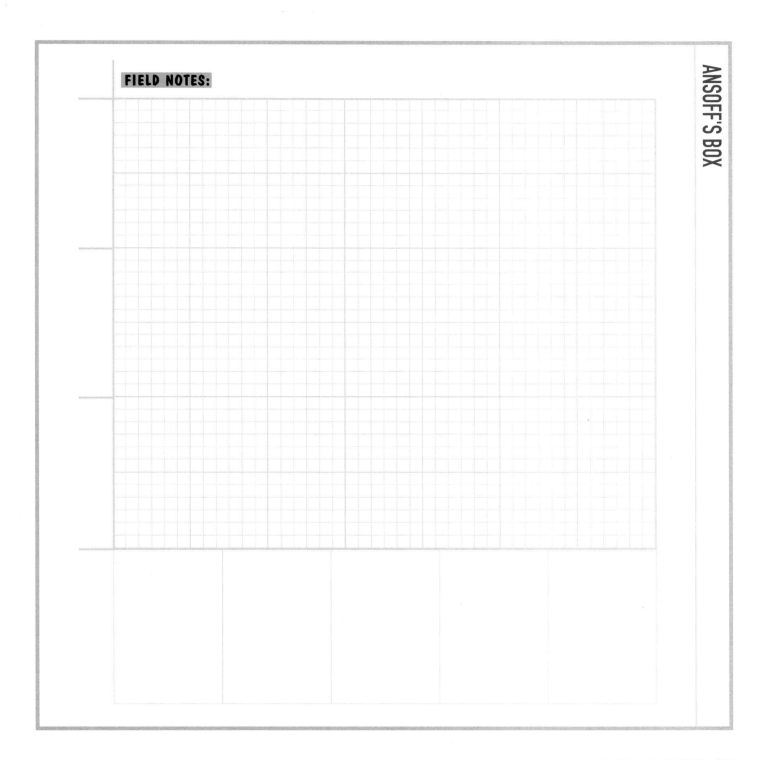

## 20. Post-acquisition Matrix

**AUTHOR: Duncan Angwin**

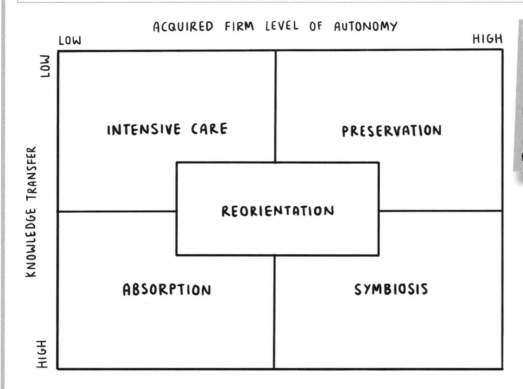

ACQUIRED FIRM LEVEL OF AUTONOMY

LOW — HIGH

KNOWLEDGE TRANSFER (LOW — HIGH)

| INTENSIVE CARE | PRESERVATION |
| ABSORPTION | SYMBIOSIS |

REORIENTATION

**RATINGS:** AIM rates corporate parenting matrices as the 18th most popular strategy framework (5%) and merger and acquisition (M&A) matrices in general at number 15 (8%). This post-acquisition matrix (PAM) captures some of the best insights from these.

**WHEN TO USE:** The PAM is best used when considering an acquisition in order to think through how the intended synergy benefits could be best achieved after the acquisition.

**COMPONENTS:** The PAM considers how much autonomy the acquired firm needs, in terms of (a) how much freedom the top management has to make strategic decisions such as capital investments and disposals and (b) how far the organizational culture needs to remain intact for the acquisition to perform well; and the extent to which knowledge transfer between both organizations is important to generating collective synergies.

**DEVELOPMENT:**

Early research on M&A assumed that good strategic and financial fit between acquirer and target would be enough to create successful deals, but disappointing outcomes caused attention to focus upon the post-acquisition integration phase as key for success and failure. Noting earlier work that suggested a fit between culture and strategy is essential for organizational effectiveness, Nahavandi and Malekzadeh's (1988) four modes of acculturation showed companies' different preferences for cultural integration may be antithetical to positive organizational performance. Later work showed the constraints that different cultural types place on merging individuals. The need to protect acquired company culture was also linked to value creation in Haspeslagh and Jemison's (1991) typology. Their work was tested and extended in Angwin and Meadows (2014) and five distinct integration styles were outlined: (i) 'preservation' – high autonomy/low knowledge transfer to protect the acquired company's sources of benefits; (ii) 'absorption' – low autonomy/high knowledge transfer so the acquired firm can be fully consolidated into the parent firm; (iii) 'symbiotic' – high autonomy/knowledge transfer, for progressive sharing of resources to achieve positive synergies; (iv) 'holding' – low autonomy/knowledge transfer, enabling rapid restructuring of the acquired company for quick turnaround in performance; and (v) 'reorientation' – medium levels of autonomy/knowledge transfer, where external-facing activities are rapidly changed and aligned to the acquiring parent, but internal activities are protected.

## Key Takeouts:

➔ What is your preferred post-acquisition integration strategy? Why?

➔ How should this strategy influence the way in which you negotiate the acquisition of the target company?

# Disney/Pixar: Maintaining animation, maximizing benefits (c. 2006)

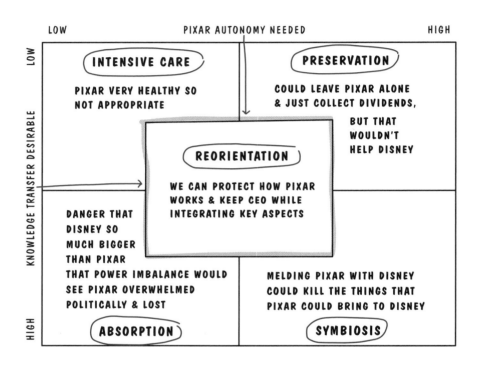

**PIXAR AUTONOMY NEEDED** — LOW / HIGH

**KNOWLEDGE TRANSFER DESIRABLE** — LOW / HIGH

**INTENSIVE CARE**
PIXAR VERY HEALTHY SO NOT APPROPRIATE

**PRESERVATION**
COULD LEAVE PIXAR ALONE & JUST COLLECT DIVIDENDS, BUT THAT WOULDN'T HELP DISNEY

**REORIENTATION**
WE CAN PROTECT HOW PIXAR WORKS & KEEP CEO WHILE INTEGRATING KEY ASPECTS

**ABSORPTION**
DANGER THAT DISNEY SO MUCH BIGGER THAN PIXAR THAT POWER IMBALANCE WOULD SEE PIXAR OVERWHELMED POLITICALLY & LOST

**SYMBIOSIS**
MELDING PIXAR WITH DISNEY COULD KILL THE THINGS THAT PIXAR COULD BRING TO DISNEY

| ① | ② | ③ | ④ | ⑤ |
|---|---|---|---|---|
| Pixar has valuable + rare assets: characters, brand loyalty among young kids and parents, talented CEO and other employees | Disney's scale + reach can help Pix grow, Pix can transfer talent to Dis and help it reach hard-to-tap markets | High absorption may destroy Pix capabilities + damage the customer loyalty that Dis wants to utilize | But if Dis doesn't integrate Pix into its network, little will be gained | Reorientation best to protect Pix capabilities, keep excellent Pix staff on board and aid speedy integration + commercialization to benefit of all |

**DRAW YOUR OWN HERE...**

1. Draw the horizontal axis first and label it 'Acquired firm level of autonomy: low/high'. Identify the extent to which the target company's culture is critical to the protection of its value-creating capability — and locate along the horizontal axis.

2. Draw the vertical axis and label it 'Knowledge transfer: high/low'. Consider the extent to which transferring knowledge (such as skills, innovation, patents) between the companies may generate added value — and locate on the vertical axis.

3. Find the intersection of your two points and you have a preferred post-acquisition integration strategy.

Creative ideas:

A. Consider and draw below your matrix the timeline of synergy benefits for your integration style — will this satisfy stakeholders?

B. Consider the pros and cons of adopting different integration strategies in terms of organizational disruption, timing of synergy benefits, risks and sustainability.

**COMMON PITFALLS:** It is easy to think that reorientation is superior to the others, as it contains elements of all styles. This is an error as no one post-acquisition integration strategy is the 'one best way' – they each aim to achieve different things. For instance, intensive care is appropriate for turning around an acquired company in the short term. The actions necessary for this would probably seriously damage the capabilities and competencies of a well-run acquisition more suited to a preservation strategy.

Another common error is to believe that the acquirer can begin with one integration strategy and then move to another. This only applies for a maintain integration strategy which, over time, may become a symbiosis strategy. Flipping between other integration strategies is likely to be harmful and value destroying.

**GOOD IN COMBINATION WITH:** Used in combination with the value chain (no. 7) the PAM can enable a finer-grained understanding of which parts of the organizations are to be combined, kept separate or discarded, particularly if one utilizes the 'value chimera' shape (a value chain with more than one 'head' connected to one body) described in the value chain section.

**MUTATION POTENTIAL:** Introducing a temporal dimension is beneficial in order to understand the time requirements of integration as well as contextual time constraints. For the latter, integrate an industry life cycle (no. 6) into your picture and for the latter the ESTEMPLE (no. 2).

**INFO FOR FURTHER READING:**
- Nahavandi, A. and Malekzadeh, A.R. (1988). Acculturation in mergers and acquisitions. *Academy of Management Review,* 13(1), 79–90.
- Haspeslagh, P.C. and Jemison, D.B. (1991). *Managing Acquisitions: Creating Value through Corporate Renewal.* New York: Free Press.
- Angwin, D.N. and Meadows, M. (2014). New integration strategies for post-acquisition management. *Long Range Planning* (available online in May, 2015).

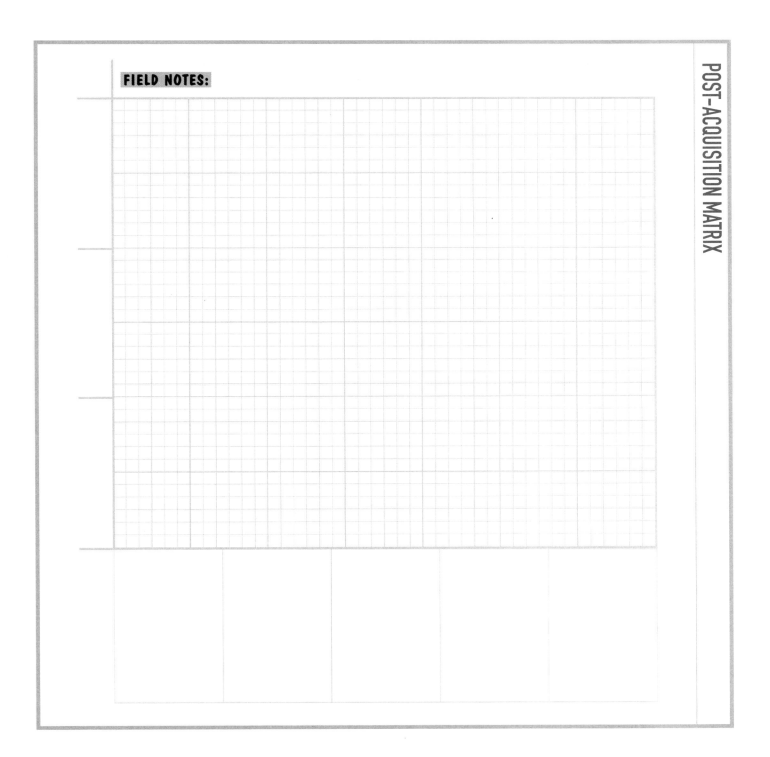

**FIELD NOTES:**

## 21. Next Practice Matrix

### AUTHORS: Stephen Cummings and Chris Bilton

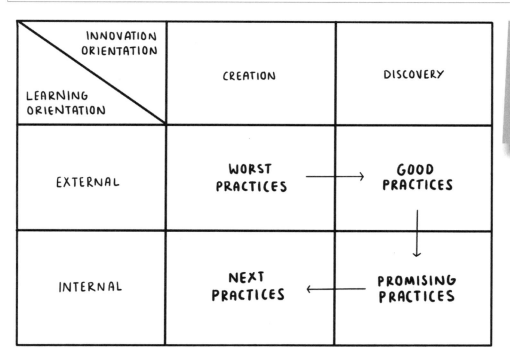

**WHEN TO USE:** A structured way of encouraging strategic initiatives other than those that simply follow the current industry leader's best practices and the diminishing returns associated with this.

**COMPONENTS:** Four different developments upon benchmarking that claim to offer superior opportunities for strategic learning and development: worst, good, promising and next practice; arranged in a matrix crossing learning orientation with innovation orientation.

## DEVELOPMENT:

Benchmarking or utilizing what is seen to be best practice became extremely popular through the 1990s. But in 2000, a McKinsey study showed that margins declined in industries where best practice was widely applied. While best practice is a useful tool for increasing efficiency, if applied at the strategic level it denudes differentiation and competitive advantage as firms homogenize by coming up to the 'bench' rather than surpassing it. Better to keep a strategic focus on what your unique and difficult-to-replicate capabilities enable you to keep adapting. Or, as Bruce Nelson from Office Depot put it, realizing that 'they can steal our ideas but they can't steal our culture'.

This realization has encouraged alternative approaches: that more can be learned from mistakes, so frankly discussing 'worst practices' can be insightful; it is better to encourage debate about multiple forms of 'good practice' than isolate one 'best' one; firms should be encouraged to promote 'promising practices' from within; and arguing that firms would do better to think about how they can 'leapfrog' current best practice using their own capabilities to reinterpret current practices and take them in new directions. C.K. Prahalad has referred to elements of his work as 'the next practice' since the 1990s, but 'next practice' was first explicitly promoted as an approach to strategy development in the 2002 book *Recreating Strategy*. In 2010, Bilton and Cummings developed these ideas into the next practice matrix (NPM).

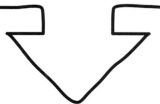

**Key Takeouts:**
→ What might next practice be for your organization?
→ How is this different from what you currently do?
→ Does this next practice reflect your organization's particular set of capabilities?

# Oakland As: Bases loaded (*c.* late 1990s)

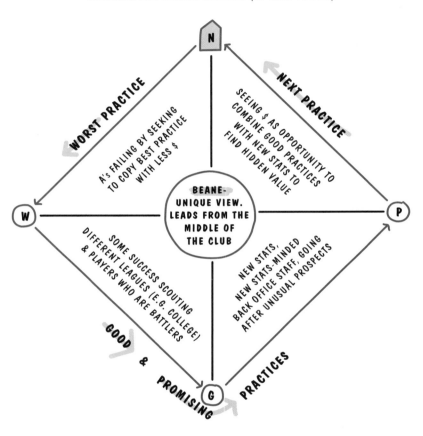

**N**

**WORST PRACTICE** — A's FAILING BY SEEKING TO COPY BEST PRACTICE WITH LESS $

**NEXT PRACTICE** — SEEING $ AS OPPORTUNITY TO COMBINE GOOD PRACTICES WITH NEW STATS TO FIND HIDDEN VALUE

BEANE- UNIQUE VIEW. LEADS FROM THE MIDDLE OF THE CLUB

**W**

**P**

SOME SUCCESS SCOUTING DIFFERENT LEAGUES (E.G. COLLEGE) & PLAYERS WHO ARE BATTLERS

NEW STATS, NEW STATS-MINDED BACK OFFICE STAFF, GOING AFTER UNUSUAL PROSPECTS

**GOOD & PROMISING PRACTICES**

**G**

| ① | ② | ③ | ④ | ⑤ |
|---|---|---|---|---|
| When Beane became GM his experience as a hailed but failed player enabled him to get to heart of things & see with new perspective | He saw that trying to follow best practice on the As' budget wasn't getting them to 1st base & challenged orthodoxy | Beane aware of promising stats practices and that As had some success with unusual or 'ugly' players who scrambled to 1st | He saw next practice as blending trad good practices with promising practices to buy players others overlooked | The As approach was unique for a time, but the challenge was staying ahead as others copied their approach |

**DRAW YOUR OWN HERE...**

1. While it makes sense to move clockwise from worst practice around to next practice, you can start in any of the first three boxes of this framework.

2. To get started, you can use the NPM as a pinboard and put up any examples of worst, good or promising practices you think of or invite examples from those you work with.

3. Having thought about and/or debated W, G and P practices, now think about, debate and draw or write up what your organization could do next to leapfrog current conventions and expectations.

Creative ideas:

A. It can be difficult to dwell on your own worst practices, so ask instead: 'What is the worst practice of anybody in our industry?'

B. Actually find an example (or project a picture) of what is considered to be current best practice and place it in front of you or the group. Make sure this gets updated over time. This is what you are trying to leapfrog.

**COMMON PITFALLS:** Reverting back to looking for 'the answer' from outside. While it might seem easier and less risky to borrow a 'solution' from somebody else, next practice thinking requires that you think beyond what is considered best practice elsewhere and utilize your own organization's particular capabilities (knowledge, culture, experience, unique perspective, etc.) to develop unique products, services and strategies for what you are going to do NEXT.

**GOOD IN COMBINATION WITH:** Using the NPM works well after going through frameworks from the first Strategy Builder blocks to determine a short list of opportunities and strengths so that next practice ideas can be directed towards, or assessed in terms of, an ability to capitalize on distinctive strengths and take advantage of emerging opportunities.

**MUTATION POTENTIAL:** Insert design thinking into the NPM by thinking about the four different types of practice in terms of the 'user experience'. For example, what is the worst user experience, and how will the user experience be made better by your next practice? When thinking through how to get to/realize your strategy for next practice/s think through how you can work with/utilize constraints, prototype quickly and build in ways of adapting and improving as you learn from the development process.

**INFO FOR FURTHER READING:**
- Nattermann, P.M. (2000). Best practice ≠ best strategy. *McKinsey Quarterly,* (2), 22–31.
- Cummings, S. (2002). *Recreating Strategy.* London: Sage.
- Prahalad, C.K. and Ramaswamy, V. (2004). Co-creation experiences: The next practice in value creation. *Journal of Interactive Marketing,* 18(3), 5–14.
- Bilton, C. and Cummings, S. (2010). *Creative Strategy: Reconnecting Business and Innovation.* London: John Wiley.

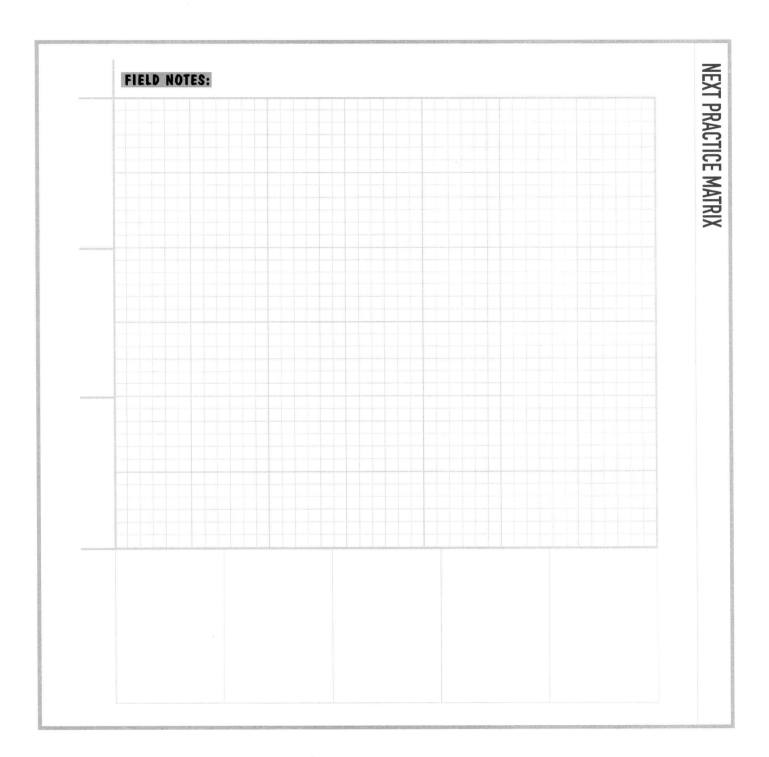

**FIELD NOTES:**

NEXT PRACTICE MATRIX

# The Best of the Strategic Growth Options Frameworks Combined – Fourth Foundation: The Growth Options Heatmap

## PURPOSE:

The Growth Options Heatmap (GOH) seeks to bring together the key insights from a range of strategic growth options frameworks to help see how relating key strengths and weaknesses to opportunities and threats enables better decision-making about appropriate future strategic goals.

## COMPONENTS:

The core is a collision matrix to enable strengths and weaknesses summarized from analysis using tools from the second and third sections of the Strategy Builder and the opportunities and threats from the first section to be set against each other to analyse their relations and relative impacts. Aspects of other frameworks in this section can be sketched, leading off from where the greatest impact 'heat' is in the matrix. Ansoff's box can be arranged at different angles leading from the greatest area of heat (e.g. if strengths and opportunities line up, product growth and market penetration may be good options; if threats and weaknesses are more obvious then diversification might make sense, as in example above). What growth into certain areas may mean for the overall portfolio can be considered, how any acquisition might be best managed can be discussed, and options for next practice innovation evaluated.

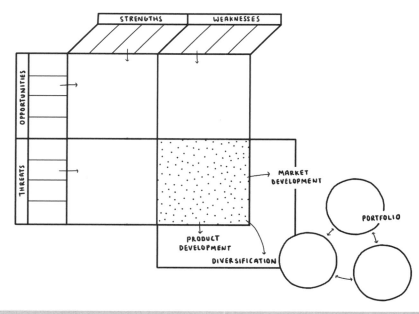

Large parts of this book were figured out during meetings that took place in London in November 2013 at a place called Shoreditch House. Shoreditch House (and its 'sister establishment', called Soho House) may be like hotels but they are more 'members' clubs with bedrooms'. Located in a converted old warehouse in East London close to a vibrant creative industries cluster, one can apply to be a local member of Shoreditch or a global member with access to a network of similar establishments around the world. Discounted memberships are available for those under 27. The top floors of Shoreditch are spaces where members meet, surf, play table tennis, work out, drink, think, eat and work. For many in this networked age, it's a much more effective approach than leasing premises in London. Product developments include a range of toiletries used in the bedrooms and member facilities and marketed more broadly, a spa, and a gentleman's barbers for the hirsute.

## Key Takeout:
→ A clearer understanding of the relative veracity of the opportunities, threats, strengths and weakness, their interrelationships and the potential impact of these things on strategic growth options. And, as a consequence, a clearer understanding of what an organization's strategy should focus on for the future.

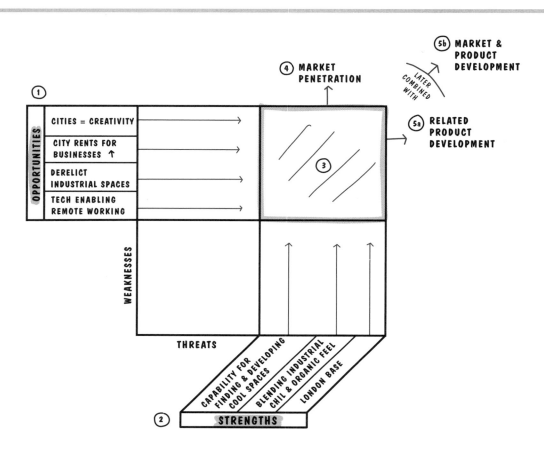

| ① | ② | ③ | ④ | ⑤ |
|---|---|---|---|---|
| Big opps — creative activity increasingly clustered in cities with high room rents & derelict industrial space; increasingly tech networked virtual workers | SH has capabilities for delivering cool alternative space to meet/relax/ work in areas where few cost-effective hotels or premises | This has created the heat for growth if desired | At this stage, there are many opportunities for lower risk/hi-return growth in further mkt penetration in other locations | As viable space for mkt penetration decreases & strengths copied by competitors, next practice prod & mkt dev should be considered |

You can download templates of the Growth Options Heatmap to aid your drawing at www.wiley/go/strategybuilder.com or try out the app at www.strategicplan.com.

# MANAGING PERFORMANCE STRATEGICALLY

**Purpose:** This final block of frameworks helps to generate a set of guiding strategic principles and goals that balance present conditions with the need to think about the future prosperity and sustainability of the organization, people and the planet.

22. **Vision** – Provides one simple overarching statement of strategic intent that orients and animates development for all members and key stakeholders of an organization.

23. **Triple bottom line** – Encourages corporate social responsibility, sustainability and a broader view of performance than conventional financial measures by promoting the measurement of social and environmental impacts of the firm's strategy.

24. **Balanced scorecard** – Shows the importance of balancing short-term financial measures with performance relating to the longer-term strategic health of the organization: maintaining differentiating capabilities, the ability to innovate, and keeping customers happy.

25. **Risk management/probability impact matrix** – A graphical means to assess and debate whether the organization's strategy is exposing it to unnecessary or overly high levels of risk.

26. **Animation–orientation matrix** – A simple check to gauge if your strategy is memorable, inspiring and providing the necessary direction to those who are charged with implementing it.

## 22. Vision

**AUTHOR: Multiple**

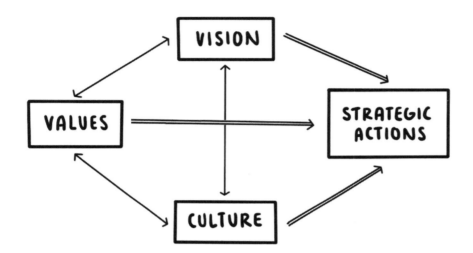

**WHEN TO USE:** To develop a simple, overarching statement of strategic intent that can orient and animate development for all members and key stakeholders of an organization.

**COMPONENTS:** Normally just a brief, memorable statement, but the adaptation of the Ashridge mission model above also focuses minds on how a vision must align with the firm's values and culture to be an effective driver of strategic action.

## DEVELOPMENT:

The bloated, poorly constructed and confusing sentences that many firms used as visions, and numerous similar things like mission, purpose and corporate philosophy that often muddied the waters further, and became the subject of derision for employees and Dilbert alike, fell out of favour in the past decade. Moreover, they are not really frameworks at all. So, how do they make our list? The concept of developing a vision as an overarching strategic goal has made a comeback as firms seek greater focus, simplicity and certainty in recessionary times, and we've learned from the worst and best examples of that first wave.

One thing we've learned is that graphical presentation of key elements of a good vision or how a vision should relate to strategy and other key aspects of a firm helps. In the book *Strategy Pathfinder*, we developed a set of key elements claiming that a good vision should be brief, authentic (or true to the nature of the firm), verifiable, inspirational, understandable and flexible (so it need not be changed if an environmental shift occurs). These elements can be used in a spidergram to test prospective visions. It is easy to see that good visions like HSBC's 'The world's local bank'; Lego's 'Inventing the future of play' and Disney's 'Making people happy' achieve on all fronts. The adaptation of the Ashridge mission model is a useful way to visualize whether a firm's vision, values and culture (see the 7-S framework, no. 16) are consistent in driving strategic development at the 'bow' of the ship.

**Key Takeout:**

→ Is your vision brief, authentic, verifiable, understandable, inspirational and flexible?

## LEGO: 'Everything [we help a kid do] is awesome' (*c.* 2014)

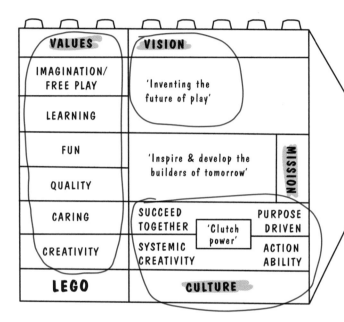

**VALUES**
- IMAGINATION/ FREE PLAY
- LEARNING
- FUN
- QUALITY
- CARING
- CREATIVITY

**LEGO**

**VISION**

'Inventing the future of play'

'Inspire & develop the builders of tomorrow'

**MISSION**

SUCCEED TOGETHER

SYSTEMIC CREATIVITY

'Clutch power'

PURPOSE DRIVEN

ACTION ABILITY

**CULTURE**

**STRATEGIC ACTIONS**

e.g.

→ OPEN INNOVATION & CROWDSOURCING e.g. 'LEGO MINDSTORMS'

→ THE PLOTLINE OF THE LEGO MOVIE

→ PRODUCT DEVELOPMENT PARTNERSHIPS WITH LIKE-MINDED ORGANIZATIONS

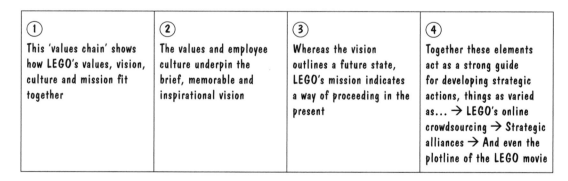

**①** This 'values chain' shows how LEGO's values, vision, culture and mission fit together

**②** The values and employee culture underpin the brief, memorable and inspirational vision

**③** Whereas the vision outlines a future state, LEGO's mission indicates a way of proceeding in the present

**④** Together these elements act as a strong guide for developing strategic actions, things as varied as... → LEGO's online crowdsourcing → Strategic alliances → And even the plotline of the LEGO movie

**DRAW YOUR OWN HERE...**

1. Leaping into writing a vision is daunting. So start by working from the outside in (what the previous page's framework encourages). List your firm's values on the bottom left of the page and an approximation of your strategic goals on the bottom right. Draft a vision above these that reflects the values and indicates a path to the goals.

2. You'll need lots of pages and lots of drafts. Despite only being a few words long, a good vision takes a lot of development and refinement.

3. Don't be discouraged if everybody else isn't stunned by the brilliance of your vision. It's a step on the road. Hand it over and ask others to improve upon it (so long as the improvements stay brief, inspirational, verifiable and so on).

Creative ideas:

A. Think pictorial symbols rather than words. If your vision was expressed in a drawing rather than text, what would it look like? Once you have pictures, convert them into words.

B. Involve people from outside the C-Suite in development, because this is who a vision has to orient and animate (no. 26). Make sure your key stakeholders from your PI matrix (no. 3) are included in the development team.

**COMMON PITFALLS:** Visions that are not brief.

Visions that are not authentic and distinctive (they could be the vision of any organization).

Visions that are not verifiable or measurable (but there are many creative ways of measuring things: social media and Google offer many new possibilities).

Visions that are not understood by those who have to implement them.

Visions that are not inspirational.

Visions that are not flexible and have to be discarded every other year.

Most bad visions are developed by committees. Most good ones come from somebody taking the lead, then being prepared to listen to criticism and adapt (but not completely).

**GOOD IN COMBINATION WITH:** We have found that the best simple test of any draft vision is to look at it alongside the animation–orientation matrix (no. 26), and ask those who have to implement your organization's strategy: Does this orient you (give you some sense of what you should do, broadly)? Does this animate you (inspire you to do it and indeed go above and beyond)?

**MUTATION POTENTIAL:** A bit like chips/French fries, a good vision goes well with anything! Once you have a good vision, write it at the top of any page with a strategy framework or strategy drawing or strategy document. This will help to remind you what you are aiming for (something that can be very easy to forget in the day-to-day rush of business and strategy-making and doing).

**INFO FOR FURTHER READING:**
- Campbell, A., Nash, L.L., Devine, M. and Young, D. (1992). *A Sense of Mission: Defining Direction for the Large Corporation*, Addison-Wesley.
- Cummings, S. and Davies, J. (1994). Mission, vision, fusion. *Long Range Planning*, 27(6), 147–150.
- Raynor, M.E. (1998). That vision thing: Do we need it? *Long Range Planning*, 31(3), 368–376.

**FIELD NOTES:**

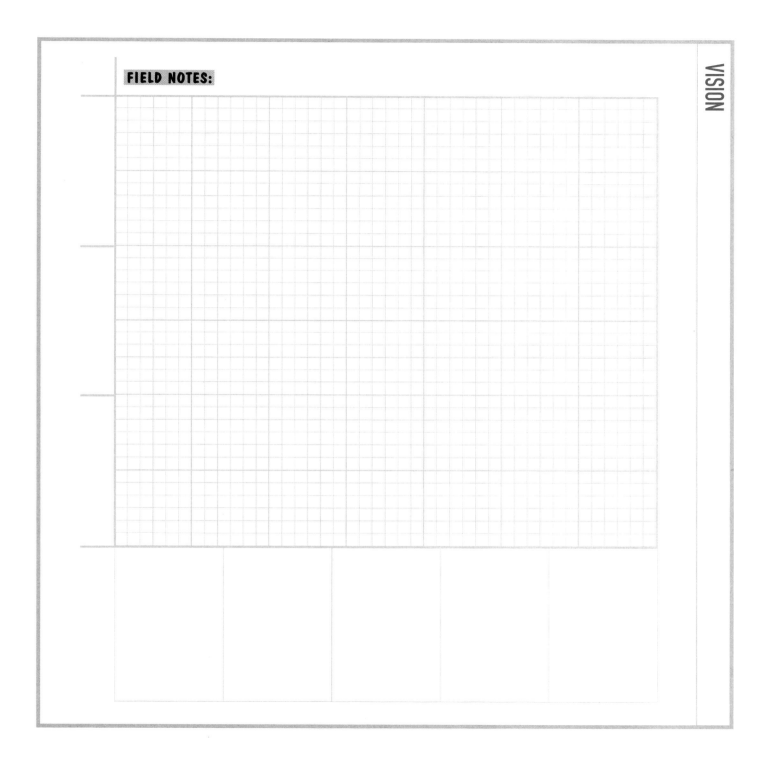

## 23. Triple Bottom Line

**AUTHOR: Multiple**

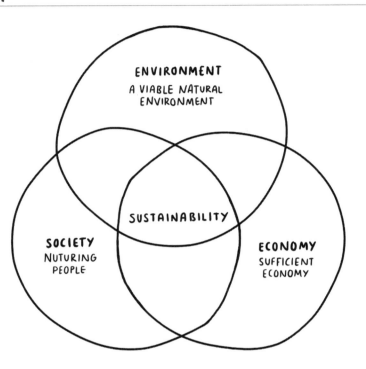

ENVIRONMENT
A VIABLE NATURAL ENVIRONMENT

SUSTAINABILITY

SOCIETY
NUTURING PEOPLE

ECONOMY
SUFFICIENT ECONOMY

**RATINGS:** The triple bottom line (TBL) is generally not classified as a tool or framework. However, it is most commonly used to promote social and environmental concerns, and these now consistently rate near the top of lists of imperatives for executives.

**WHEN TO USE:** To develop a broader view of strategic performance, and subsequently broader strategic goals, than conventional financial measures would promote by considering the social and environmental impacts and responsibilities of an organization's strategy.

**COMPONENTS:** Three intersecting circles: one in which to record conventional economic goals; one for goals relating to impacts on the natural environment; and one that encourages goals relating to the development of people and the broader community.

## DEVELOPMENT:

In 1981, Freer Spreckley proposed that organizations could report on social and environmental performance, in addition to the measure of revenue less costs traditionally shown on the bottom line of a financial statement, in a work called *Social Audit – A Management Tool for Co-operative Working*. In 1995, John Elkington developed a phrase reflective of these three bottom lines: 'people, planet, profit'. This was adopted as the title of Shell's first 'sustainability report' in 1997. However, the phrase 'triple bottom line' (TBL) was coined by John Elkington in the 1997 book *Cannibals with Forks*.

Interestingly, it has recently been discovered that something similar was in the minds of those who first promoted management as a professional endeavour: when Frederick Taylor's ideas were rebranded as scientific management by a legal team concerned to promote the 'conservation movement' at the beginning of the 20th century. The team took a US railroad company to court on behalf of shippers facing continual price rises and claimed that they could better conserve resources and reduce costs rather than increase prices through better management. The performance principle of the conservation movement was 'the greatest good for the greatest number for the longest time'. TBL became the dominant approach in public sector full cost accounting in 2007 following its endorsement by the UN, most financial institutions now incorporate a TBL approach, and in the private sector a commitment to corporate social responsibility or sustainability now implies a commitment to some form of TBL reporting.

## Key Takeout:

→ Will your set of strategic goals encourage you to achieve a good balance of environmental, social and economic responsibility?

# EcoPower: Four cables (c. 2014)

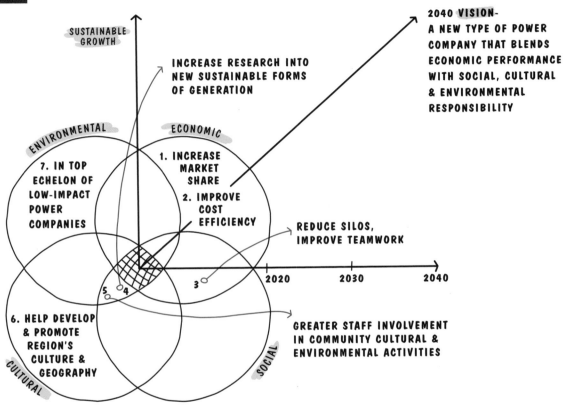

SUSTAINABLE GROWTH

2040 VISION-
A NEW TYPE OF POWER COMPANY THAT BLENDS ECONOMIC PERFORMANCE WITH SOCIAL, CULTURAL & ENVIRONMENTAL RESPONSIBILITY

INCREASE RESEARCH INTO NEW SUSTAINABLE FORMS OF GENERATION

ENVIRONMENTAL

ECONOMIC

7. IN TOP ECHELON OF LOW-IMPACT POWER COMPANIES

1. INCREASE MARKET SHARE

2. IMPROVE COST EFFICIENCY

REDUCE SILOS, IMPROVE TEAMWORK

2020     2030     2040

6. HELP DEVELOP & PROMOTE REGION'S CULTURE & GEOGRAPHY

CULTURAL

SOCIAL

GREATER STAFF INVOLVEMENT IN COMMUNITY CULTURAL & ENVIRONMENTAL ACTIVITIES

| ① | ② | ③ | ④ | ⑤ |
|---|---|---|---|---|
| EcoPower needed a way to focus minds out into the longer term & a way of showing how their strategic goals were linked | They added the preservation & development of their region's distinctive cultural heritage to the TBL | This resulted in 4 strategic goal 'arenas': economic, social, environmental & cultural | 3 other long-term goal sets that related to the intersections between these arena were defined = 7 goals towards the 2040 vision | Other docs that link to this one outline shorter-term five-yearly targets with respect to each of these 7 goals |

The identity of this organization has been disguised.

**DRAW YOUR OWN HERE...**

1. A good way of beginning to draw the TBL is by drawing the outline of the three circles and placing each of your current strategic goals (or what you think these should be) in the appropriate circles or intersections.

2. Think through or debate whether this set looks balanced.

3. If not, how might you adjust and move them or develop different or additional goals? What might they be, and what would the impact of pursuing them be on the others?

Creative ideas:

Rather than using the circles, draw a three-legged spidergram of the three performance dimensions and explore the implications for each of pursuing different goals.

**COMMON PITFALLS:** Thinking that softer environmental and social achievements can't be measured. Something as simple as an engagement survey, if well defined, or what people are posting about your organization on social media, or newspaper stories, or the Houses of Parliament, can provide measurable data if you think creatively.

Being too vague. Related to the last point, if you are going to track environmental and social performance, then measure it against clearly defined targets.

Getting so carried away with the social and environmental thinking that you forget to take care of the economic. As they say in flight safety announcements, 'If you don't secure your oxygen mask first you won't be able to help those around you.'

**GOOD IN COMBINATION WITH:** Combined with traditional accounting practices, the TBL can turn straight financial analysis into more nuanced strategic thinking, discussion, judgement and decision-making and lead to the creation of a small set of high-level strategic goals that can underpin a good vision (no. 22).

**MUTATION POTENTIAL:** There's really nothing to stop you adding in other categories of performance beyond the now conventional three. In New Zealand, organizations owned by the indigenous Maori have added in a fourth bottom line: the preservation and development of cultural interests. While some may split hairs and say this could be subsumed into the social category, this fourth column inspires and gives a clearer sense of purpose and vision, so why not use it as a framework for developing strategic goals?

**INFO FOR FURTHER READING:**

- Cummings, S. and Bridgman, T. (2014). *The Origin of Management is Sustainability.* Published as part of Best Paper Proceedings for The Academy of Management Conference, Philadelphia, August, 2014.
- Elkington, J. (1997). *Cannibals with Forks: the Triple Bottom Line of 21st Century Business.* John Wiley & Sons.
- Porter, M.E. and Kramer, M.R. (2006). The link between competitive advantage and corporate social responsibility. *Harvard Business Review*, (84): 78–92.

**FIELD NOTES:**

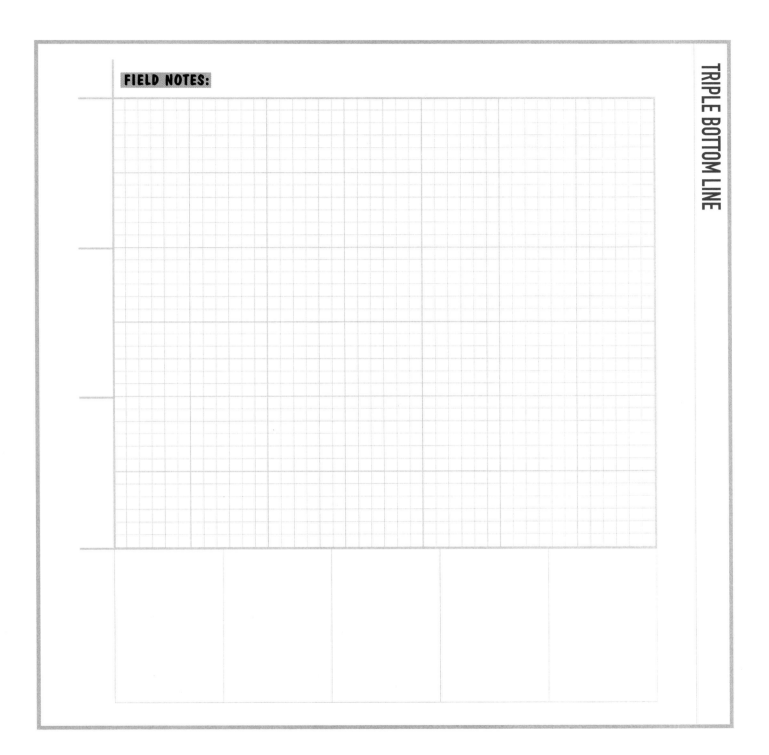

## 24. Balanced Scorecard

## AUTHOR: Robert Kaplan and David Norton (inspired by Art Schneiderman)

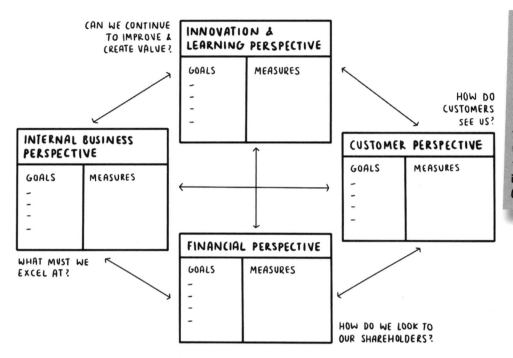

CAN WE CONTINUE TO IMPROVE & CREATE VALUE?

**INNOVATION & LEARNING PERSPECTIVE**

GOALS | MEASURES

**INTERNAL BUSINESS PERSPECTIVE**

GOALS | MEASURES

WHAT MUST WE EXCEL AT?

HOW DO CUSTOMERS SEE US?

**CUSTOMER PERSPECTIVE**

GOALS | MEASURES

**FINANCIAL PERSPECTIVE**

GOALS | MEASURES

HOW DO WE LOOK TO OUR SHAREHOLDERS?

**RATINGS:** Bain's most popular strategy tool globally, number one in the US until recently and tied with vision as the tool 'most satisfied with'. Not rated by AIM. Number six in the most popular strategy tools by the Aston study and a much more recent development than those tools rated above it. Eighth equal and rising in China (37%).

**WHEN TO USE:** To think through balancing short-term financial measures with performance relating to the longer-term strategic health of the organization.

**COMPONENTS:** Two sets of 'scales' representing the need for balance between short-term financial performance and longer-term investment in maintaining capabilities (the vertical plane), and how customers perceive us and what we strive to excel at (the horizontal plane).

## DEVELOPMENT:

The aim of the balanced scorecard (BSC) is the presentation of financial and non-financial measures so that their individual and collective value to the firm can be seen on a page or in a single report. To create a simple cross or diamond shape to the framework, three categories are traditionally used in addition to a financial perspective: how the customer views the firm; internal business processes and perspectives; and how the firm learns and innovates. Designing a BSC requires the identification of a small number of goals in each of these areas and measures against which progress can be charted. Firms have used a mix of financial and non-financial measures to track progress for many years but the term 'balanced scorecard' was developed by Art Schneiderman in 1987. Schneiderman participated in an unrelated research study in 1990 led by Robert Kaplan for management consultancy Nolan-Norton, and during this he outlined his work on performance measurement. Kaplan and David Norton subsequently developed the idea and published a 1992 *Harvard Business Review* article, 'The balanced scorecard – measures that drive performance'. The article proved popular and was quickly followed by another in 1993 ('Putting the balanced scorecard to work') and a book, *The Balanced Scorecard: Translating Strategy into Action*, in 1996. As the Bain and other surveys show, despite not really being a strategy development framework (it is more a goal-setting tool and is best used in this manner), the BSC is now very much a part of the strategic management landscape and in many organizations it is used to set the direction towards which a firm's strategy aims.

**Key Takeout:**

➔ Do you have a set of balanced strategic goals that will guide your success in both the short and the long term?

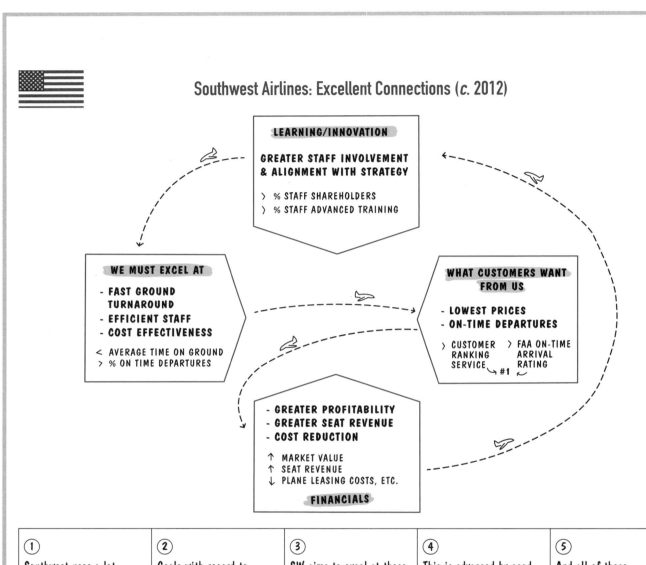

## Southwest Airlines: Excellent Connections (*c.* 2012)

**LEARNING/INNOVATION**

**GREATER STAFF INVOLVEMENT & ALIGNMENT WITH STRATEGY**

> % STAFF SHAREHOLDERS
> % STAFF ADVANCED TRAINING

**WE MUST EXCEL AT**

- FAST GROUND TURNAROUND
- EFFICIENT STAFF
- COST EFFECTIVENESS

< AVERAGE TIME ON GROUND
> % ON TIME DEPARTURES

**WHAT CUSTOMERS WANT FROM US**

- LOWEST PRICES
- ON-TIME DEPARTURES

> CUSTOMER RANKING SERVICE ↳ #1
> FAA ON-TIME ARRIVAL RATING

- GREATER PROFITABILITY
- GREATER SEAT REVENUE
- COST REDUCTION

↑ MARKET VALUE
↑ SEAT REVENUE
↓ PLANE LEASING COSTS, ETC.

**FINANCIALS**

| ① | ② | ③ | ④ | ⑤ |
|---|---|---|---|---|
| Southwest uses a lot of simple BSCs to help inform staff of strategy and what they are contributing to | Goals with regard to customer service are simple: lowest prices + on-time arrivals. | SW aims to excel at these things, which requires efficient, engaged staff who understand the importance of these goals | This is advanced by good training + enabling staff to own shares and see how things fit together to the benefit of all | And all of these connections enhance the achievement of financial goals: cost reduction, market value and revenue |

**DRAW YOUR OWN HERE...**

1. Start out on the horizontal and on the right-hand side with some words or pictures depicting what customers expect of you. If you are not sure, ask someone or seek out what has been expressed on the internet.

2. On the left, outline how you will match this by achieving and exceeding these expectations.

3. Outline your short-term financial goals in the northern node, then seek to balance these with a set of longer-term goals aimed at maintaining and developing human capabilities.

Creative ideas:

Make the BSC more strategic by bringing in elements from earlier frameworks. Make the western node of the BSC into a value chain (no. 7) shape and insert the main primary activities you must excel at and how they are linked. Make the eastern node the eastern part of the five forces (no. 5), charting buyer behaviour and expectations.

**COMMON PITFALLS:** Diving too deeply into the detail too quickly. Draw in broad terms first, developing an understanding of each of the four points of the BSC compass before seeking to develop lists of specific goals for each.

Too many goals. While five or six goals may not seem like too many for each node, when you multiply that by the four points of the BSC, that could add up to 26 strategic goals. Ask yourself if you really want that many. If not, make sure you limit yourself to perhaps three goals for each of the four nodes.

Being beholden to BSC goals because you worked so hard to agree on them. If the environment changes, you must change your BSC. Don't let the BSC stifle innovation!

**GOOD IN COMBINATION WITH:** The BSC is not really a comparative or analytical tool like most of the frameworks outlined in this book. Despite this, people often use it to make strategy at the expense of using better strategic thinking tools. The BSC is a goal-setting and business-reporting tool with which strategic progress can be measured. Hence it is best used after a strategic analysis to record the insights and goals that have stemmed from this process.

**MUTATION POTENTIAL:** People often use a BSC and a TBL (no. 23) to record strategic goals, which can lead to duplication and confusion as they do similar things. It can be useful, therefore, to deliberately meld the two frames. The north box can double as the economic circle, the south box can contain social goals, and environmental responsibility can be recorded as a horizontal slice that runs through what customers expect and an element that we must excel at.

**INFO FOR FURTHER READING:**
- Kaplan, R. and Norton, D. (1992). The balanced scorecard – measures that drive performance. *Harvard Business Review*, 70(1), 71–79.
- Kaplan, R. and Norton, D. (1993). Putting the balanced scorecard to work. *Harvard Business Review*, 71(5), 134–142.
- Voelpel, S.C., Leibold, M. and Eckhoff, R.A. (2006). The tyranny of the balanced scorecard in the innovation economy. *Journal of Intellectual Capital*, 7(1), 43–60.

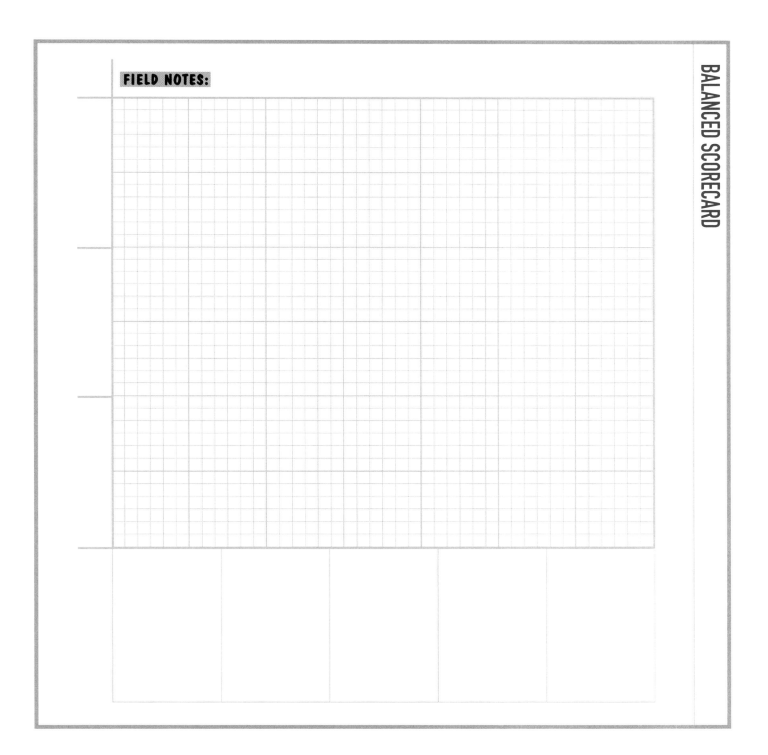

**FIELD NOTES:**

## 25. Risk Management/Probability Impact Matrix

### AUTHOR: Unknown

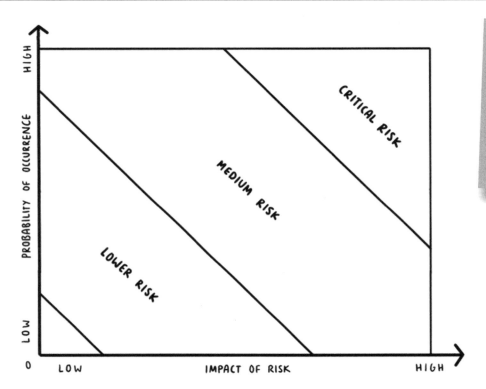

**RATINGS:** Not rated by AIM. Aston study rates risk analysis the fifth most popular strategy tool. Risk management is always a major concern in executive surveys. Risk analysis is rated the seventh most popular strategy tool in China by the He. et al (2012) study (46%).

**WHEN TO USE:** To assess and debate whether the organization's strategy is exposing it to unnecessary or overly high levels of risk.

**COMPONENTS:** Probability of occurrence is a continuous scale but can be categorized as high/medium/low and attributed numeric values. Impact of risk is also a continuous scale but can be attributed categories. This means the figure could be a grid with numeric scores attached or a conceptual space as presented above. Locating risks on the matrix allows judgement to be made about what is the acceptable level of overall risk.

## DEVELOPMENT:

Risk management has a long history in both the finance and strategy literatures. In a nutshell, risk management is about the distribution of future outcomes as a result of internal decisions and the actions of external factors.

The probability/impact matrix aims to help the user identify and analyse risk factors in order to allow an organization to respond to perceived risk factors for a given strategy, in the best interests of overall organizational objectives. The key message is not that risks should be avoided or even reduced, but that they should be seen for what they are and managed accordingly.

**Key Takeouts:**

➔ What are the risks that could impact on our strategic development?

➔ Is this risk profile manageable?

➔ Do your opportunity benefits outweigh the risks, or is change to the strategy needed?

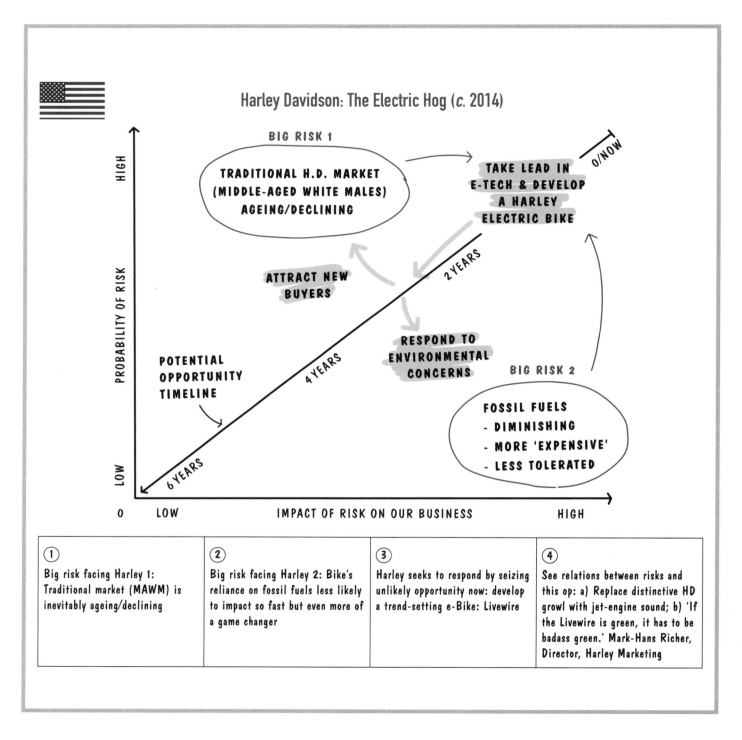

# Harley Davidson: The Electric Hog (*c.* 2014)

**BIG RISK 1**

TRADITIONAL H.D. MARKET
(MIDDLE-AGED WHITE MALES)
AGEING/DECLINING

TAKE LEAD IN
E-TECH & DEVELOP
A HARLEY
ELECTRIC BIKE

0/NOW

ATTRACT NEW
BUYERS

2 YEARS

PROBABILITY OF RISK — HIGH / LOW

POTENTIAL
OPPORTUNITY
TIMELINE

4 YEARS

RESPOND TO
ENVIRONMENTAL
CONCERNS

**BIG RISK 2**

FOSSIL FUELS
- DIMINISHING
- MORE 'EXPENSIVE'
- LESS TOLERATED

6 YEARS

0   LOW                IMPACT OF RISK ON OUR BUSINESS                HIGH

| ① | ② | ③ | ④ |
|---|---|---|---|
| Big risk facing Harley 1: Traditional market (MAWM) is inevitably ageing/declining | Big risk facing Harley 2: Bike's reliance on fossil fuels less likely to impact so fast but even more of a game changer | Harley seeks to respond by seizing unlikely opportunity now: develop a trend-setting e-Bike: Livewire | See relations between risks and this op: a) Replace distinctive HD growl with jet-engine sound; b) 'If the Livewire is green, it has to be badass green.' Mark-Hans Richer, Director, Harley Marketing |

**DRAW YOUR OWN HERE...**

**1.** List the main risks associated with your strategy in terms of: (1) organization; (2) demand; (3) competition; (4) supply risks.

**2.** Estimate for each their probability of occurrence (either by marking the chart or by attributing a value) and their potential impact upon the organization.

**3.** Locate each risk on the chart and then consider the overall distribution of risks — is the level of overall risk acceptable in terms of the outcomes intended by your strategy?

Creative ideas:

**A.** The matrix can also be used to represent opportunities at the same time, so that risks can be assessed directly in relation to emergent opportunities.

**B.** It might also be used dynamically in order to show how the positioning of risks and opportunities may change over time using arrows, or with a number of diagrams in a succession.

**COMMON PITFALLS:** A classic problem with this matrix is 'spurious precision'. If numeric values are ascribed to specific risks, they can seem concrete in nature when they may in fact be impossible to determine with any great accuracy.

Focusing purely upon risks can be rather disheartening, so the idea of matching with opportunities can provide a more balanced picture.

No simple matrix can provide a complete view of a complex situation, so use the matrix as a stimulus for debate and further analysis. It should not become a yoke.

**GOOD IN COMBINATION WITH:** The matrix can be used alongside Ansoff's box (no. 19) and blue ocean strategies (no. 10) to ensure that the optimism of new growth strategies is tempered with an appreciation of potential risks. The matrix can also be used in conjunction with financial planning tools if specific values are used for risks. These may be factored into cash flow projections.

**MUTATION POTENTIAL:** One can consider 'how manageable' risks are as a third dimension on the matrix. A simple dial or traffic light colour coding next to each noted risk, to show how easily managed the risk could be, can usefully feed into contingency planning and strategic objectives.

**INFO FOR FURTHER READING:**

- Baird, I.S. and Thomas, H. (1990). What is risk anyway? Using and measuring risk in strategic management. In: Bettis, R.A. and Thomas, H. (eds) *Risk, Strategy and Management. Greenwich:* JAI Press.
- Miller, K.D. and Bromiley, P. (1990). Strategic risk and corporate performance: an analysis of alternative risk measures. *Academy of Management Journal*, 39, 91–122.
- Ruefli, T.W., Collins, J.M. and Lacugna, J.R. (1999). Risk measures in strategic management research: auld lang syne? *Strategic Management Journal*, 20(2), 167–194.

**FIELD NOTES:**

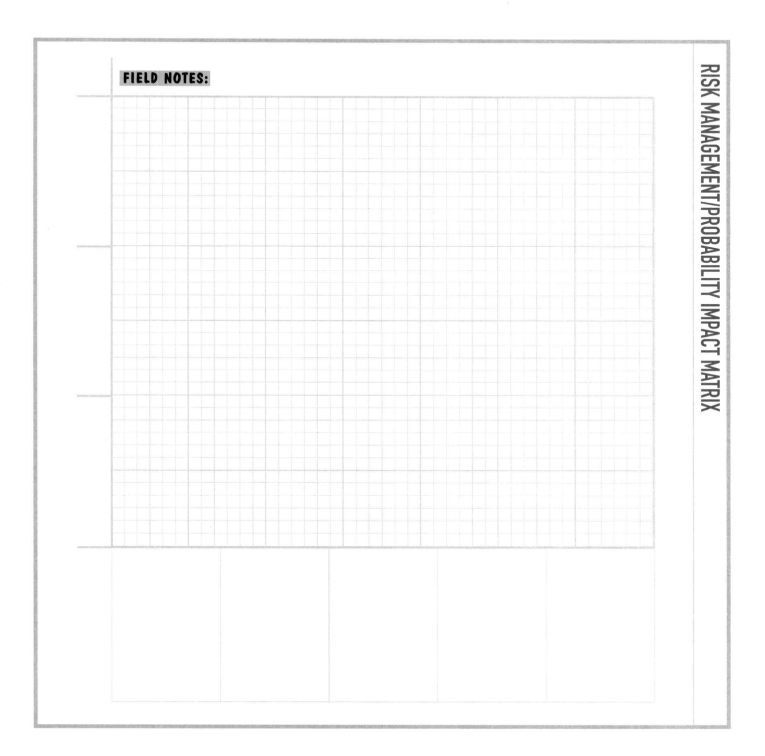

## 26. Animation—Orientation Matrix

### AUTHOR: Stephen Cummings and David Wilson (based on an idea by Karl Weick)

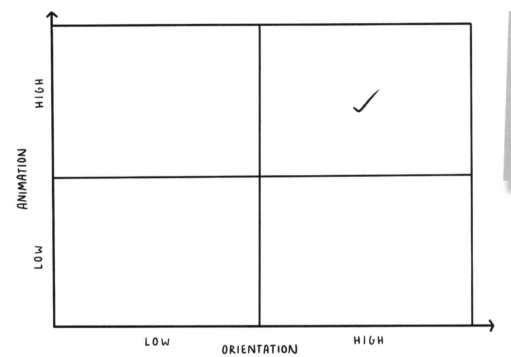

**WHEN TO USE:** As a simple check to gauge if your strategy is memorable, inspiring and providing the necessary direction to those who are charged with implementing it.

**COMPONENTS:** A 2 × 2 matrix that uses Karl Weick's two 'substitutes for formal strategic planning', orientation and animation, on its *x*- and *y*-axes.

## DEVELOPMENT:

The idea that a good strategy both orients and animates people in an organization was developed by organizational psychologist Karl Weick in a 1989 chapter entitled 'substitutes for strategy'. Here Weick utilized a famous story of a platoon of Hungarian soldiers lost in the Alps on a training exercise to show how a segment of a found map (which was later found to be a map of the Pyrenees) still helped get the soldiers moving, gave them hope and gave them a sense that they knew where they were heading.

Stephen Cummings and David Wilson turned this idea into a matrix in the book *Images of Strategy*. Their argument was that while the world was too complex to say what a good strategy for all firms *is*, it was possible to say what a good strategy *does*: it orients and animates. Hence, the matrix is a good framework for discussing and checking where your organization is after a strategy development process. Many organizations have a plan that outlines an orientation, but their staff lack enthusiasm to achieve and exceed this. Some organizations contain highly animated staff, but lack a clear sense of collective direction. The aim is that the strategy you have built both orients and animates. If it doesn't, it's back to the drawing board!

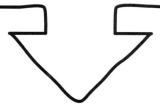

### Key Takeouts:
→ Is your current strategy animating and orienting the people who have to implement it?

→ If not, how could you develop and communicate it better?

# Philips: Strategic Simplicity (*c.* 2009)

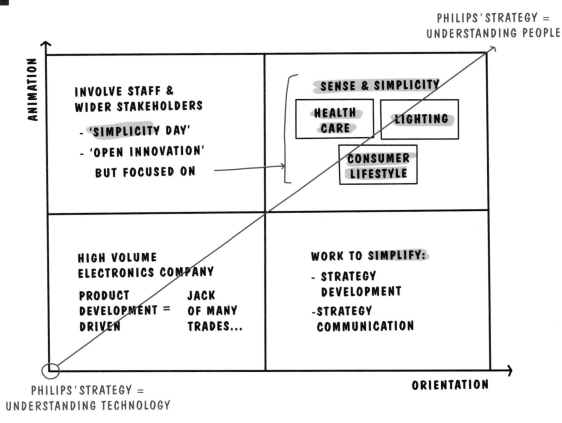

PHILIPS' STRATEGY =
UNDERSTANDING PEOPLE

ANIMATION

**INVOLVE STAFF &
WIDER STAKEHOLDERS**

- **'SIMPLICITY DAY'**
- **'OPEN INNOVATION'**
  BUT FOCUSED ON

**SENSE & SIMPLICITY**

HEALTH
CARE

LIGHTING

CONSUMER
LIFESTYLE

**HIGH VOLUME
ELECTRONICS COMPANY**

**PRODUCT
DEVELOPMENT =
DRIVEN**

**JACK
OF MANY
TRADES...**

**WORK TO SIMPLIFY:**

- **STRATEGY
  DEVELOPMENT**
- **STRATEGY
  COMMUNICATION**

ORIENTATION

PHILIPS' STRATEGY =
UNDERSTANDING TECHNOLOGY

| ① | ② | ③ | ④ | ⑤ |
|---|---|---|---|---|
| Philips was a highly successful company in the 20th century but change was required for the 21st | Strategy development trad based on following tech developments left the company disparate & unclear of focus | Seek to reorient by simplifying organization, strategy development and strategy comms | Reanimate by involving staff in initiatives like a day devoted to thinking about how to simplify their work | Strategy reorganized around understanding people rather than tech, in just three clear divisions |

**DRAW YOUR OWN HERE...**

1. The animation–orientation (AO) matrix is one framework that sometimes you don't need to embellish much at all. It's there to provoke reflection and discussion, so just draw up the framework on a board or a page.

2. Get people to point to where they think your organization is strategically, asking them to provide reasons as they do so. Note these.

3. Discuss/note ways that you could move upwards and rightwards.

Creative ideas:

A. So, you've arrived in the top right box. Make a note of all the threats that could lead to you drifting back out of high orientation and animation. Outline potential strategies that could prevent this drift towards de-orientation and de-animation from happening.

B. Draw these strategies in as thickening borders around the top right box acting as barriers from exiting it.

**COMMON PITFALLS:** Seeking to be too exact. Don't get too hung up on, or argue about, where the organization in focus is on either scale. The framework is much better used to stimulate broad and general discussion.

You are probably not the crucial stakeholder. While you might be oriented and animated by a strategy you have developed, unless you are the only person involved in its implementation (highly unlikely unless you are a sole trader, and even then...) then you need to ask others if they feel oriented and animated.

**GOOD IN COMBINATION WITH:** The AO matrix is usefully used at the 'top and tail' of any strategy development process. Ask people at the start where they would place the current strategy in these terms, then ask how the strategy could be made more orienting and animating. Seek to improve according to this list. Then, towards the end of the process, ask again. If you are not moving upwards and/or rightwards then you are not building things correctly.

**MUTATION POTENTIAL:** As a communication and review tool, you can insert an agreed animating and orienting vision in the top right of the top-right box, then ask people to identify and insert the frameworks or development processes that they felt really helped move the organization's orientation and animation upwards and rightwards. Keep this page and make sure to utilize these frameworks again in the next strategy building process.

**INFO FOR FURTHER READING:**
- Cummings, S. and Wilson, D. (2003). *Images of Strategy*. London: John Wiley & Sons.
- Weick, K.E. (1983). Misconceptions about managerial productivity. *Business Horizons*, 26(4), 47–52.
- Weick, K.E. (1987). Substitutes for strategy. In: Teece, D. (ed.) *The Competitive Challenge*. New York: Harper & Row, pp. 211–233.

**FIELD NOTES:**

## The Best of the Managing Performance Strategically Frameworks Combined — Fifth Foundation: The Balanced Goals Envelope

### PURPOSE:

To bring together key insights from a range of strategic goal development frameworks to help present these goals graphically, enable the evaluation of their collective balance, and encourage better strategic discussion and analysis about future direction.

### COMPONENTS:

The BGE places a box for capturing and animating an orienting vision and/or set of values in the middle of an envelope with different strategic goal aspects on the north, south, east and west sides. These are an amalgam of elements from the TBL, the BSC and the RSIM. The framework encourages 'pushing the envelope' on all sides with goals that are balanced rather than a set of goals that are all in the same quadrant.

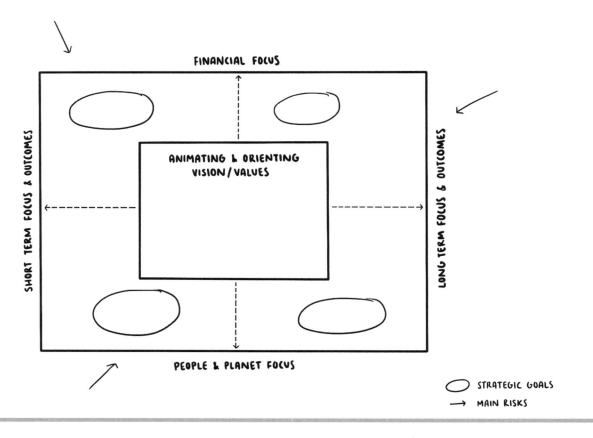

## Maersk (c. 2014)

Maersk is a Danish business conglomerate based in Copenhagen with interests primarily in the transportation and energy sectors. It is the world's largest container ship and supply vessel operator and employs over 100,000 people. In 2014 it introduced a new 'sustainability strategy' that would take a broad view of stakeholders and proactively seek to mitigate longer-term risks. It was titled 'Unlocking growth for society and Maersk', which outlined three key priorities in addition to a continued focus on responsible financial conduct: energy efficiency; investing in education; and enabling trade. The Balanced Goals Envelope applied to Maersk depicts this approach graphically.

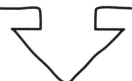

**Key Takeout:**

→ We have a clear vision of our strategic purpose and a set of balanced goals that will lead to its achievement and sustain the organization and its stakeholders.

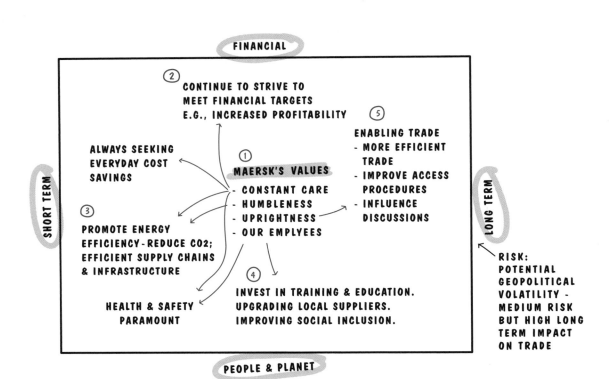

**FINANCIAL**

② CONTINUE TO STRIVE TO
MEET FINANCIAL TARGETS
E.G., INCREASED PROFITABILITY

⑤ ENABLING TRADE
- MORE EFFICIENT
TRADE
- IMPROVE ACCESS
PROCEDURES
- INFLUENCE
DISCUSSIONS

ALWAYS SEEKING
EVERYDAY COST
SAVINGS

① MAERSK'S VALUES
- CONSTANT CARE
- HUMBLENESS
- UPRIGHTNESS
- OUR EMPLYEES

**SHORT TERM**

**LONG TERM**

③ PROMOTE ENERGY
EFFICIENCY - REDUCE CO2;
EFFICIENT SUPPLY CHAINS
& INFRASTRUCTURE

④ INVEST IN TRAINING & EDUCATION.
UPGRADING LOCAL SUPPLIERS.
IMPROVING SOCIAL INCLUSION.

HEALTH & SAFETY
PARAMOUNT

RISK:
POTENTIAL
GEOPOLITICAL
VOLATILITY -
MEDIUM RISK
BUT HIGH LONG
TERM IMPACT
ON TRADE

**PEOPLE & PLANET**

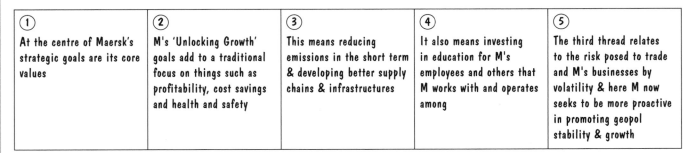

| ① | ② | ③ | ④ | ⑤ |
|---|---|---|---|---|
| At the centre of Maersk's strategic goals are its core values | M's 'Unlocking Growth' goals add to a traditional focus on things such as profitability, cost savings and health and safety | This means reducing emissions in the short term & developing better supply chains & infrastructures | It also means investing in education for M's employees and others that M works with and operates among | The third thread relates to the risk posed to trade and M's businesses by volatility & here M now seeks to be more proactive in promoting geopol stability & growth |

You can download templates of the Balanced Goals Envelope to aid your drawing at www.wiley/go/strategybuilder.com or try out the app at www.strategicplan.com.

# PART THREE
# REALIZATION

We have shown how strategy can be drawn to reflect unique strategic influences, options and developments – and that this has many advantages over the conventional box and line drawings found in textbooks or the screeds of numbers, text and generic infographics that have become the norm in conventional business practice. As you followed Part Two of this book, we hope you developed a taste for enhancing your building of strategy through pictures. While learning to draw strategy by utilizing classic frames that have stood the test of time is extremely beneficial, there is, we believe, a further advanced level of drawing strategy – that is, the development of unique and individualized, but easy-to-communicate and recall, images that outline a particular organization's strategy or some dimension of this.

We call this approach 'stratography'. It is not a new word. It has a variety of definitions, 'things belonging to an army', or the 'art of directing an army', but the term is now hardly ever used. We use it here in relation to the second sense listed in the previous sentence, but also as it is reflective of the first known use of the word strategy: the Ancient Greeks created the position of 'strategos' (a combination of *stratos* (= army) and *agin* (= to lead) – run together the combined word means to lead an army as it spreads out across the ground). This was a new leadership position created around 500 BC in the fledgling democracy of Athens. Ten 'strategoi', one for each of the 10 tribes of Athens, would be elected as the city's military and political leaders.[46] And we also use it because of the connotation provided by 'graphy' (also descended from Greek), meaning a descriptive science and the production of images.

We know that people start making judgments about the value of a presentation and whether they should engage or disengage within the first seven seconds. So how would you present your organization's strategy? A big wordy document? A ream of PowerPoints? The first two parts of this book have demonstrated the value of graphic images as a powerful way to develop, present and recall strategy. And in this final part we outline two routes towards better stratography, or the effective graphic realization and communication of strategy, in this third part of *Strategy Builder*.

# WELL-BUILT STRATEGIES, SIMPLY CONVEYED

The first approach we offer here is a template based upon the five generic 'combination' frameworks we developed in Part 2: the Environmental Ecosystem, the Competitive Spidergram, the Capability Radar, the Growth Options Heatmap and the Balanced Goals Envelope. This template is shown in Figure 3.1. It contains space for using the ecosystem frame, or other frameworks from the ecosystem section of Part 2, to outline environmental opportunities and threats in the top-left corner. And space for utilizing positioning and capability frameworks, or the generic spidergram and radar, for determining capabilities and weaknesses, beneath this. In the centre is space for bringing these aspects together into a confrontation matrix or heatmap in the centre. And, importantly, given that strategy development frequently does not result in the determination of specific actionable

STRATEGY BUILDER: Strategy on a Page

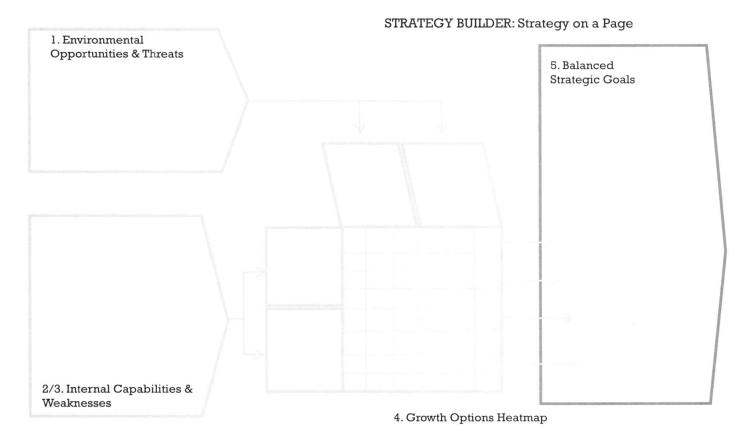

1. Environmental Opportunities & Threats

2/3. Internal Capabilities & Weaknesses

4. Growth Options Heatmap

5. Balanced Strategic Goals

**Figure 3.1** Strategy Builder 'Strategy on a Page' Template

objectives, there are spaces on the far right of the page for noting strategic goals that strike a balance between financial and people development concerns and short- and long-term objectives.

Having surveyed what cartography, graphics, aesthetics, cognition and optics have concluded with regard to the best ways to communicate complex relations and directions simply, and 15 years of our own practice in this regard, we describe the development of this 'Strategy on a Page' template according to six principles of good stratography. In outlining these principles and explaining the development of the template we shall also illustrate how good-strategy graphics relating to your particular organizational concerns can be expressed by referring

to good-practice stratography examples that we have found or been involved in developing, and compare these examples to not-so-good (i.e. bad) practice.

It is not difficult to find bad attempts at drawing strategy. While all of the classic frameworks we have listed in this book, and many more besides, encourage drawing, as we have already described, the presentation of these frameworks tends to discourage actual creative drawing; and furthermore, when managers and others seek to draw with them, things can get very messy and very confused very quickly. An example is provided in Figure 3.2. And in our experience such graphical representation is commonplace (Google 'strategy drawing' or 'strategy map' and you'll see many similar

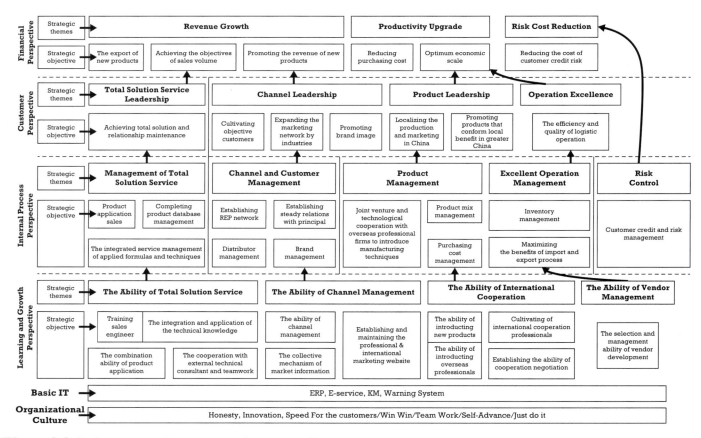

**Figure 3.2** Bad stratography: strategy drawn poorly

images). Whenever we show it to our MBA or Exec Education participants they respond with knowing sighs. As an example of poor practice we shall also refer back to this picture when we outline our six principles of good stratography.

This brings us to the second approach to stratography that we wish to promote here: 'freestyle'. While it can be extremely useful to use a shared template grounded in the best strategy frameworks, the classics and some of the latest best thinking, you can also do it your own way. Having gained the confidence to build and communicate strategy through drawing, there is nothing to stop you taking what you've learned and developing your own style and approaches. However, in so doing,

we believe that the six stratographic principles are useful general ground rules in presenting strategic ideas graphically. And, in addition, the good-practice examples we outline may provide inspiration as to how stratography can be done differently while adhering to these principles.

In both modes, either following the Strategy Builder 'Strategy on a Page' template or developing your own freestyle approach, in keeping with all that we have written thus far, we suggest that conveying a strategy using graphics is greatly advanced if it can be done as simply as possible. The ideal, and the aim of this final part of the book, is to realize and communicate your strategy simply and effectively.

# SIX STRATOGRAPHIC PRINCIPLES

In the following pages we outline six principles of good stratography that align with the latest science relating to graphical representation. The first four may be associated with mechanical movements:

1. **Arresting and focusing** the eye on the page.

2. Helping the eye to **spread** across a terrain.

3. Enabling the eye to **seek out connections.**

4. Facilitating the eye to **zoom in and out**, between micro and the macro levels, to draw key linkages.

The last two relate more to cognitive and otherwise sensory principles:

5. **Mimesis** or following common human patterns and behaviours.

6. **Synaesthesis** or encouraging the engagement of more than one sense.

As we discuss these principles, we examine a number of examples of stratography in action from the corporate world and classic documents often used to describe these principles in fields such as cartography, optics, psychology and illustration. And we explain the development of the one-page Strategy Builder template for developing and communicating a strategy founded on the best strategy frameworks developed over the past 50 years. Indeed, as we go through, it is useful to keep in mind those frameworks that we outlined in Part 2 of the book, as reviewing these principles will probably help you to understand why you found particular frameworks outlined in Part 2 more appealing than others. It is likely that your

favourites appealed to a good many of the principles we are about to outline.

## 1. Good stratography attracts and focuses the eye

Because we are bombarded by so much visual information, our eyes are kept busy and often become overwhelmed and jaded. In the first instance, good stratography must gain the attention of the viewer. It must have 'eye appeal'. It must be quickly perceived to be interesting or useful and able to be quickly comprehended. Put another way, it must have a use or interest value greater than the perceived effort it will take to extract that interest or use. Given this, key elements for stopping the eye and encouraging it to focus on a graphic are listed below:

- **Clarity of purpose** – a clear view of what the graphic is seeking to do, and not trying to do too much. As we outlined in Part 2, one of the main reasons that the application of most graphical strategy frameworks does not work as well as it should is a lack of clarity in the mind of the user about what the framework is specifically for.

- **Aesthetics** – clear lines and strong colours, but not too many of either. There has never been a popular rainbow-coloured strategy framework, or one with more than eight main elements, for good reason.

- **Novelty** – this helps to attract a second glance, but too much can make a graphic appear irrelevant. One reason that the generic strategy frameworks that we featured earlier do not excite as much interest as they might is that they are continually presented in the

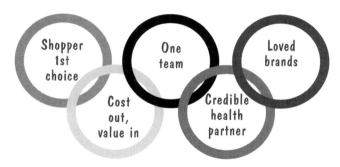

**Figure 3.3** From bullet points to Olympic rings

same uniform ways. By contrast, many of the worked examples in Part 2 take some artistic licence, and illustrate using metaphor.

- **Utility** – conveying a sense that the viewer could quickly take something interesting from it and do something with it. Your strategy graphic should have almost immediate utility impact for the viewer/user. Does it make them think they should and can do something to contribute?

A good real-life example of this first principle in practice is shown in the simple picture in Figure 3.3. It is taken from a regional office of a multinational food group. Five strategic objectives are depicted, but not in the standard bullet pointed list.

Aesthetically, the Olympic rings are a well-known positive symbol and visually interesting. Because of this, and the novelty of seeing objectives in this format, the viewer is drawn to look inside the rings rather than perhaps ignoring the contents of a standard bullet point list. It conveys these five objectives in a powerful but functional manner. Looking further into the optical effects of this graphical representation, one can see how the eye is drawn first to the strongest colour – the black – and the overarching objective of acting as

'one team'. This is further enhanced by the degree of whitespace in between the text of the 'one team' and the circle surrounding it. From here, the eye scans around (generally to the red – the next strongest colour at top right) to the blue, bottom left, to note the other four objectives in a manner that will add a further dimension to the objectives and make them far easier for employees and other stakeholders to recall. An important related characteristic is that there are only five rings. It is worth noting that strategic objectives often lead to confused implementation on account of their being too numerous – people just cannot remember them all!

By contrast, the bad practice example we showed earlier on page 210 exhibits little novelty, little variation of line, colour, text or form and is cluttered, very complex and unclear in terms of direction and purpose. It does little to attract and focus the viewer in any particular way.

In keeping with this principle, we have tried to arrange the key elements distilled from the 26 frameworks incorporated into the Strategy Builder on our 'Strategy on a Page' template in a way that focuses and attracts without overwhelming the viewer with detail. We've sought to limit it to the five key Builder 'foundations', and emboldened the space for balanced goals on the right to remind the user that this is what your drawing and writing on this page are aimed at (see Figure 3.4).

The Environmental Ecosystem's similarity to a human eye and the Ecosystem's placement on the template can be useful in this regard. We know that eyes in pictures attract the viewer's eyes (the Mona Lisa might be the most readily recalled example). Hence the ecosystem graphic will likely be where your eye is drawn to on the 'Strategy on a Page'. This is where you will probably begin to doodle, and its placement in the top-left corner has been done for a reason… which we shall explain in more detail in respect of Principle 2.

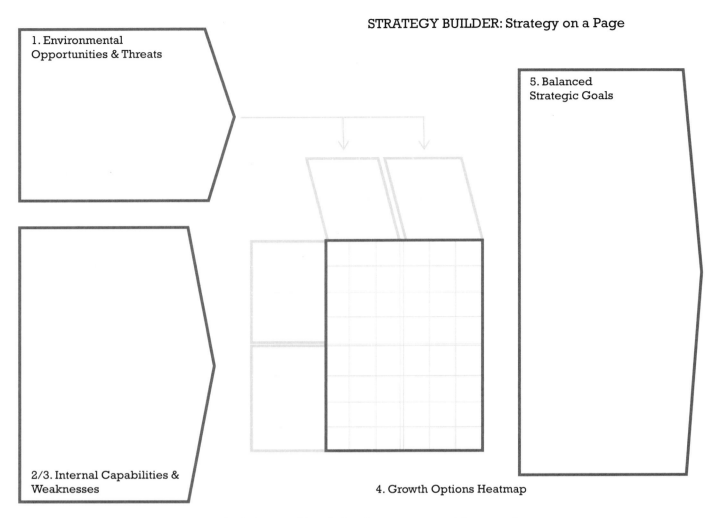

1. Environmental Opportunities & Threats

5. Balanced Strategic Goals

2/3. Internal Capabilities & Weaknesses

4. Growth Options Heatmap

**Figure 3.4** Strategy on a Page: Principle 1 — Simplicity that attracts and focuses the eye

## 2. Good stratography spreads the eye

The Western eye is acculturated to scanning a page hierarchically from the top left corner across and down the page, or clockwise from left to right, down and back around. It follows that good stratography in business contexts where this is, or is becoming, the prevailing culture (it is increasingly more common for Chinese characters to be recorded and read across rather than down the page) will work with, rather than against, this grain (although in some cultures adjustment will be necessary). Enabling the eye to move in this comfortable manner, to quickly get an understanding of the presentation of the terrain and the key relationships, really enhances the effectiveness of stratography.

Up went the coal cars.
Up went the flat cars.
Up went the little red caboose.

One day the train
started up a mountain.
Up went the big black engine.
Up went the boxcars.
Up went the oil cars.

**Figure 3.5** Principle 2 in action: The Little Red Caboose. Sourced from http://www.imaginarymuseum.org/MHV/PZImhv/WoodPowerMaps1993.html

Denis Wood's *The Power of Maps* (1992) illustrates the value of this with reference to a well-known illustration by Tibor Gergely in the children's book *The Little Red Caboose*.[47] The second half of the book, the beginning of which is marked by the picture in Figure 3.5, brings a mountain, and its defining characteristics, into the foreground of the story. What immediately grabs the reader upon viewing this illustration is the train about to make it to the top, with all eyes in the picture also leading to it (and, as we described earlier, it helps that the front of the engine is reminiscent of a human eye). The viewer's eye then rolls down the mountain and into the context – where the train has come from. Of course, this context is important too, but it is best absorbed after you have understood that this story is now about the train's relationship to and ascent of the mountain.

A simple example of this 'effective spreading' principle in action in a piece of stratography is shown in Figure 3.6, which is taken from a recent Procter & Gamble (P&G) Annual Report and website. This takes an extremely large and complex company's growth strategy and distils it into

**P&G Growth Strategy:** Touching and improving more consumers' lives in more parts of the world more completely

**WHERE TO PLAY:**
1. Grow leading, global brands and core categories
2. Build business with underserved and unserved consumers
3. Continue to grow and develop faster-growing, structurally attractive businesses with global leadership potential

**HOW TO WIN:**
1. Drive Core P&G Strengths in consumer understanding, brand building, innovation and go to market
2. Simplify, Scale and Execute for competitive advantage
3. Lead change to win with consumers and customers

**Figure 3.6** Principle 2 in action: P&G's graphic spreads the eye

a simple and memorable image that leads the eye from the top left corner, enables the viewer to search to and from the field of play to how to win on that field. This allows different readers to dive down to explore different levels of detail underneath each of the statements, and mirrors the classic left-to-right movement of the Value Chain. But it adds value by enabling the viewer to think through the reciprocity of actions from right to left as well.

While the P&G graphic may seem a little mundane, it is important to note that it is unusual. Despite some of the now obvious advantages of communicating strategy by incorporating individualized graphics along with text, very few firms currently do this. Indeed, in the survey we mentioned at the beginning of Part 1 of this book, it was found that, out of 250 of the world's largest and most respected companies, the P&G example was the only one where a picture was used to describe a strategy and made public on its website.

Related to this, our 'Strategy on a Page' template is designed so that the viewer may be first drawn

to the ecosystem figure in the top left corner. It then encourages the viewer to move towards key aspects relating to the Competitive Spidergram and the Capability Radar (many state or not-for-profit organizations may choose to skip the spidergram to focus on the capability radar – our Strategy Builder app, available at strategicplan.com, enables this step too). Key opportunities, threats, strengths and weaknesses are then carried downwards and rightwards through the growth options confrontation matrix and onwards to the strategic objectives that should be the outcome of a strategy development process (see Figure 3.7).

In light of this principle – that good stratography should smoothly spread the viewer's eye across the page in a calm manner so that the person can follow the flow of the relevant information – we can see that one of the most damning graphical characteristics of the bad practice example in Figure 3.2 is that the upward arrows are fighting against the direction in which the user's eye wants to go, which further adds to the frustration of the viewer experience.

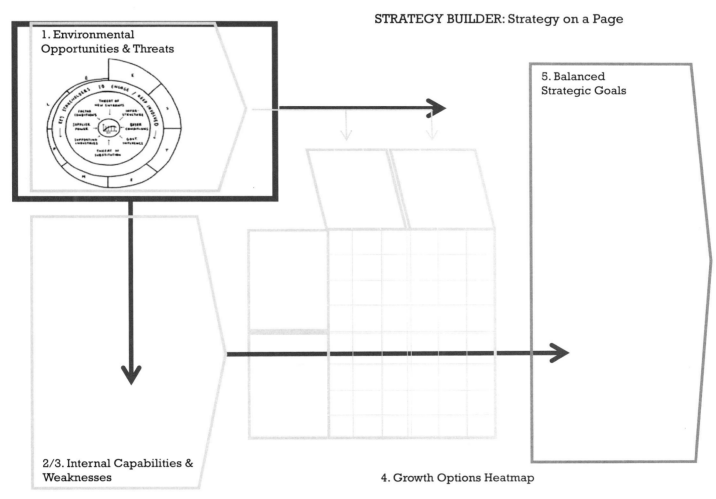

STRATEGY BUILDER: Strategy on a Page

1. Environmental Opportunities & Threats

5. Balanced Strategic Goals

2/3. Internal Capabilities & Weaknesses

4. Growth Options Heatmap

**Figure 3.7** Strategy on a Page: Principle 2 – Spread the eye

## 3. Encouraging the eye to wander, engage and find relations

Having attracted the attention of viewers, focused and then spread their eye across the page, a very good stratographical representation will begin to do two more things simultaneously. It will draw in the eye, keeping it engaged in the picture; and it will begin to loosen the eye up, too, to make the viewer suspend preconceived beliefs and ways of proceeding and seek new patterns. While this sounds unusual, look at the two examples in Figure 3.8 and decide which one causes your eye to be drawn into the figure and encourages you to look around, and which one seems to repel it?

The adaptation of a painting by Bridget Riley (at the top of the figure), draws you in. Then, almost immediately, you feel your eye wandering as it looks for patterns, lighting up different parts of the brain as you go. Written languages and graphs and charts that follow a regular, predetermined pattern (e.g. right, down one, left, right, down one, left…) and cover most of the available surface do not have the same effect.

Unfortunately, most attempts to communicate strategy have an effect more similar to the image shown at the bottom of Figure 3.8. When cigarette manufacturers were first required to print health warnings on their packets, they were very clever about designing statements like

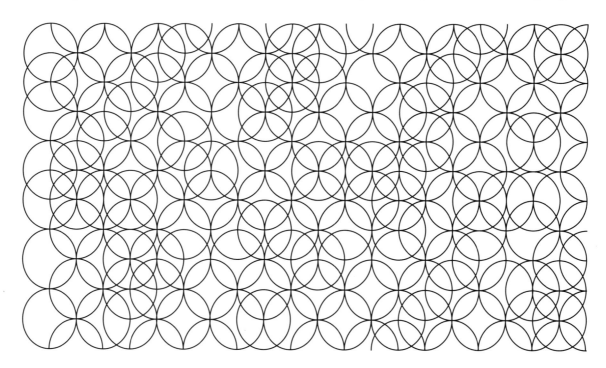

**SURGEON GENERAL'S WARNING: SMOKING CAUSES LUNG CANCER, HEART DISEASE, EMPHYSEMA, AND MAY COMPLICATE PREGNANCY**

**Figure 3.8** Good and bad practice examples of graphics encouraging the eye to wander and find relations

these that both conformed to the fledgling regulations but were not particularly easy to absorb. However, as governments and other regulating bodies have become increasingly savvy about this practice, tobacco companies have had to print bigger, bolder and less wordy warnings. Now many countries require a warning far less removed from concrete experience of the illnesses caused by smoking, and far more likely to have an impact on the viewer: pictures of those diseases or degradations.

So, why does the image at the top draw in the eye while the warning below seems to be pushing it out? It has to do with space and what we might call an irregularity which is not too irregular. Good graphical representations like these include a lot of white or neutral or negative space, generally irregularly proportioned but in ways that patterns can easily be sought and found. This helps to bring viewers in and encourages them to start looking for relationships because it is part of the way our brain works – always seeking patterns and connections. In the same way that knowledge management or creativity gurus tell us that 'slack' is required to encourage new and productive reservoirs of tacit knowledge and patterns of thinking, graphics need to contain 'slack' too, in the form of enough space to enable the reader to find themselves and other connections. The top picture exhibits these characteristics. The image below it, with its heavy and close borders and its cramped and regular font (all caps, and little differentiation between the space between words and letters within words), makes it a struggle to read. You can almost feel the image trying to push your eye away.[48]

Look back at that bad practice example of a drawn strategy that we showed in Figure 3.2 on page 210 and you will see that it does the same thing: its crowdedness and lack of white space, the regularity of the boxes and the monotony of the crowded text all in the same font repel the eye and make it less likely that those who have to implement the strategy it is seeking to communicate will engage with it.

By contrast, on the Strategy Builder website (www.wiley.com/go/strategybuilder.com) you can observe the drawing that Alan Mulally did outlining his view of the Ford strategy, which so impressed, and seemed so novel to, the journalists who were interviewing him that they asked if they could reproduce it in their article. The centrepiece of the typed strategy statements draws the eye in, but the handwriting around the edge tempts one to look out around the edge and then back in again, looking for relationships between one and the other.[49] One is drawn to the bubble with 'The Plan' written inside it, but then one can move clockwise or anti-clockwise, in the order the notes are written, or not. In the bottom right, a more formal list aims to pull everything together. It is an engaging representation of a strategy that makes the viewer want to get involved and find out more. In a more formal way, BECA's strategic action development template achieves a similar effect (see Figure 3.9). BECA is a professional services consultancy specializing in construction and related industries (their most high-profile project is likely the Marina Bay Sands complex in Singapore). The template helps key actions, and desired outcomes from those actions, to be seen in relation to key stakeholders or capabilities (Clients, Reputation, People) wander across to Key Success Measures and back to check and better understand their fit into the desired strategic pattern or flow (NB. we've replaced the actual figures with x's).

Similarly, our 'Strategy on a Page' template contains some shapes and areas as prompts, but plenty of white space to encourage engagement and the seeking of relationships that may reinforce or be seen to jar with one another as the user looks at things and the links between them as they are drawn or viewed, as the arrows in Figure 3.10 illustrate.

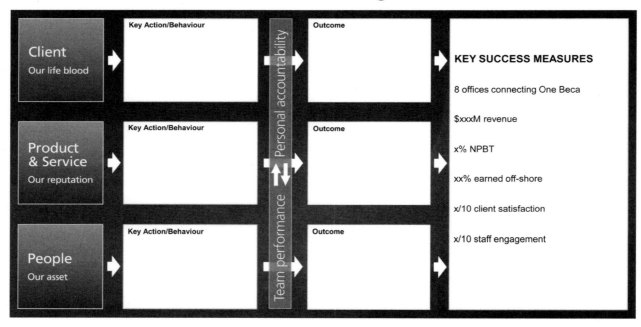

Figure 3.9  BECA's strategic action development template

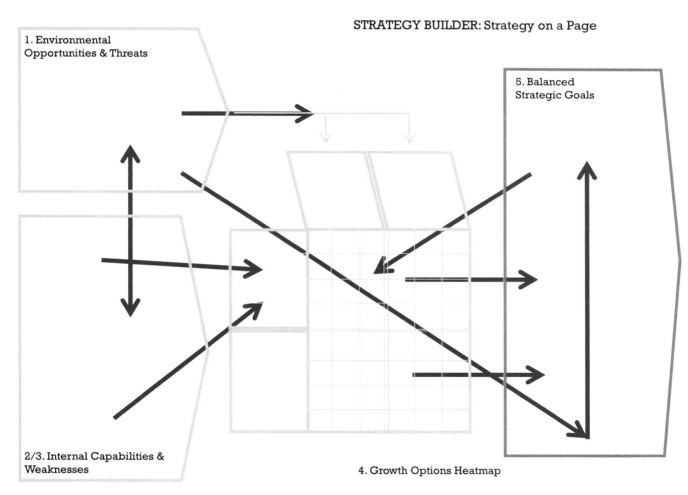

STRATEGY BUILDER: Strategy on a Page

1. Environmental Opportunities & Threats

5. Balanced Strategic Goals

2/3. Internal Capabilities & Weaknesses

4. Growth Options Heatmap

**Figure 3.10** Strategy on a Page: Principle 3 – Encouraging the eye to find relations

## 4. Good stratography facilitates zooming in and out

Why is Google Maps so useful (and addictive!)? Why are Prezi presentations easier to follow than traditional PowerPoint equivalents? One answer is that users love being able to zoom in and see the detail and zoom out and see this detail in a wider context. So often the presentation of strategy does not allow for this.

The ability to see the micro and the macro, the big picture and the detail, the complex and the simple, is a particularly important aspect of effective strategic action. Good stratography should aid this. Because incorporating too much detail can turn people off or paralyse them, good stratography should focus solely on the few dimensions necessary to aid decision-making in a particular arena.

Certainly, while three dimensions may enable us to better represent reality, we find it much easier to work with a two-dimensional map or graphic. And, within two dimensions, a useful general rule is to aim for no more than seven colours, no more than seven directions or seven value categories and not to introduce too many different shapes. By simplifying complexity in this way, we contribute to the achievement of the first three eye movements described above, and we facilitate a fourth: the ability to see both the micro and macro, to see a particular detail that may relate specifically to a particular part of the system while seeing the system as a whole. To move in and out as it were, on a vertical plane – like a zoom lens.

An exemplar of this characteristic is Harry Beck's London Underground map, which we discussed in Part 1. While it is far less geographically accurate than the map

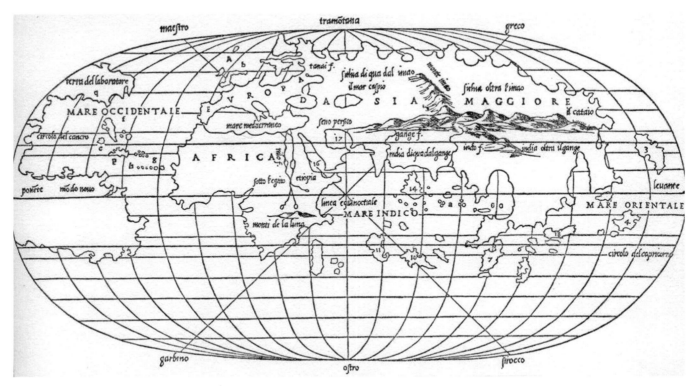

**Figure 3.11** Bordone's *Isolario* 16th-century woodcut world map. Sourced from http://www.raremaps.com/gallery/detail/31432?view=print

it replaced – the actual location of objects has been manipulated to aid visibility and recall – it is a far more effective decision-making aid.

The simplifications incorporated into Beck's diagram enabled travellers to quickly plan, discuss and take action, picking out particular lines while easily seeing key relationships between lines and the Underground as a whole. Measures of the Beck map's value include the way in which it has slipped into the very fabric of London life, an icon that affects behaviour and language, and the way that it has been copied all over the world (from New York to Moscow to China), and adapted for the London Underground itself as its network has expanded.[50] Thanks to the white space within the map people have been able to 'get into it' and develop it for different purposes.

As Edward Tufte explains, people respond to this macro/micro effect, they love to be able to see the big picture and personalize the data.[51] Similarly, Karl Weick argued that having the ability to see both the actual complexity and interconnectedness of things in a simple big picture could increase confidence and reduce stress. Indeed, any device that enables this (be it a new World Map for 16th-century explorers – see Figure 3.11 – or Google Maps for today's travellers) is thus extremely endearing and engaging.[52]

Unfortunately, most strategic plans are not so endearing. They are either so generalized as to have little real meaning or resonance to employees on the ground, or they go into such detail and are so complex and thickly worded that people can't readily zoom in to see how they relate to themselves or zoom out to see where they are in relation to the big picture. Figure 3.12, by way of contrast, is a good example of stratography that does exhibit this zoom principle. It is British-based multinational supermarket giant Tesco's 'strategy steering wheel'.

This unique wheel form attracts the viewer, with the eye drawn into the cool blue centre and the macro mission that underpins it all: 'every little helps'. The strong red of the Community arc then focuses the viewer on the top left corner of the image with the primary focus on the customer, which goes into more detail (you can find full colour versions of this illustration and others on the Strategy

**Figure 3.12** Tesco's 'steering wheel'. (Source: Tesco PLC, 2008)

Builder website). The eye is then steered clockwise around the circle from left to right, top to bottom and back around to relate all of the other segments back to the customer perspective. The eye is then able to walk in and out of the middle circle from macro to micro and back again.

To aid this, the wheel was combined with other multi-modal graphical and textual tools, such as individual store updates with traffic lights that show green, amber or red on each of the 20 slices within the five arcs, and individualized 'shopping lists' that describe in simple terms current areas of focus in terms of the wheel's elements, so that employees can incorporate them into their daily practices. Together, these visual aids helped bridge the macro–micro divide that is so often a problem in strategy communication: How can we relate the big picture to the everyday smaller activities that employees undertake? As former CEO Sir Terry Leahy (a prime mover behind the wheel) said: 'Tesco doesn't want one leader. We want thousands of leaders who take initiative to execute [our] strategy.'[53]

The steering wheel grew out of a classic Kaplan and Norton balanced scorecard approach that began to be developed in the 1990s. This heritage can be seen in four of the arcs representing customers, finance, operations and people. However, this initiative to capture Tesco's strategy in a simple and effective graphical manner for staff and other stakeholders was taken to another level when Tesco developed its own geometry to represent it and a fifth distinctive arc about their community. This changed the approach from being a generic management framework to a living and guiding example of stratography that oriented and animated the organization. The shape, colours and simplicity (five general arcs each with

contributing spokes that may change over time) added up to a memorable and meaningful image that can be reinterpreted and adapted over time. This was important for driving the huge multinational's strategy and keeping initiatives co-ordinated.

A key part of this is being able to zoom into each of the five segments and other aspects of the wheel to look in more depth at what these elements mean. Figure 3.13 shows examples of how the Wheel has been developed in different ways by the organization, to enable (on the left) different divisions or regions or particular employees to discuss what the different elements mean to them and how they can get involved to improve things. On the right-hand

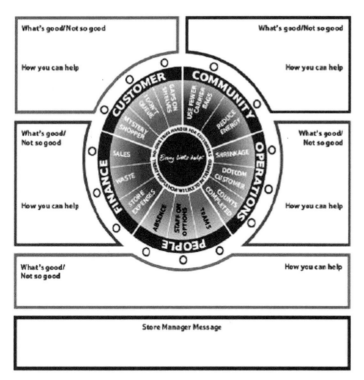

**Figure 3.13** Tesco's steering wheel extension and a 'shopping list'[54]

side is an example of a series of 'shopping list' extensions of the wheel that pick out parts of the big picture and provide more micro detail about what exactly they meant.

By contrast, the bad practice example in Figure 3.2 has so many indistinguishable elements (64!) that the prospect that one might go deeper into any of them would fill most people with dread.

In keeping with this fourth stratographic principle, our template is divided into just five macro parts, but each part can be the subject of more detailed extrapolation, with more detailed expositions drawing on some of the key frameworks that contribute to each foundational block to explain the detail behind what is presented on an overarching single-page strategy graphic (Figure 3.14).

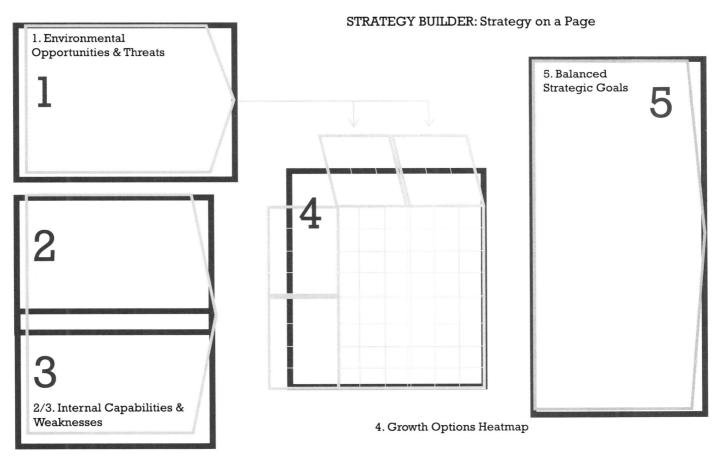

STRATEGY BUILDER: Strategy on a Page

1. Environmental Opportunities & Threats

1

2

3

2/3. Internal Capabilities & Weaknesses

4

4. Growth Options Heatmap

5. Balanced Strategic Goals

5

**Figure 3.14** Strategy on a Page: Principle 4 – Encouraging the eye to zoom in and out

## 5. Mimesis: good stratography relates to human actions and directions

Not only do graphic depictions of space and relationships have an advantage over text in engaging the eye, enabling it to roam, pick out relationships between things and move in and out, they also have the advantage of appealing to 'mimesis': in other words they can mirror the different directions people might take in real life or objects and activities that they can relate to.

Strategic planning documents, presented as text, can only go left to right and top to bottom, they can't mimic any other direction. (This unilateral movement is also the case with classic strategy frameworks in their generic un-customized forms like the microeconomic Theory of the Firm (input–process–output) and the Value Chain.) The mimetic dimension helps learning and retention by connecting cognition to physiology.

The famous map of Napoleon's fateful Russian campaign by Charles Joseph Minard (shown in Part 1, Figure 1.1), may be the best-known example of using mimesis to deliver a complex story in a simple and compelling way. The narrowing beige line shows the gradual decline of his force from 422,000 when crossing the Russian border to 100,000 when it gets to Moscow. The black line traces the demise in retreat set against the declining temperatures of the Russian winter (bottom thin line). Only 10,000 men will cross back into Poland. Napoleon is spent. Words alone could not capture this left-to-right and then right-to-left movement in a way that enables one to so readily see antecedents and relationships between actions and leave such an indelible mark on the memory. Numbers are less effective communicators in this respect, too, as, in the words of organizational psychologist Karl Weick: 'People who examine [only] the numbers are unable to reconstruct [in reality or in their minds] the actual events that produce those numbers.'[55]

With graphical representations, three pathways to market can be drawn as three arrows; going upmarket can be shown as going above where we might draw the market now, and by doing so the drawing will be more closely linked to our experience of the world. Indeed, mimesis means that simple pictures can transcend language. If a man points left anywhere in the world, he is universally understood to mean left.

When Rob Fyfe became CEO of Air New Zealand in 2005, he wanted a wider range of employees and other stakeholders to feel connected to the company's emerging strategy and understand how it related to their everyday jobs. A multidisciplinary team of 15 employees was empowered to simplify and make memorable the company's new strategy. They chose to do so by drawing and writing it out in a series of 'doodles' that could be taken on tour as part of a 'roadshow' in order to explain it and involve people more effectively in the organization's strategy. An example is reproduced in Figure 3.15. The novel use of common office objects like post-it notes and coffee cup stains attracts and focuses the eye while making the drawing appear much less daunting, more 'relatable' and more human than a normal strategic planning document: as if you were sitting at a desk or coffee table with a colleague as they are explaining it.

The Air New Zealand employees that we spoke to were universally positive about the effect of the roadshow drawings. In the words of one senior operations manager (who was a sales manager at the time): 'It was one of the most compelling pieces of work to come out of the exec office and nothing like what I had seen at the airline before, or indeed expected. For a "foot soldier" in sales like myself it provided a very clear and unified vision of what needed to be achieved and why. To survive we were going to have to be different and do things differently – and the strategy drawings "walked the talk".'[56]

That's a clear advantage of drawings over text and numbers or good drawings over bad (i.e. uniform, boring and cluttered) drawings: they can represent not only the talk of strategy, but also the walk: the actual actions required. In the 'Strategy on a Page' template, we've drawn on the very relatable images of a distillery or coffee filter or loom, with the opportunities, threats, capabilities and weaknesses being concentrated,

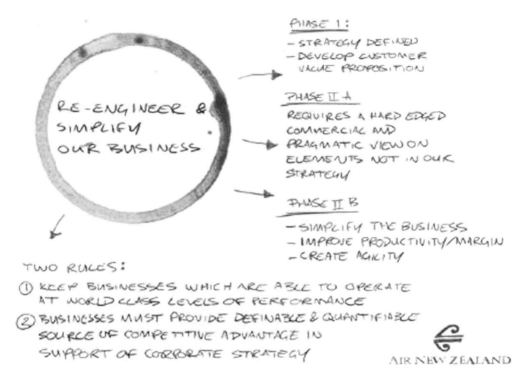

Figure 3.15 One of Air New Zealand's 2005 strategy roadshow images

funnelled and woven through the confrontation matrix, as sand through an hourglass, into clear strategic goals (Figure 3.16).

## 6. Synaesthesis: good stratography unites different senses and behaviours

One of main communication advantages of a drawing our map is that it can be multi-modal – it generally contains both pictures and text. Multi-modality generally enhances the ability to communicate meaning. Good multi-modal graphical representations of space also have a 'synaesthesic' effect; that is, they develop their relationships with the reader from the initial 'eye contact' onwards to draw in and engage other senses which then

start working together to give the image greater meaning. A good map makes you want to touch it; trace what you see with your finger; maybe even talk to the person you're with about it and hear what they have to say – whether they see what you see. If you've ever been in London, you may recall just how tactile the Tube map is: it invites you to trace your route with your finger, to share your perspective on it with your travelling companions, and to annotate it with reminders and doodles particular to individual aims and goals. And as with any map, once you have added to it physically, you (and your co-customizers) have a greater mental connection with it.

Consequently, a good graphical representation of a strategy does more than just depict. It can also aid communication, network and integrate senses within a

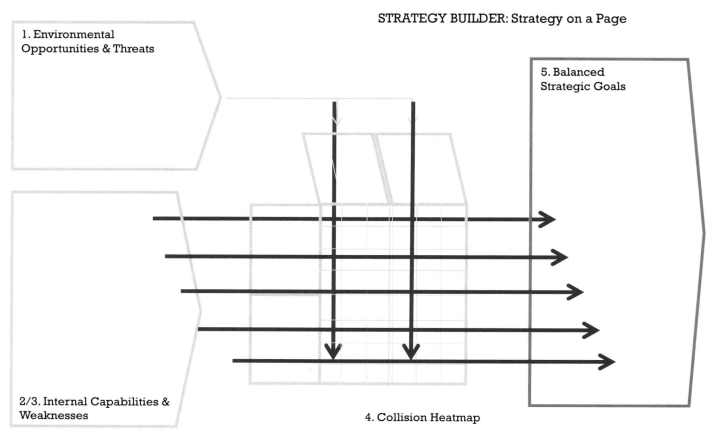

1. Environmental
Opportunities & Threats

5. Balanced
Strategic Goals

2/3. Internal Capabilities &
Weaknesses

4. Collision Heatmap

**Figure 3.16** Strategy on a Page: Principle 5 – Drawing on relatable human patterns

person or between people. A story outlined by Karl Weick to illustrate this point reflects these social functions:

*The young lieutenant of a Hungarian detachment in the Alps sent a reconnaissance unit into the icy wilderness. It began to snow immediately, and unexpectedly continued to snow for two days. The unit did not return. The lieutenant feared that he had dispatched them to death. However, on the third day the unit came back. Where had they been? How had they made their way? 'Yes,' they said: 'We considered ourselves lost and waited for the end. We did not have any maps, compasses or other equipment with which to ascertain their position or a probable route out. But then one of us found an old tattered map in a seldom used pocket. That calmed us down. The map did not seem to quite fit the terrain but eventually we discovered our bearings. We followed the map down the mountain and after a few wrong turns eventually found our way.' The lieutenant borrowed the map and had a good look at it. 'This isn't a map of the Alps,' he said. 'It's a map of the Pyrenees.'[57]*

There has been much debate about just how apocryphal this story is, but people certainly identify with it. It illustrates how pictures are useful not only because they represent reality, but also because they draw people in, encourage people to communicate, and provide both a template and the confidence to inspire decision-making and action. Thus, graphical representations (which can never be perfect matches with reality) may not get people to their destination in a straightforward manner, but they can get people moving, and when people are animated and begin to combine their energies and actions, new vistas emerge, new communication arises and new possibilities come into view. These enable the next decisions to be calibrated with better information and a clearer orientation to emerge.

Through this we can better understand how strategic endeavour was greatly advanced in the 15th and 16th centuries through the advent and spread of maps like Geradus Mercator's. While such maps were not completely accurate representations of reality, they provided guidelines and inspired greater confidence to act. Just a sense that you have some shared idea of the lay of the land can focus minds and consequently encourage and inspire decisive actions where there might otherwise have been procrastination or circular debate.

Because of their eye appeal, mimetic potential, their openness, their ability to draw people in and their capacity to simultaneously enable macro and micro thinking, picturing the 'terrain', a strategy for crossing it and what winning would look like is a great device for bringing people together. One can tell when one has hit upon an interesting graphical representation on a whiteboard: it becomes a focal point, a skeleton, or a repository for ideas. Indeed, scientific research tells us not only of the value of pictures over the printed word, but also of the spoken word over the printed word in communication. Subsequently, stratography that people want to speak to, draw on, debate, add to or adapt, covers, or unites, all the bases.

A nice example of this principle in practice comes from an electricity company we have worked with (hence the cable running through Figure 3.17, which shows just a portion of the whole image – the whole image spreads out to develop a picture of future strategies and desired states). The overriding objective of the exercise was to provide a greater sense of aiming out strategically to longer-term aspirations – towards goals in 20 years' time – rather than getting bogged down debating next month's targets. It was decided that some pictorial representation of this would help and a cross-section working group was brought together to tackle this. The group gravitated to the triple bottom line framework and added in a fourth line: the maintenance and development of their culture. With the involvement of an artist they took this concept and developed objectives to be achieved for the short-term (early iterations of which you can see in Figure 3.17) and longer-term goals by 2030.

The artist's initial sketches (which are shown here) would gradually be enhanced with a screen version that incorporated 'click-throughs' so viewers could dive down into parts of the diagram to find greater detail on the goals, approaches and people responsible for each area and goal. And more stylized computer-generated versions were developed for corporate publications directed at external stakeholders. But partway into the development process, the working group decided that there was something about the initial hand-drawn working sketches that they liked and wanted to retain internally. The fact that these didn't look 'finished' or 'polished' or 'sanitized' encouraged people to see them as an organic, living document. The 'homely' style made people think that 'I could draw something like that' rather than a strategy that was distant, remote and created by a 'higher power'. The hand-drawn ribbons conveyed movement and encouraged the viewer to trace how they came together and integrated with one another towards the various stations and termini. So, the hand-drawn style, which was initially just a way of the artist quickly capturing the working group's thoughts, became their stratographic 'house style'. We thought long and hard about how to incorporate this principle into our Builder template. While the prospect of drawing a strategy on a blank page may appeal to some (probably those who are keener on that second 'freestyle' mode that we encouraged at the start of this part of the book), for most it's hard to get started without some prompts. Subsequently, we've incorporated images that relate to some of the five foundations of

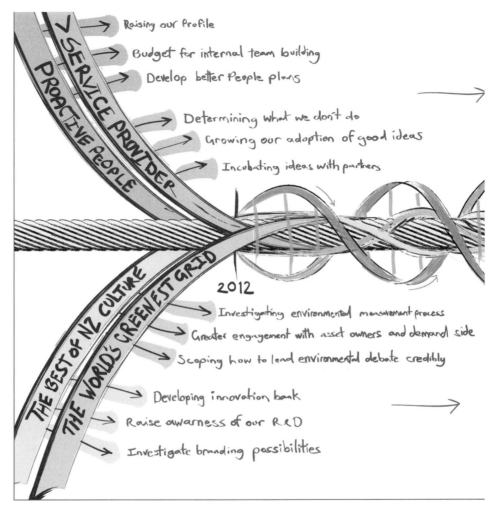

**Figure 3.17** A hand-drawn picture can be more tactile and engage the senses more that a computer generated one

the Strategy Builder approach to inspire users, but not so much by following them, or copying them, but rather by tracing their general flow while drawing and writing their own ideas, and perhaps different favoured frameworks from each section, to represent their own unique strategic situations (Figure 3.18).

Returning us right back to where this book started (the global experiment that showed the power of pictures over text in strategy representation), the principles of stratography

we have outlined here all work together to enable a good graphical representation of a strategy to be 'mnemonic': easier to remember and act upon than conventional modes of developing and communicating strategy.

Being able to 'stick' in the mind is important in strategy development, but especially important with regard to strategy implementation, where the 'rubber meets the road'. Because, despite our belief in, and adherence to, annual planning cycles and the like,

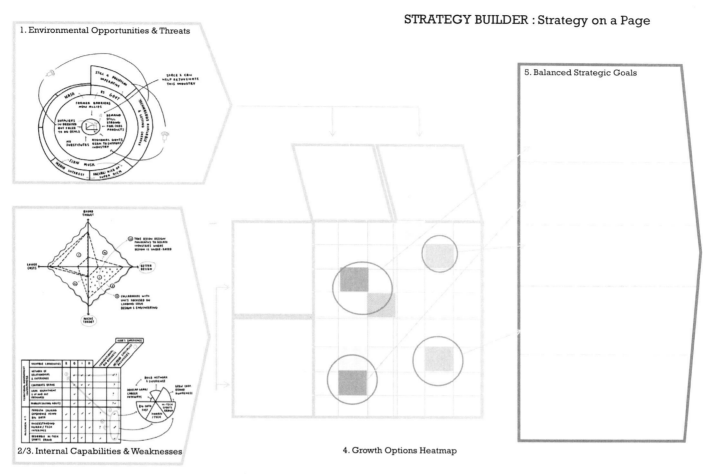

1. Environmental Opportunities & Threats

5. Balanced Strategic Goals

2/3. Internal Capabilities & Weaknesses

4. Growth Options Heatmap

**Figure 3.18** Strategy on a Page: Principle 6 – Seek to engage more than one sense

strategy is being enacted in real time all of the time. Hence, there are very few opportunities for people to refer back to the plan or policy details in the flow of everyday business life before acting. Consequently, it helps greatly if people can retain a broad working picture of the strategy they are supposed to be contributing to and, most importantly, how they contribute to it.

If a stratographic image – be it your own which you have drawn freestyle or one following the 'Strategy on a Page' template – has arrested and focused the viewer, easily spread their eye across its main elements, drawn the user in and helped them to engage and see and find patterns, aided the viewer to zoom into specific situations while seeing the big picture, brought other senses into play, then it will surely be remembered by far more of those whom you have to work with to implement that strategy than would have been the case if it was developed and communicated via a conventional medium – such as that wordy and dense strategic plan sitting on your top shelf.

# GET BUILDING

## How to be a Part of the Strategy Development Revolution

This is the place in a book where you might expect to find a conclusion that summarizes the key points. But we know what can happen. You read a book to the finish, put it down, go to sleep and start dreaming about how you've been changed by it, only to get up in the morning and do everything the same way you did it the day before. So, instead of a restatement or a conclusion, we are going to finish with a plan of action: six of the best ways to get building and communicating strategy by drawing it – not just thinking (and then forgetting) about doing so.

## A 6 point plan to get building: Remembering, Drawing, Passing, Promoting, Editing and The Arrow

### 1. Remember the strategy pictures you especially liked

We began *Strategy Builder* by reporting on how little the people who are charged with implementing a strategy can remember about that strategy when it is communicated using conventional methods. The revolution *Strategy Builder* promotes is built upon recognizing how much more engaged in strategy people can be if that strategy is developed and conveyed through drawing. Drawings and pictures, done well, are far easier to recall and interact with.

Thinking back through *Strategy Builder*, which particular pictures do you recall? Can you see the map of Napoleon's march? The strategic goal in the black Olympic ring? LEGO's 'value chain'? Barcelona's 7-Ss? DELL's classic re-thinking of the conventional path to market? Tesco's steering wheel? Or something else?

Whatever two or three pictures most resonated with you, keep them in mind, pin them to the wall and let them inspire you to draw your own stratography.

### 2. Just *draw it*

In recalling those pictures that you particularly liked and thinking about situations in organizations you work in or know, you're likely to think about drawing their strategic situations and options. Don't just think about drawing it – just draw it.

This would be greatly aided by carrying around something to draw with at all times. With other media (books, magazines, documents) being increasingly digitized you can often be caught short at that moment you are inspired to draw by not having a pen or a piece of paper. While you can draw pretty well on tablets now with some very clever apps, there's still something about scratching a pen or pencil on a real live piece of paper (authors, composers and artists often carry around notebooks to capture thoughts and ideas as they occur). There are many beautiful notebook and diary options available now. Point two of this plan says get one, carry it with you at all times, and use it liberally.

## 3. Pass the ball

There can be few things more pensive than a restart in an under-8s soccer match. (You can read their minds. They're thinking: there are so many options, what should I do? Our best player is marked? Now what? To heck with it, I'm just kicking it!) And few things as joyous and dynamic as when the ball is finally kicked.

Likewise, don't dwell too long on those pictures you've drawn. Pass them on to others. Don't wait until the boss is available or for the perfect moment in that key meeting to arrive. Pass your pics to colleagues, customers, that guy you're talking to in the airport lounge. And let them have a go at adding to it or changing it. You will learn a lot. A momentum may even build.

A strategy drawing should be viewed as a prototype that is open to innovation and improvement. A strategy picture shared can lead to your insight being 'squared'.

## 4. Promote drawing spaces and opportunities

Over the past year we and Visory (the company responsible for most of the great illustrations throughout this book) have been involved in a number of projects working with Sport New Zealand focused on how their strategy processes and those of the organizations and teams they advise can be simplified and more effectively communicated.

In the process, Simon Scott, one of the principals of Visory, has developed something of a workspace there. Due to space pressures, this isn't really an office: it's more a piece of glass for drawing on in a corridor. It's been a great surface for Simon to draw on, but more interestingly, he has begun to notice how, over time, others have started to come by and use the glass to do their own drawings and have their own discussions. It has started to become an organic feature of how people think.

We have noticed how similar boards and spaces in shared areas also attract ideas, conversations and insights in other organizations. While these boards can remain blank for a time (often people don't like to be the first to draw), once the first drawings are scratched, things take off. If those whiteboards in your meeting rooms aren't used so much anymore, move them into the hallway or near the water cooler or coffee machine. Then see what happens.

## 5. Edit

Don't let things get over-complicated. While it is great to involve and learn from others, as the complexity of interconnection increases, you have to be continually editing to ensure that things don't get overwrought.

A key aspect that has influenced our development of this book (reducing 26 frameworks down to five 'best of' foundations, the design of our 'Strategy on a Page' template, etc.), and which should also influence the development of any of your attempts to capture strategy graphically in your own style, is 'the rule of seven'.[58]

This rule of seven was first discovered by scientists trying to ascertain why it was so difficult to develop a computer that could beat a chess grandmaster. Rather than thinking in individual squares and pieces, they found that grandmasters divided the board into seven main combinations depending on the state of the game. While the seven zones might change depending on the state of play, and some might organize in fewer than seven 'chunks' (the process is referred to as 'chunking'), it was never more than seven.[59]

This notion of chunking is true in other fields, from professional musicians to everyday life issues.[60] Large local authorities encounter problems when they move from seven- to eight-digit phone numbers as the memory difficulty that people face when making such a move is exponential. One way around this is to encourage remembering a number in pairs (e.g. 34 55 61 20), thus requiring the memorization of just four bits of information. Indeed, it is not for nothing that none of the most popular management frameworks of the past five decades has had more than seven components. One easy way to improve the reception of the bad practice example of a strategy picture depicted (Figure 3.2 on page 210) would be to arrange its 64 components into seven or fewer easy-to-distinguish chunks.

Consequently, as you remember, draw, pass and promote strategy graphics, make sure to keep editing: combine down into memorable and manageable chunks as you go.

Remember
Draw
Pass
Promote

## 6. It only takes one arrow to start a revolution

The real-life examples that we looked at to help illustrate the six principles of stratography also adhere to the 'rule of seven'. In so doing, we hope that they might be memorable enough to inspire your own strategy drawings. However, while these stratographic exemplars and the other examples and pictures in *Strategy Builder* are fully formed and often polished in appearance, we believe it is the principles that underpin them rather than the polish that are key – and these principles can be kicked off and played around with in relation to your organization at any time and in any place.

All that is required to begin building a more effective and easy-to-communicate strategy for you and your organization's future is a pencil, some basic frameworks and principles, a scrap of paper and one or more inquiring minds. The start of the revolution in your organization could be as simple as an arrow drawn on a whiteboard linking a box called your business to customers in an interesting way…

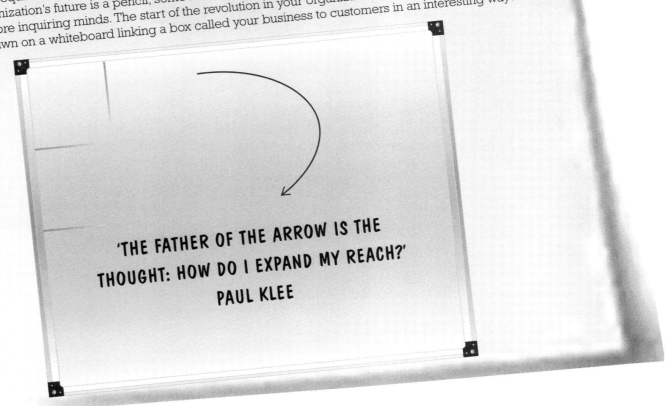

'THE FATHER OF THE ARROW IS THE
THOUGHT: HOW DO I EXPAND MY REACH?'
PAUL KLEE

## Back of the envelope, back to the future for Business Schools?

Over the past decade we have searched for good examples of stratography, and they are few and far between. One can understand, therefore, why the *Fortune* journalists mentioned earlier might have been so surprised and enamoured by Ford's CEO's drawing strategy: it is certainly not the norm nowadays. Correspondingly, the idea that drawing might be taught on an MBA sounds novel. But it might not have turned out this way.

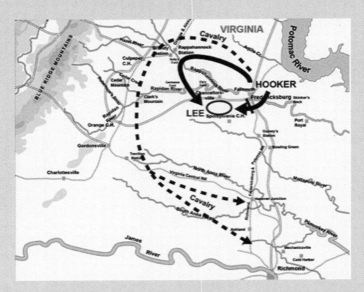

It is largely forgotten that the first business school established in a university was very nearly launched at Washington College (now Washington and Lee University) by College President Robert E. Lee.[61] On 8 January 1869, Lee presented a report to Washington College's Board of Trustees outlining a plan for a business school as part of a range of initiatives he and his team were sponsoring in relation to the college's commitment to 'practical education'. A committee chaired by Lee had been considering this for some time, and Lee tabled the proposed curriculum. Many subjects would not appear out of place at a business school today, but not the last one: mathematics, book-keeping and penmanship, correspondence and the correct use of the English language, geography, technology, law, economy, history and biography, modern languages, geometry and drawing.

Lee's plan was approved, but he became seriously ill just a few weeks later, and without him as its champion the business school did not come to pass. Modern business schools trace their lineage back to institutions established nearer the turn of the 20th century, and the reports that led to the standardization of a business curriculum around one agreed model in the 1950s, where the experts involved were of quite a different type from Lee's practical band.[62]

But the General was onto something. The ability to think 'geometrically' and to draw ideas and strategic initiatives should be a part of every good manager's arsenal. This book has attempted to combine his and many others' ideas in such a way to encourage many more managers to build and communicate strategy not just by saying, writing and tabling it: but also by drawing it.

# ENDNOTES

1. The data and findings from this experiment are reported on in Cummings, S., Angwin, D. & Daellenbach, How Graphical Representation Helps Strategy Communication, *SMS (Strategic Management Society) Special Conference*, Sydney, December 2014.

2. This compelling definition comes from Robert Grant: Grant, R.M. (2010). *Contemporary Strategy Analysis and Cases: Text and Cases*, John Wiley & Sons, Chichester, UK. It is certainly the definition that in our experience most animates and orients (in the terms of our framework no. 26) strategy students and managers alike.

3. Kaplan, R.S. and Norton, D.P. (2005). The office of strategy management. *Harvard Business Review*, 83(10), 72–81.

4. See, for example, Levie, W.H. and Levie, D. (1975). Pictorial memory processes. *Educational Technology Research and Development*, 23(1), 81–97; Anghileri, J. (2005). *Children's Mathematical Thinking in the Primary Years*. New York: Continuum International Publishing; and Foos, P.W., and Goolkasian, P. (2005). Presentation format effects in working memory: The role of attention. *Memory and Cognition*, 33(3), 499–513. Despite a recent dalliance with the idea that people have fundamental learning differences, that some are visual learners others are audio learners etc., mostly stemming from Howard Gardner's book *Frames of Mind* (Gardner, H. (1983). *Frames of Mind: The Theory of Multiple Intelligences*. New York: Basic), latest research suggests there is little evidence for this (Pashler, H., McDaniel, D., Rohrer, D. and Bjork, R. (2008). Learning styles: Concepts and evidence. *Psychological Science in the Public Interest*, 9(3), 105–119). While there may be some variance in terms of preferences, all humans benefit from multi-modality (Chanlin, L. (1997). The effects of verbal elaboration and visual elaboration on student learning. *International Journal of Instructional Media*, 24(4), 333–339; Chanlin, L. (1998). Animation to teach students of different knowledge levels. *International Journal of Instructional Media*, 25(3), 166–175; Hull, G.A. and Nelson, M.E. (2005). Locating the semiotic power of multimodality. *Written Communication*, 22(2), 224–261).

5. See, for example, Kaplan, S. (2011). Strategy and PowerPoint: An inquiry into the epistemic culture and machinery of strategy making. *Organization Science*, 22(2), 320–346.

6. Better writers than us have bemoaned the influence of PowerPoint, and particularly over-simplified bullet-points within PowerPoints – for example, Tufte, E.R. (1990). *Envisioning Information*. New York: Graphics Press; Tufte, E.R. (2001). *The Visual Display of Quantitative Information*. New York: Graphics Press; and Tufte's essay 'The cognitive style of PowerPoint: pitching out corrupts within', www.edwardtufte.com/tufte/powerpoint.

7. Crawford, M. (2009). *The Case for Working with Your Hands*. London: Penguin, published in the US as Crawford, M. (2009). *Shop Class as Soulcraft: An Inquiry into the Value of Work*. New York: Penguin. See also, Sennett, R. (2007). *The Craftsman*. London: Penguin Allen Lane.

8. Volvovski, J., Rothman, J., Lamothe, M. and Macaulay, D. (2012). *The Where, the Why, and the How: 75 Artists Illustrate Wondrous Mysteries of Science*. San Francisco, CA: Chronicle Books.

9. *Fortune* (2009). Fixing up Ford, May 25, 41–47.

10. Norridge, J. (2008). *Can We Have our Balls Back Please: How the British Invented Sport*. London: Penguin.

11. Miller, J.J. (2011). *The Big Scrum: How Teddy Roosevelt Saved Football*. HarperCollins p. 211; see also the website: http://archive.org/stream/stnicholas05unkngoog#page/n30/mode/2up/search/foot-ball.

12. Mortimer, G. (2012). *A History of Football in 100 Objects*. Serpent's Tail. Mortimer represents Pozzo's contribution with a stick of chalk from p. 107ff.

13. Khurana, R. (2007). *From Higher Aims to Hired Hands: The Social Transformation of American Business Schools and the Unfulfilled Promise of Management as a Profession*. Princeton, NJ: Princeton University Press.

14. Earlier schools of commerce in Portugal and Scotland (both established around the same time as those countries attained their own respective diplomatic, economic and intellectual heights) also incorporated graphical subjects such as cartography and geometry, probably influenced by an association with a similarly stochastic disciplines or practices: military leadership and international relations.

15. Hunter, P. and O'Shannasy, T. (2007). Contemporary strategic management practice in Australia: 'Back to the Future' in the 2000s. *Singapore Management Review*, 29(2), 21–36.

16. Levie and Levie, (1975), ibid; Foos and Goolkasian, (2005), ibid.
17. Weick, K. (1983). Misconceptions about managerial productivity. *Business Horizons,* 26(4), 47–52.
18. Massironi, M. (2001). *The Psychology of Graphic Images: Seeing, Drawing, Communicating.* Psychology Press, Hove, UK, p. 138.
19. Minard, C.J. (1869). Figurative map of the successive losses in men of the French army in the Russian campaign 1812–1813. Retrieved from http://en.wikipedia.org/wiki/File:Minard.png.
20. Andrade, J. (2010). What does doodling do? *Applied Cognitive Psychology*, 24(1), 100–106.
21. Gibson, E. (2009). 'How a doodle serves your noodle'. *Businessweek*, 6 April, 18.
22. It is worth remembering that these are clever people looking at the most simple strategy and seeking to reproduce it just minutes after they have read it. It is highly likely that your organization's strategy is more complicated and that your people have far greater distractions than these subjects.
23. Keyser, B., Hayakawa, S.L. and Keysar, B. (2012). The foreign-language effect: Thinking in a foreign tongue reduces decision biases. *Psychological Science*, 23(6), 661–668.
24. Garland, K. (1994). *Mr. Beck's Underground map.* London: Capital Transport Publishing; Ovenden, M. (2011). *Transit Maps of the World.* London: Penguin.
25. Luffman, 1838.
26. For a review of this debate, see Cummings, S. and Wilson, D. (2003). *Images of Strategy.* John Wiley & Sons, Chichester, UK, chapter 1.
27. Pascale, R.T. (1996). The 'Honda effect'. *California Management Review*, 38(4), 80–91.
28. Nattermann, P.M. (2000). Best practice does not equal best strategy. *The McKinsey Quarterly*, 2: 22–31.
29. Evans, J. (2008). Electronic publishing and the narrowing of science and scholarship. *Science* (321)5887, 395–399.
30. Garfield, S. (2009). *Mini: The True and Secret History of the Making of a Motor Car.* London: Faber & Faber.
31. Wilson, J. (2010). *Inverting the Pyramid: The History of Football Tactics.* Hachette, London, p. 313.
32. Porter, M.E. (1991). Towards a dynamic theory of strategy. *Strategic Management Journal*, 12(2), 95–117.
33. Garfield, S. *Mini*, ibid, p. 265.
34. Martin, R.L. (2009). *Design of Business: Why Design Thinking is the Next Competitive Advantage.* Boston: Harvard Business School Press.
35. Weick, K. (1983). Misconceptions about managerial productivity, ibid.
36. Wilson, J. (2010). *Inverting the Pyramid*, ibid.
37. Abschied von. Sindelar. In: *Pariser Tageszeitung* v. 25.01.1939, p. 3; http://www.guardian.co.uk/football/2007/apr/03/sport.comment3; see also Wilson, p. 62. Perhaps the only thing that stood between Sindelar winning a famous World Cup victory for Austria in 1934 was the strategizing of Vittorio Pozzo, whom we discussed in earlier in this chapter.
38. Cummings, S., Daellenbach, U., Davenport, S. and Campbell, C. (2013). 'Problem-sourcing': a re-framing of open innovation for R&D organisations. *Management Research Review*, 36(10), 955–974.
39. Dye, R. and Sibony, O. (2007). How to improve strategic planning. *McKinsey Quarterly*, 3: 40–48.
40. Volvovski, J., Rothman, J., Lamothe, M. and Macaulay, D. (2012). *The Where, the Why, and the How*, ibid.
41. Massironi, M. (2001) *The Psychology of Graphic Images*, ibid.
42. March, J.G. and Sutton, R.I. (1997). Organizational performance as a dependent variable. *Organization Science*, 8(6), 698–706.
43. Whittington, R. (2012). Big strategy/small strategy. *Strategic Organization*, 10(3), 263–268.
44. Financial Reporting Council. (2009). *Consultation on the Revised UK Corporate Governance Code.* London: Financial Reporting Council, p. 13.
45. Stern, S. (2010). 'Investors want you to tell a better story'. *Financial Times*. Retrieved December 8, 2010, from http://www.ft.com/cms/s/c3bcd18e-6cdb-11df-91c8-00144feab49a.
46. Cummings, S. (1993). The first strategists. *Long Range Planning*, 26(3), 133–135; Cummings, S. (1995). Pericles of Athens–Drawing from the essence of strategic leadership. *Business Horizons*, 38(1), 22–27.
47. Wood, D. (1992). *The Power of Maps.* London: Guilford Press.
48. For more on this phenomenon, see, Tufte, E.R. (1990). *Envisioning Information.* New York: Graphics Press; and Tufte, E. R. (2001). *The Visual Display of Quantitative Information.* New York: Graphics Press.
49. Taylor, A. (2009). 'Fixing up Ford'. *Fortune*, May 25, 41–47.
50. Ovenden, M. (2011). *Transit Maps of the World.* London: Penguin.
51. Tufte, E.R. (1990) *Envisioning Information,* ibid; and (2001) *The Visual Display of Quantitative Information*, ibid.
52. Weick, K. (1983). Misconceptions about managerial productivity. *Business Horizons*, 26(4), 47–52. Quoted on p. 49-50.
53. Retrieved from http://blogs.hbr.org/hbr/kaplan-norton/2008/09/tescos-approachto-strategy-co.html (Kaplan, R.S. and Norton, D.P. (2008). Tesco's approach to strategy communication, September 2).
54. Source: Tesco plc, 2008 and as above, ibid.

55. Weick, K. (1983). Misconceptions about managerial productivity, ibid.

56. As quoted in Cummings, S. and Angwin, D. (2011). Stratography: The art of conceptualizing and communicating strategy. *Business Horizons*, 54(5), 435–446.

57. Weick, K.E. (1987). Substitutes for strategy. In: Teece, D.J. (ed.) *The Competitive Challenge: Strategies for Industrial Innovation and Renewal*. Cambridge, MA: Ballinger, pp. 211–233.

58. Miller, G.A. (1956). The magical number seven, plus or minus two: Some limits on our capacity for processing information, *Psychological Review*, 63(2): 81–97.

59. Chase, W.G. and Simon, H.A. (1973). Perception in chess. *Cognitive Psychology*, 4, 55–81.

60. Levitin, D.J. (2011). *This is Your Brain on Music: Understanding a Human Obsession*. New York: Atlantic Books; Gobet, F., de Voogt, A.J. and Retschitzki, J. (2004). *Moves in Mind: The Psychology of Board Games*. Hove, UK: Psychology Press.

61. Lee, R.E., Jr. (1905). *Recollections and Letters of General Robert E. Lee*. New York: Doubleday, Page, & Co.; Marsh, C. S. (1926). General Lee and a school of commerce. *Journal of Political Economy*, 34(5), 657–659.

62. Gordon, R.A. and Howell, J. (1959). *Higher Education for business*. New York: Columbia University Press; Pierson, F.C. (1959). *The Education of American Businessmen*. New York: McGraw-Hill.

# IMAGE CREDITS

- Page 9 Blank chalkboard – Koosen/Shutterstock.com & Hand Drawn ABC Elements/ Illustration of a set of hand drawn sketched and doodled ABC letters – Benchart/Shutterstock. com
- Page 13 Minard's Napoleonic invasion of Russia. Retrieved from http://en.wikipedia.org/wiki/File:Minard.png
- Page 15 Punch cartoon (1909). Sourced from http://britton. disted.camosun.bc.ca/punch.html
- Page 16 Beck's Underground map (1933) © TfL from the London Transport Museum collection
- Page 17 Luffman's famous 'Invasion map' (1803). Sourced from http://www.mapforum.com/04/luffman.htm
- Page 21 Adapted from figure Massironi's *Psychology of Graphic Images*, ibid. Drawn by Rebecca Walthall.
- Page 24 Vector light bulb – Vector/Shutterstock.com
- Page 215 Originally from the Little Red Caboose, 1953, by Marian Potter, illustrated by Tibor Gergely, reproduced in Dennis Wood, The Power of Maps, 1992. This version taken from http:// www.imaginarymuseum.org/MHV/PZImhv/ WoodPowerMaps1993.html
- Page 216 Sourced from P&G Annual Reports circa 2010 – adaptations by the authors.
- Page 220 Figure used by permission of BECA, New Zealand.
- Page 222 Bordone's *Isolario* 16th-century woodcut world map. Sourced from http://www.raremaps.com/gallery/ detail/31432?view=print
- Pages 223 & 224 Sourced from Tesco Annual Reports and associated documents circa 2008.
- P227 Air New Zealand's 2005 Strategy Roadshow image sourced from Air New Zealand's Publically Available Strategy Roadshow Document, 2004. We have used this image before in Cummings, S., & Angwin, D. (2011). Stratography: The art of conceptualizing and communicating strategy. Business Horizons, 54(5), 435–446.
- Page 230 Excerpt of working drawing by Visory. Used with permission.
- P238 Map by Hal Jespersen, www.posix.com/CW. Sourced from http://en.wikipedia.org/wiki/File:Chancellorsville_ Hooker%27s_Plan.png

## Frameworks

- 2. ESTEMPLE – Adapted from Duncan Angwin, Stephen Cummings and Chris Smith, *Strategy Pathfinder*. Chichester: Wiley, 2011.
- 3. Power/interest matrix – Adapted from Abraham Mendelow, Setting corporate goals and measuring organizational effectiveness – a practical approach. *Long Range Planning*, 16(1), 70–76, 1983.
- 4. Diamond of international competitiveness – Adapted from Michael E. Porter, *Competitive Advantage of Nations*. London: Macmillan, 1990. Figure 3.5, p. 127.
- 5. Five forces of industry – Adapted from Michael E. Porter, *Competitive strategy: Techniques for Analyzing Industries and Competitors*. NY: Simon & Schuster, 1980.
- 7. The value chain – Adapted from Michael E. Porter, *Competitive strategy: Techniques for Analyzing Industries and Competitors*. NY: Simon & Schuster, 1980.
- 8. Generic strategy matrix (GSM) – Adapted from Michael E. Porter, *Competitive Advantage: Creating and Sustaining Superior Performance*. NY: Free Press, 1985. Figure 1.3, p. 12.
- 10. Blue ocean strategies – Adapted from W. Chan Kim and Rene Marbourgne, *Blue Ocean Strategy: How to Create Uncontested Market Space and Make the Competition Irrelevant*. Cambridge, MA: Harvard Business School Press, 2005.
- 11. Co-option/the value net – Adapted from Adam Brandenburg and Barry Nalebuff, *Co-option*. NY: Currency Press, 1996.
- 14. Dynamic capabilities – Adapted from David J. Teece, Explicating dynamic capabilities: the nature and microfoundations of (sustainable) enterprise performance. *Strategic Management Journal*, 28(13), 1319–1350, 2009.
- 15. Design thinking – Diagram developed by authors with Terry Bowe, Kieran Nolan, Simon Scott, Hadley Smith, Rebecca Walthall.
- 16. 7-S framework – Adapted from R. Pascale and Anthony Athos, *The Art of Japanese Management*. NY: Warner Books, 1981.
- 17. Confrontation matrix – Adapted from H. Weihrich, The TOWS matrix – a tool for situational analysis, *Long Range Planning*, 14(2): 54–66, 1982.

- 18. General Electric/McKinsey screen – Adapted from H. Igor Ansoff, *Corporate Strategy*. NY: McGraw Hill, 1965. Figure 6.1, p. 99.
- 20. Post-acquisition matrix – Adapted from Duncan Angwin and Maureen Meadows, New Integration Strategies for Post-Acquisition Management. *Long Range Planning*, (forthcoming, available online in May, 2015).
- 21. Next practice matrix – Adapted from Chris Bilton and Stephen Cummings, *Creative Strategy: Reconnecting Business and Innovation*. Chichester, UK: Wiley, 2010.
- 22. Vision – Diagram developed by authors. Contains elements from the Ashridge Mission Model, from Campbell, A., Nash, L. L., Devine, M., & Young, D., *A Sense of Mission: Defining direction for the large corporation*. London: Addison-Wesley, 1992.
- 24. Balanced scorecard – Adapted from Robert S. Kaplan and David P. Norton, The Balanced Scorecard: Measures that Drive Performance, *Harvard Business Review*, Vol. 70(1), 71–80, 1992.
- 26. Animation–orientation matrix – Adapted from Stephen Cummings and David Wilson, *Images of Strategy*. Chichester: Wiley, 2003.

**FIELD NOTES:**

**FIELD NOTES:**

**FIELD NOTES:**